DICTIONARY OF FRENCH TOOLS & MATERIALS

DICTIONARY OF FRENCH TOOLS & MATERIALS

A bilingual sourcebook for home-owners in France

ENGLISH–FRENCH
FRENCH–ENGLISH

By Richard Wiles

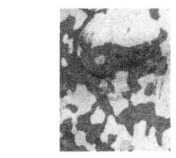

Plátanos Publications

DICTIONARY OF FRENCH TOOLS & MATERIALS

First published by Plátanos Publications 2016

Copyright © Richard Wiles 2016

The right of Richard Wiles to be identified as the author of this work has been asserted in accordance with sections 77 and 78 of the Copyright, Designs and Patents Act 1988.

All rights reserved.

No part of this book may be reproduced by any means, nor transmitted, nor translated into a machine language, without the written permission of the publisher.

Condition of Sale
This book is sold subject to the condition that it shall not, by way of trade or otherwise, be lent, re-sold, hired out or otherwise circulated in any form of binding or cover other than that in which it is published and without a similar condition including this condition being imposed on the subsequent publisher.

The publisher and author can accept no legal responsibility for any consequences arising from the application of information, advice, or instructions given in this publication.

ISBN: 978-1-5262-0141-6

Compiled, written and designed by Richard Wiles
Edited by Tania Taylor – www.thenorthernwriter.co.uk

À chaque oiseau, son nid est beau
To every bird, its own nest is beautiful

CONTENTS

INTRODUCTION	14
SOCIAL MEDIA	16
ABOUT THE AUTHOR	17
VIVE LA DIFFÉRENCE!	18
Welding, soldering & brazing	20
Trowels & floats	21
Hammers	24
Nails	26
Screws	27
Paintbrushes	28
Plumbing systems	30
Pipe & fittings	31
Electricity supply	38
Sanitation	41
Plasterboarding	42
Roughcast & render	43
Bricks	44
Blocks	46
Sand, gravel & materials in bulk	47
Timber	48
DICTIONARY OF TERMS ENGLISH-FRENCH	51
BUILDING	53
Additives/treatments for mortar & concrete	54
Wood treatments	55
Bricks & blocks	55
Masonry & aggregates	56
Paving	58
Plastering & filling	58
Plasterboarding	59
Partition walls & ceilings	60
Frames	60
Tools for assembly of partitions	60
Sheet materials	61
Beams & supports	61
Insulation, ventilation & damp-proofing	61
Adhesives	62
Rainwater drainage	63
Sanitation	63
Roofing	63
Tools & equipment	64
Hand tools	64
Roofer's tools	64
Saws & blades	65
Trowels & floats	65
Projectors of cement & thick coatings	65
Measuring & marking	66
Hammers & hatchets	66
Masonry chisels	66
Crowbars	67
Equipment, powered	67
Power tools & accessories	67
Drills & screwdrivers	67
Drill bits	67
Files & grinders	68
Saws	68
Planes & routers	68
Sanders	68
Scaffolding, ladders & steps	68

Equipment & accessories	69	Tiling materials	84
Manual construction equipment	69	Preparation for walls & ceilings	84
		Primers & undercoats	85
		Paint	86
CARPENTRY & JOINERY	71	Paint for decorative effects	87
Carpentry tools	72	Stain, varnish, oil & wax	87
Carpenter's hammers	72	Wallpapers & wallcoverings	88
Wood chisels & gouges	72	Decorating tools & materials	89
Measuring & marking	72	Masking tape	89
Clamps	72	Dust sheets & protective accessories	90
Saws	73		
Planes, rasps & scrapers	73	Decorating tools & accessories	90
Drills	74		
Carpentry equipment & accessories	74	Tools for special paint effects	91
Lathes & accessories	74	Wallpaper paste	91
Wood	74	Carpet & vinyl floorcoverings	91
Sheet materials	75		
Construction timber	75	**ELECTRICITY**	95
Woodstrip flooring, floorboards & panelling	75	Electric sheathing & accessories	96
Mouldings & beadings	75	Mouldings & trunking	96
Wood varieties	76	Accessories: mouldings & trunking	97
Stairs & stair parts	77		
		Trunking	97
DECORATING	79	Mouldings	97
Decorating tools	80	Skirting boards	97
Paintbrushes	80	Conduit	97
Rollers, paint pads & sprayguns	81	Cable & wire	98
		Flex & power cords	98
Paperhanging tools & equipment	82	Conduit & cable fixings	98
		Junction boxes	99
Tiling tools	83	Mounting boxes	99
Tiles	84	Switches & sockets	100

Plugs & lampholders	101
Consumer units	101
Circuit breakers	102
Light bulbs & tubes	102
Fuses	103
Electrical accessories	103
Electrician's tools	104

IRONMONGERY & HARDWARE 107

Adhesives	108
Adhesive tapes	111
Adhesive tools & equipment	113
Abrasives	113
Fixings	114
Nails	114
Screws	115
Plugs	116
Accessories for plugs	118
Nuts & bolts	118
Screw hooks, pegs & eyes	119
Fixing & assembly	120
Riveting & stapling	120
Security	121
Hinges	123
Shutter accessories	124
Door accessories	125
Window accessories	126
Mosquito nets	126
Rope, webbing, chain & cable	127
Accessories for rope, webbing, chain & cable	128
Storage & transport: tools & materials	129
Ladders & stepladders	130
Workbenches & accessories	130
Draughtproofing; weatherseal	130
Wheels & castors	131
Furniture fittings	132

METALWORK 135

Metal	136
Types of metal	136
Metal sections	136
Metalwork hand tools	137
Accessories for metalwork hand tools	138
Metalwork power tools	138
Accessories for metalwork power tools	139
Metalwork accessories	139
Soldering, welding & brazing	140
Arc welding	141
MIG welding	141
Gas welding	141
Metalwork abrasives	142

PLUMBING & HEATING 145

Pipe & tube	146
Plumbing connectors	146
Solder fittings	146
Plastic fittings	147
Compression fittings	147
American system fittings	148
Automatic push-fit fittings	149
Connections for washing machine & dishwasher	149
Valves & stop taps	149
Regulation of water pressure	150
Multilayer system	150
PER system	151

Waste water drainage	152
PVC pipe & connectors	152
Pumps	153
Bathroom	153
Showers & shower trays	153
Baths & bidets	155
Whirlpools, spas & saunas	155
Accessories for showers & baths	156
Toilets & washbasins	156
WC cistern mechanisms	157
Bathroom taps	158
Kitchen	158
Kitchen taps	158
Kitchen sinks	159
Electric heating	159
Auxiliary heaters	160
Central heating	161
Boilers & accessories	162
Wood heating	163
Production of hot water	164
Air conditioning & ventilation	165
Water treatment	166
Plumbing & heating tools & accessories	166
Gas & accessories	168

REFERENCE	171
Numbers	172
Fractions	173
Percentages	173
Decimals	173
Property	174
Trades	176
Colour	177

Letters of the alphabet	312
Useful words & phrases	312
Coming soon from Plátanos Publications	314
Also by the author	315
Acknowledgements	316

DICTIONARY OF TERMS FRENCH-ENGLISH   **179**

The contents listing in French

ABBREVIATIONS USED

f feminine noun
m masculine noun
pl -x plural form
adj adjective

SOMMAIRE

PRÉFACE	14
MÉDIA SOCIAL	16
À PROPOS DE L'AUTEUR	17
VIVE LA DIFFÉRENCE!	18
Soudage & brasage	20
Truelles & taloches	21
Marteux	24
Clous/Pointes	26
Vis	27
Brosses/Pinceaux	28
Systèmes de plomberie	30
Tuyau & raccords	31
Fourniture d'électricité	38
Assainissement	41
Plaque de plâtre	42
Crépi & enduit	43
Briques	44
Blocs	46
Sable, gravier & matériaux en vrac	47
Bois	48
DICTIONARY OF TERMS FRENCH-ENGLISH	179
MAÇONNERIE	181
Additifs/traitements pour mortier & béton	182
Traitements du bois	183
Briques & blocs	183
Maçonnerie & granulats	184
Pavage	186
Plâtrage & de remplissage	187
Plaque de plâtre	188
Cloisons & plafonds	188
Ossatures	188
Outils pour l'assemblage des cloisons	189
Matériaux en feuille	189
Les poutres & les supports	189
Isolation, la ventilation & l'imperméabilisation	190
Adhésifs	191
Évacuation des eaux pluviales	191
Assainissement	192
Toiture	192
Outils & équipement	193
Outils à main	193
Outils de couvreur	193
Scies & lames	194
Truelles & taloches	194
Projecteurs de ciment & d'enduits épais	194
De mesure & de marquage	195
Marteaux & hachettes	195
Ciseaux de maçon	195
Pieds de biches	196
Équipement motorisé	196
Outils électriques & accessoires	196
Perceuses & visseuses	196
Forets/mèches	196
Limes & meuleuses	197
Scies	197
Rabots & defonceuses	197
Ponceuses	197

Échafaudage, échelles & escabeaux	197	Outillage du carreleur	215
Équipement & accessoires	198	Matériaux de carrelage	216
Matériel chantier manuel	198	Carreaux	216
		Préparation des murs & plafonds	217
MENUISERIE	201	Apprêts & sous-couches	218
Outils de menuiserie	202	Peinture	219
Marteaux de charpentier	202	Peintures décoratives	220
Ciseaux à bois & Gouges	202	Lasure, vernis, huile & cire	220
Mesure & traçage	202	Papier peints & revêtements muraux	221
Serre-joints	203	Outils & matériaux de décoration	222
Scies	203	Masquage	222
Rabots, râpes & grattoirs	203	Bâches & accessoires de protection	222
Perceuses	204	Outils & accessoires de décoration	223
Matériel de menuiserie & accessoires	204	Outils pour les effets spéciaux de peinture	224
Tours & accessoires	205	Colle à papier peint	224
Bois	205	Moquette & sol vinyle	224
Panneaux de bois	205		
Bois de charpente	205	**ÉLECTRICITÉ**	227
Parquet, plancher & lambris	206	Gaines & accessoires électriques	228
Moulure & baguettes	206	Moulures & goulottes	228
Varietiés de bois	207	Accessoires: moulures & goulottes	229
Escaliers & balustrades	207	Goulottes	229
		Moulures	229
DÉCORATION	211	Plinthes	229
Outils de décoration	212	Tubes	229
Pinceaux	212	Câble & fil d'installation	230
Brosses	212		
Rouleaux, tampons de peinture & pistolets à peinture	213		
Outillage du tapissier	214		

Câble souple & cordon d'alimentation	230
Fixation des gaines & câbles	231
Boîtes de dérivation	231
Boîtes d'encastrement	231
Interrupteurs & prises	232
Fiches électriques & douilles	233
Tableaux électriques	234
Disjoncteurs	234
Ampoules & tubes	235
Fusibles	236
Accessoires électriques	236
Outils d'électricien	237
QUINCAILLERIE & VISSERIE	241
Adhésifs	242
Ruban adhésifs	246
Outils pour adhésifs	247
Abrasifs	247
Fixations	248
Clous	248
Vis	250
Chevilles	251
Accessoires pour des chevilles	252
Boulonnerie	252
Crochets, pitons & gonds de fixation	254
Fixation & assemblage	254
Rivetage & agrafage	254
Sécurité	256
Charnières & paumelles	258
Accessoires pour volets	259
Accessoires de porte	260
Accessoires de fenêtre	261
Moustiquaires	261
Corde, sangle, sandow, chaîne & câble	262
Accessoires: corde, sangle, sandow, chaîne & câble	263
Stockage & transport: les outils & les matériaux	263
Escabeaux & marchepieds	264
Établis & accessoires	265
Calfeutrage	265
Roues & roulettes	266
Ferrures de meubles	266
FERRONNERIE	269
Métal	270
Types de métal	270
Sections métalliques	270
Outils à main ferronnerie	271
Accessoires pour outillage à main ferronnerie	272
Outils électriques ferronnerie	272
Accessoires pour outils électriques ferronnerie	273
Accessoires ferronnerie	273
Soudage & de brasage	274
Soudure à l'arc	275
Soudure MIG	275
Soudure à gaz	275
Abrasifs ferronnerie	276
PLOMBERIE & CHAUFFAGE	279
Tuyaux & tubes	280
Raccords d'alimentation	280
Raccords à souder	280
Raccords en plastique	281

Raccords sans souder bicône	281	Production d'eau chaude sanitaire	298
Raccords sans souder américains	282	Climatisation & ventilation	299
		Traitement de l'eau	300
Raccords sans souder automatique	283	Outils & accessoires pour la plomberie & le chauffage	301
Raccordements pour machine à laver & lave-vaisselle	283	Gaz & accessoires	302
Vannes & robinets d'arrêt	283	**RÉFÉRENCE**	305
Régulation de la pression de l'eau	284	Les numéros	306
		Les fractions	307
Multicouche système	284	Pourcentages	307
PER système	285	Les decimaux	307
Évacuation des eaux	286	Propriété	308
Tubes & raccords en PVC	286	Metiers	310
Pompes	287	Couleur	311
Salle de bains	288	Lettres de l'alphabet	312
Douches & receveurs	288	Mots & expressions utiles	312
Baignoires & bidets	289	Bientôt de Plátanos Publications	314
Balnéos, spas & saunas	290		
Accessoires pour douches & baignoires	290	Également par l'auteur	315
		Remerciements	316
WCs & lave-mains	290		
Mécanismes & evacuation WC	291	**DICTIONARY OF TERMS ENGLISH-FRENCH**	51
Robinetterie de salle de bain	292	The contents listing in English	
Cuisine	293		
Robinetterie de cuisine	293	**ABBREVIATIONS USED**	
Eviers de cuisine	293	*f* feminine noun	
Chauffage électrique	294	*m* masculine noun	
Chauffage d'appoint	294	*pl* -x plural form	
Chauffage central	295	*adj* adjective	
Chaudières & accessoires	296		
Chauffage au bois	297		

Introduction

HOW THE BOOK WORKS

"This book is, I hope, highly informative, but it certainly reflects what you'll actually encounter in stores when out shopping, or what you'll read on the websites or in the brochures of suppliers – wrinkles and all."

A cursory riffle through the pages of this book will tell you that it is by no means a conventional dictionary. I'll put my hands up and admit that it's a bit quirky in places, and downright geeky in others – after all, I've spent more than six years trawling the websites and brochures of manufacturers and suppliers *en France* to produce this comprehensive and, dare I say, *définitif* guide to buying tools and materials. It's been something of a labour of love. A previous bilingual dictionary I compiled on French building terms was carried out with the aid of my brother and niece, but with this one I have no-one to blame but myself.

In many cases, there's no direct, or at least neatly succinct, translation between French and English for items, and so you may discover a more lengthy English entry than you'd find in an ordinary dictionary.

Margin for error
As in the UK – and I imagine in other countries worldwide – it's not unknown for the French to adopt abbreviations, acronyms, Anglicisms, Americanisms, and even colloquialisms, in their descriptions and classifications of tools and materials – and they're as prone as we Brits to perpetrating howlers in spelling, punctuation and grammar, and other shameful bastardisations of *la langue française*.

For example, when researching the subject of woodwork saws for this book, I came upon the *scie à chantourner* (coping saw,

Introduction

or fretsaw) misspelled *scie à chantonner*, which translates as 'humming saw'. Incidentally, the electric version of this tool, the scroll saw, is called both *scie à chantourner* and *scie à défilement*. On the subject of saws, the word commonly used for a jigsaw, (*sauteuse*) also translates as 'deep skillet', for sautéing, and so you should always prefix it with *scie* to avoid confusion.

There are also words in this book that are unlikely to appear in most traditional French dictionaries: words such as *circulateur* (circulating pump), for example; or words whose relevance is vague, such as *fourrure* (fur or pelt), which refers to a furring strip, used to level floor or wall timbers.

Some words and phrases will almost certainly raise a titter, because they reveal the French often daft humour: for example, *colle à bois en biberon* (wood glue in a baby's bottle). Beware of mixing these two up.

Sourcebook
What makes this book not only a dictionary, but also a sourcebook, *Vive La Difference!* is a chapter that explains the anomalies that exist between the UK and France – items that don't exist in both, or that appear radically different.

On the assumption that you might find this tome valuable to consult while out on a shopping expedition, there is also a wodge of blank pages distributed through the sections, entitled Appendix (*Appendice*), designed to encourage you to make notes, observations and comments that you can refer to later in the privacy of your own ruin – although I'm afraid you'll have to supply your own pencil.

Main categories
I've divided the contents of the dictionary into the seven main categories that cover all aspects of home renovation: Building, Carpentry & Joinery, Decorating, Electricity, Ironmongery & Hardware, Metalwork, and Plumbing & Heating. Within these

Introduction

categories, there are sub-divisions that list the tools and materials applicable to those disciplines. There's some repetition, of course, because certain items can be employed in more than one category.

At the end of the book, you'll also find a guide to translating the names of trades people, a list of words connected with property and property-buying, how to pronounce the letters of the alphabet in French, some useful words and phrases – plus an aid to that notoriously difficult aspect of learning the language: numbers.

This book is the first in the *La Source!* series of French-English dictionaries from Plátanos Publications. See page 314 for details of upcoming titles.

ONLINE CHIT-CHAT

Readers are invited to join in the online conversation on tools and materials in France by visiting (and hopefully 'Liking') the La Source Bilingual Dictionaries Facebook page, and following us on Twitter: @LaSourceBooks

Here you'll be able to help create a forum where you can exchange advice and information with like-minded individuals, submit entries that may woefully have been omitted from these pages (but will later be included in a reprint), upload photographs of your favourite tools, or proudly (or otherwise) display pictures of your French renovation projects.

Richard's personal website, which contains a full *résumé* of his career and details of published titles, is:
www.richardwiles.wix.com/richardwiles

ABOUT THE AUTHOR

Richard Wiles is a professional author and editor. Born in Newcastle upon Tyne, Northumberland, in 1954, he drifted southward via spells in the Lake District, Cheshire, London, Surrey and Kent, before settling in East Sussex, where he has spent most of his adult life.

He gained his knowledge of home renovation from his early career on the national magazines *Do It Yourself*, *Homemaker* and *Ideal Home*, and the partwork publications *Jobmate*, *Do It Right* and *Fix It* in the mid-1970s and 1980s, later establishing himself as one of the UK's foremost DIY columnists and authors. He regularly contributed to magazines such as *Traditional Homes* and *Period Living*, and has written and edited more than a dozen books on home interest topics.

His connection with France began in the late 1990s, when he bought a 13-acre farm in the Limousin region, renovated its rundown barn and kept llamas – the subject of his bestselling humorous travel genre books, *Bon Courage!* (2003/13) and *Bonne Chance!* (2006). He turned his attention to offering practical advice for other ex-pats in articles for the magazines *Living France*, *Everything France*, *Destination France*, *The Connexion*, *Homes Overseas* and *Living Abroad*, and in books including the *Dictionary of French Building Terms* (Summersdale 2006).

Having moved on from the Limousin, he is now, with the aid of his long-suffering brother, 'The Count', in the throes of renovating a ramshackle hill-top property in the beautiful Lot department, in the Midi-Pyrénées region of France, where he is writing *La Source!*, the third book in his travel series, and further titles in his series of French-English dictionaries.

When not involved in home-related matters in France, Richard can be found immersed in his passion for hot-air ballooning, and edits *Aerostat*, the bi-monthly journal of the British Balloon & Airship Club.

VIVE LA DIFFÉRENCE!

"It's highly unlikely that you'll turf up in France – a raw and unsophisticated *rosbif* (or 'roast beef' as the French affectionately nickname the Englishman) – gaze around you despairingly and think: "What the heck is all this stuff?"

In the majority of cases, the tools, equipment and materials you'll encounter in France will be recognisable for what they are: a length of rough sawn timber, for example, couldn't really be anything else (although it may be dyed a garish custard yellow, and its dimensions will be different to those you're used to in Blighty). By the same token, you'd be hardly likely to stare at a sheet of plasterboard and scratch your head trying to identify it (although, again, get your tape measure out and you'll find its dimensions are fractionally different to the same animal in the UK). A nail, after all, is invariably just a nail... this is true, but the cunning French apply two names – *clou* and *pointe* – to what appear to be the same thing. The same confusion exists with paintbrushes: *brosse* and *pinceau*, feminine and masculine respectively. So it's these items, and others, that perhaps require a little explanation.

Unfamiliarity
Some French-bred items, however, are radically different in shape to their cousins across the Channel, which could prompt the unwary Brit to do a double-take. Take the bricklaying trowel, for instance: you won't find the same pointy tool in France as you would back at home. And the humble hammer: the French one is perhaps an unfamiliar looking object, although obviously a hammer – but why is it that rather clumpy shape?

Of course, there's no reason why you need to go entirely native and adopt the French way unquestioningly: for example,

I personally have an aesthetic aversion to the French *ossatures*, aluminium frames that are used to construct what appear to be somewhat flimsy partition walls. It's true that they're used in the UK, too (often in commercial installations), although probably not to the same extent, but in my humble opinion there's nothing to beat a stout timber stud partition: wood seems especially more at home in an older house or barn conversion, even if it will be clad both sides with plasterboard.

This chapter, therefore, should not be considered as an exhaustive description of every single tool and type of material you're likely to come across when wandering the lengthy aisles of a French DIY megastore – compiling that would be an endless folly! – but is intended to offer clarity on the main differences.

Siege Mentality
People are often tempted to import old familiar British goods to their French abode: foodstuffs in particular. My good friend The Yorkshireman was known, in his early days as an ex-pat Brit, to maintain a 'siege cupboard' of goods that he considered essential, which included Marmite, Heinz Tomato Ketchup, and of course Yorkshire Tea bags. After periodic trips to the UK, he often returned to the land of the ubiquitous *baguette* with a car boot full of bog-standard sliced white bread, proclaiming "there's nowt in France that'll make a decent toast, lad".

That was more than a decade ago, however, and things have changed somewhat: most *supermarché* feature an English section tacked onto the end of an aisle, containing staunch British goods, including Coleman's English Mustard, Branston Pickle, McVitie's Digestive biscuits, Bisto gravy, and, naturally, curry pastes and other spicy morsels alien to refined French tastebuds. There are also numerous online and physical shops in France purveying British consumable goods.

However, while such home comforts can be a nice treat when living in a strange land, a touch of cosy homeliness, I'd advise against bringing certain home renovation materials to France in the misguided belief that the British type is somehow better/easier to work with/cheaper in the long run. French plumbing pipe, to give just one example, is the dimensions it is for good reason: the walls of copper pipe are thicker than those of UK pipe because the water pressure *en France* is generally higher than in the UK.

Successful UK stockist of DIY tools and materials, Screwfix, also deliver their Anglocentric ranges to European destinations, including France – so it is possible to renovate your French home in uncompromisingly British style. But why? My advice is: go native.

What now follows is a potted review of the main areas of difference and disparity between French and English home-improvement products.

Welding, soldering & brazing
Soudage et brasage

The topic of welding, soldering and brazing is a minefield that I won't linger over too long. The French perversely use the terms *soudure* (*f*) and *soudage* (*m*) for both soldering and welding, although they are distinctly different methods of joining metal components.

Soldering uses a low-melting point alloy, solder, to join items of less fusible metal, whereas in welding the metal parts are heated to the point of melting, then fused by pressing or hammering. Brazing, *brasage* (*m*), like soldering, uses an alloy to join components, although at a much higher temperature.

Gas metal arc welding, commonly known by its sub-types metal inert gas (MIG) welding and metal active gas (MAG) welding, is a process in which an electric arc forms between a consumable wire electrode and the metal components, which heats the components, causing them to melt and join.

The French love welding, but it's not really a process employed by home renovators. This dictionary, therefore, lists the main items you'll find readily available. Those of you lured by this technique will need to perform some serious research.

Trowels & floats
Truelles & taloches

truelle f; taloche f

In the motherland we tend to lump together under the all-encompassing title 'trowel' those hand tools used for bricklaying, pointing mortar joints, floor-screed laying, plastering, joint coverage between plasterboard sheets, and filling holes and cracks in walls. With the exception of sometimes calling that big flat, floor-screed-laying trowel a 'float' (short for 'floating trowel'), the classification is neatly concise. Not so in France, where *maçons* (builders) call the tools of their trade either *truelles* or *platoirs*. (You'll also find *platoir* spelt *platroir*, for indeterminate reasons, but for the sake of clarity, I'll use the version without the 'r'.)

The main distinction between these classifications is that a *truelle* fulfils the same function as the UK trowel, a metal-bladed tool with a cranked handle, ranging in size from the pointing trowel with a 100mm long, triangular steel blade to the bricklaying trowel with triangular blade in excess of 200mm long. The *platoir*, on the other hand, is akin to the UK float, a tool with a 280–450mm long, rectangular flat steel blade (sometimes with a pointed or rounded end).

However, it's not as simple as that, since French trowels don't have precisely the same shaped blades. With English trowels the edges are straight, while on French ones the edges are curved. Trowels from both countries (apart from the cheapest varieties) invariably have blades that are bevelled along the length of their top face.

The French bricklaying trowel, *truelle à brique* (used for laying and cutting bricks), has an oval blade, although commoner types are triangular: the *truelle ronde* (rounded tip) and the *truelle italienne* (pointed tip). The blade of the 'Paris' pattern brickie's trowel has a rounded rear edge; that of the 'Nord-Belge' pattern is straight.

British brickies generally use the same bog-standard bricklaying trowel for laying breezeblocks, but the French have

Vive La Différence!

a special tool: the square-bladed *truelle carrée* (or *truelle italienne carrée*), also used for laying hollow bricks, is roughly equivalent to the UK's bucket trowel (for scraping those last dregs of mortar from the bottom of a bucket, where a pointy tool just won't reach!).

The *truelle ronde* is also known as *truelle italienne ronde* (and sometimes, even more confusingly, *truelle cazzuola ronde*, whereby 'cazzuola' is Italian for 'trowel'); the Italian pattern trowels invariably have blades of tempered steel rather than riveted stainless steel.

In terms of pointing trowels, French and English types are broadly similar but the *truelle langue de chat* (cat's tongue) has a slim blade with a rounded rather than a pointed tip. This tool is also the nearest equivalent to the British gauging trowel.

The UK jointing trowel has a direct French sibling, the slim bladed *truelle à joint* – two blade profiles, flat (~ *plat*) and half-round (~ *demi-ronde*) – as does the corner or angle trowel, the *truelle d'angle* (~ *intérieur* and ~ *extérieur* for interior and exterior angles respectively). A useful oddity, which has no UK equivalent, is the *truelle triangulaire*, a small tool with three equal straight sides, which is used to access difficult spaces.

As to whether the French have the edge on the Brits when it comes to the practicality of their trowels, I cite the experience of my builder friend Jean Le Grand (Big John), a man widely regarded as living, breathing, sleeping and eating

> **FLICK OF THE WRIST**
>
> The bulbous, pizza-shovel blade of the *truelle à brique* can also hold more than the average dollop of pug, meaning bricklaying can, theoretically at least, be carried out at a quicker pace, with need to reload less frequently. Bear in mind, however, that one needs considerable wrist power to maintain the scooping action required to wield such a prodigious tool. My brother, the Count, and I both suffered identical long-term repetitive strain injuries after rebuilding a metre-thick stone wall that had, for reasons of having only mud joints, deemed fit to collapse.

bricks: discovering the veritable trove of trowels on sale in Mr. Bricolage, when helping me renovate my stone barn, he invested in a set, vowing never again to use a British trowel. The shape of the blades made them easier to manipulate, he reckoned, and the tools combined the good balance and snug grip essential when manhandling masonry all day.

When it comes to tools for plastering, the French *platoir à enduire* is a similar beast to the UK plasterer's trowel, sometimes appended with *inoxidable* (or *inoxydable*, the correct spelling) to denote a stainless steel blade, or *en acier trempé*, tempered. Rectangular bladed, they're sometimes described as *platoir rectangulaire*.

If you're looking for a notched trowel for applying tiling adhesive or mortar in neat furrows, you'll find it described as a *platoir à enduire denté* or *platoir italien à dent carreé* (with square teeth) or *à dent triangulaire* (with triangular teeth). The longer, narrower steel float used for smoothing plaster, mortar or concrete, which typically has one curved, pointed end, is known as the *platoir à bout ovale*.

> **SCRAPE**
> Another French gizmo that's extremely useful to the budding plasterer, the *truelle berthelet* is a trowel with one smooth and one notched long edge for scraping excess plaster, particularly against a door or window frame, and spreading tile adhesive respectively.

Wooden-, plastic- or polyurethane-bladed plasterer's floats – for spreading on small amounts of finish plaster, smoothing plastered coats or smoothing floor screeds – are not called *platoirs*, but *taloches* (from the verb *talocher*, to 'whack'). They are rectangular, or incorporate a pointed end for access into corners and tight spaces. A *taloche* is also commonly used as a hawk, since no such tool seems to be indigenous in France.

Vive La Différence!

Hammers
Marteux

marteau (pl -x) m

Looking for something to hit the *clou* on the *tête*? Then you should know that French hammers are vastly dissimilar to the type you'll find in B&Q, Homebase, or other British DIY institutions. There is no native French hammer that compares with the ubiquitous claw hammer, although it does appear as an import, variously known as *marteau arrache-clou* or *marteau de coffreur* (nail-puller or packer's hammer), and sometimes as the *marteau americaine*. The French equivalent – in terms of having a nail-pulling claw at the back – is the *marteau d'emballeur*, while the *marteau électricien* (electrician's hammer; not a category that exists in the UK) incorporates a dinky little claw at the back.

Most standard French-born hammers conform to a single pattern, consisting of a rectangular head with square-section striking face, and a wedge-shaped pein at the back. The pein is offset rather than being symmetrical, a feature that has been the cause of numerous heated discussions between hammer aficionados: however, no one seems certain where the pein originated (but see one hopelessly romantic explanation, left).

The wedge-shaped style of pein is common with German

> **EIFFEL INSPIRATION**
> While the 'notched' design of the French hammer could simply be to improve the balance of the tool, a more picturesque notion – and one that I'll happily accept as fact – is that the shape was developed during the construction of the Eiffel Tower in Paris, which began in 1887. The off-centre pein was said to have come into its own when setting rivets that were hard to get at. Bearing in mind there are two-and-a-half million rivets holding up the 18,000-plus parts of the iron lattice tower, it's certainly plausible that an enterprising *forgeron* might have invented a tool specifically for the job.

Vive La Différence!

and Swedish pattern hammers, but the French version is the only one to have the offset pein.

There is no obvious visual distinction between hammers for carpentry and those for metalwork, such as there is with the UK's carpenter's cross pein hammer and engineer's ball pein hammer. You may find, although rarely, a *marteau boule 'anglais'* or *'américain'*, the names used to describe a conventional engineer's hammer.

Apart from imported tools, to all intents and purposes, a French *marteau menuisier* (carpenter's hammer) looks identical to a *marteau rivoir* (riveting hammer). Although they may look the same, numerous sizes and weights of hammer are made, from the equivalent of a delicate, wooden-handled pin hammer to a weighty general-purpose hammer.

> **TAKE YOUR PICK**
> I could cite many instances of disparity between England and France when it comes to tools, equipment and materials, but there are also items that simply don't exist in the UK. Among the numerous hammers with pick-like peins favoured by French builders and roofers (notably the *martelette*, or slater's hammer; the *marteau à briques*, or brick hammer; and the *hachette de plâtrier*, or lath/drywall hammer), there's an extremely useful tool that's rarely found in the UK: a small, hand-held pick, the *décintroir à pic*, which has a curved head in various patterns, combining pick and chisel blades, or two chisel blades set at right-angles.

Builder's hammers more or less conform to the same pattern as their English cousins; the *massette* or *marteau de maçon* is identical to the club (or lump) hammer, while the *masse couple* is the same, long-handled tool as the sledgehammer.

Nails
Clous/Pointes

clou m; pointe f

More confusion exists when buying nails in France. Not because they're radically different to UK types, but because they seem to be interchangeably called *clous* (the masculine noun for 'nail') or *pointe* (the feminine noun for a 'tack' or *petit clou*). So, you may be forgiven for thinking that an ordinary nail is a *clou* and a small nail is a *pointe* – but this is not necessarily the case.

Size is not everything when it comes to nails, it seems, since some stockists can't seem to decide what to call them. Take a look at Castorama's website, for example, and you'll find listed under the heading *Clous* a vast range of *pointes*. Point.P also hedge their bets by giving us both terms.

No matter, though; it's my advice to ignore the label and choose by the shape, size and quality of nail you want: as a potted guide to the most popular Brit nails in their French guises: the ordinary wire nail is often called *clou de Paris*; the oval wire nail, *clou* (or *pointe*) *à tête d'homme*; the round wire nail, *clou à tête plate*; the lost-head nail, or brad, is *clou à tête perdue* or *sans tête*. It's quite logical, really. The trusty old clout-nail is *clou à tête diamant*; the masonry nail *clou à beton*; and the twisted-shank nail *clou torsadé*. Beware of some lax stockists, who perversely don't append a fully descriptive name to their products, instead calling them rather vaguely *clous spécial* (special nails): in cases such as this you simply have to go by the shape of the nail.

Commonly found in France is the *pointe striée béton acier zingué*, a zinc-plated nail for hard materials (e.g. concrete,

> **PANEL GAME**
> The French differ from the Brits with regard to plasterboard fixings, since they invariably attach the sheets to metal ossatures (frameworks) rather than timber studs, and therefore use screws. You're unlikely to find a plasterboard nail in France.

stone, brick), and for frame fixing; it's not widely available in the UK, but known as a ribbed nail, which incorporates vertical 'striations' along part of the shank.

Upholsterer's tacks, or square section brads, are rather colourfully called *semences de tapissier* (*semence* meaning seed, or sperm). The U-shaped wire staples commonly used in fixing fencing wire or cables, or in roofing, are not known by the French word for 'staple' (*agrafe*), as you may have innocently expected, because this refers only to the type of staple used to fasten together sheets of paper. Instead, they're called *crampillons*, and sometimes known as *conduits*.

Nails are also described by the material from which they're made, and any treatment they have undergone. For example: *acier poli* (polished steel); *acier trempé* (tempered steel); *acier nickelé* (nickeled steel); *acier galvanisé* (galvanised steel); *acier zingué* (zinc-plated steel); *acier inoxydable* (stainless steel); *laiton* (brass); *acier laitonné* (brass-plated steel); *cuivre poli* (polished copper); *acier vieilli* (antiqued steel).

Screws

Vis
vis f

There's less confusion when choosing screws than there is with nails. The French type are basically identical to the British type. Screw heads are invariably cross pattern: predominantly Posidriv or Torx, although you will also find Phillips represented. They're commonly described as *vis empreinte cruciforme*, or more specifically ~ *empreinte posi* or ~ *empreinte torx*.

You will also find slot-headed screws, although they're less common in France than they are in the UK, and usually reserved for woodwork applications. In fact, it seems that they're becoming far less popular in Britain as well, with the European cross-head pattern becoming predominant. Slot-headed screws are described as *vis empreinte fendue* (which translates as 'split' or 'cleft').

Countersunk heads are indicated as *vis à tête fraisée*, with the head pattern usually appended after. As with nails, screws are also generally described by the material from which they're made – e.g. *inox* (stainless steel), *laiton* (brass), *acier zingué* (galvanised steel) – or the material they're intended to be used with (e.g., *vis agglo*, a chipboard screw; *vis à bois*, a woodscrew; *vis plaque de plâtre*, a plasterboard screw).

Paintbrushes
Brosses/Pinceaux

brosse f; pinceau (pl –x) m

In some cases radically different in shape to UK paintbrushes, French types are either termed *brosses* or *pinceaux* (feminine and masculine nouns respectively). In the UK there's a relatively small selection of rectangular, flat brushes to choose from – with size being the main influence on choice – but in France there's a bewilderingly vast range.

The distinction between types is not always obvious. Often terms seem interchangeable, and there's inconsistency between manufacturers. The French verb *brosser* means 'to brush', so the link to *brosse* is obvious. The word that applies specifically to a 'paintbrush' (as defined in a dictionary) is, however, *pinceau*. This does not mean you won't find paintbrushes sold under either name.

The main physical difference between paintbrushes in France is shape: they're either flat, rectangular stock (like most UK types) or round stock (mainly found only in the form of artist's paintbrushes in the UK). I once thought I'd cracked the code ("Eureka! A *brosse* is rectangular; a *pinceau* is round") until I noticed that some suppliers, notably the superstore Castorama, mix the terms. (Confusingly, they also describe some rectangular brushes as *queue de morue*, codfish tail, or *queue anglaise*; but let's not go there at this juncture!).

Another big supplier, Leroy Merlin, have opted to call all their paintbrushes *pinceaux*, adding *plate* (flat) for rectangular types. Point.P, in their interactive, online catalogue, can't seem to decide either, so lump all their brushes together under both names.

So what do you choose when there seems no precise destination between flat and round bristles? Round stock brushes are usually (but not always) a more petite format suited to painting smaller areas, such as delicate wood mouldings, door and window frames. Flat-bristled brushes are typically larger and more efficient at painting broader areas, such as flat panels, walls and ceilings.

To complicate matters further, French paintbrushes are also sold according to the type of material they're intended to be used with: flat or round types are labelled and frequently colour-coded as to their suitability for *peinture glycéro* (oil-based paint such as gloss or eggshell), *peinture acrylique* (water-based paint such as emulsion), or *vernis* and *lasure* (varnish and lacquer).

As in the UK, you have the further choice between natural or synthetic bristles, or a combination of the two. Natural hairs, such as *soie de porc* (hog's hair) produce the finest finish, while those with synthetic bristles, such as nylon, are tougher and longer lasting.

> **IN THE ROUND**
> Round stock brushes are uncommon in the UK, while they're widely used in France: if you've never tried one, I recommend giving them a go. They're far more versatile when painting the delicate glazing bars of window frames, enabling you to dispose of the need for an angled cutting-in brush. Having painted both sides of more than a dozen three-paned casements in my Limousin barn conversion, I'd opt for a French round stock paintbrush any day.

Plumbing systems
Systèmes de plomberie

The main difference between a French plumbing installation and a British one is that the water supply is fed direct from the mains rather than indirectly from a storage tank in the loft. Because the water pressure in France can be quite high – a pressure of 6 bar is not uncommon – it's usual to regulate the incoming water supply pressure at the entry point using a pressure reducing valve. The resultant pressure is then about 3 bar (1 bar = 1 atmosphere, which is about 14.5lb per square inch), around 45lb per square inch. Because of this, smaller pipe sizes can be used for both hot and cold supplies.

From the mains supply pipe, water is distributed throughout the house by a manifold (*nourrice*) for each of the hot and cold circuits. The manifold is basically a length of pipe, typically with three, four or six outlets, each with its own quarter-turn stop tap. Manifolds can be connected end-to-end to incorporate more outlets for larger circuits. It's normal to have one set of manifolds per floor.

Hot and/or cold pipes from the manifolds feed fittings such as the kitchen sink (*evier*), shower (*douche*) or bath (*bagnoire*), wash basin (*lavabo*), toilet (*WC*) and washing machine (*machine à laver*). In the UK, most washing machines and dishwashers tend to draw hot water from the hot water system in the house. Machines in France, however, are invariably cold fill only – they draw in only cold water and heat it to the required temperature. If you've

> **NO PRESSURE THEN...**
> Although the water pressure in France is predominantly high, this is not universally the case. Remote rural supplies are evaluated by pressure and if your renovation project is located in an area where pressure is in the doldrums, you could find your planning application is refused. It would require applications from several households before the water company would even contemplate the costly job of upgrading the infrastructure.

signed up for an economy evening water heating tariff with EDF, it's economical to run such machines during these designated hours.

Water for taps and shower is normally heated by a mains fed electric hot water cylinder (*chauffe-eau*), typically of around 100, 150, 200 or 300 litre capacity. The insulated cylinder has a diaphragm that absorbs the expansion of the water as it is heated, and incorporates a pressure relief valve. Unlike most British hot water cylinders, which function by gravity and are normally sited in the bathroom beneath a tank in the loft, the French *chauffe-eau* can be positioned virtually anywhere, even in a cellar, and is frequently housed in the garage or utility room (*buanderie*).

> **POWER TO YOUR SHOWER**
> Because of the excellent water pressure in France, you won't necessarily need to install an electric power shower, since you can easily get the 'power shower effect' just from mains pressure.

The central heating boiler – typically an appliance of monster proportions compared to our compact UK models – is also frequently housed in the garage or utility room. Usually separate pipe runs provide an even flow of water to each of the individual fittings, e.g. so that a washing machine can be used at the same time as the shower without dire consequences, but in practice a simple tee connecter (*un té*) can be fitted on one supply pipe to serve, e.g. a wash basin and toilet.

Pipe & fittings
Tuyau & raccords

tuyau m; raccord m

Ostensibly, there is not a major difference between French and English plumbing materials, but on closer inspection you'll discover some variations that would make it awkward and unwise to mix the two. Unless you've amassed a large stock of UK fittings you're

Vive La Différence!

loathe to part with, the best option is simply to use French-sourced materials from the outset, particularly when connecting to existing services, so avoiding any potential mismatch.

Copper pipe *tuyau cuivre*

In France, copper pipe is measured nominally by its outside diameter in millimetres, rising in 2mm increments: 8, 10, 12, 14, 16, 18, 20, 22mm, and then 28, 32 and 40mm. The 8mm diameter pipe is mainly used for plumbing in taps, with main pipe runs being run in the 14mm size.

Copper pipe has a wall thickness of 1mm to cope with the higher water pressure that predominates in France, compared to the typical 0.6–0.9mm wall thickness of British pipe – another reason why importing UK pipe is a false economy. You will frequently see pipe sizes in France listed by their internal followed by external diameter – e.g. 10 x 12mm, 12 x 14mm and 14 x 16mm.

Some sources recommend using specific copper pipe sizes for certain fittings (see chart opposite), e.g. 8mm (toilet), 10mm (washbasin), 12mm (shower) all fed from a 16mm pipe from a *nourrice* (manifold). Reducers aren't necessary because French pipe 'nests', i.e. one size fits into the next. One school of thought is that 8mm is needed to reduce the noise of the WC cistern filling in a high water pressure, while another asserts that smaller diameter pipe is used so that if the toilet is flushed while the shower is in use, it causes less draw on the cold feed resulting in less of a temperature change.

> **UNHEALTHY MIX**
> Another good reason not to opt for a hybrid British-French set-up is when those unforeseen bursts and other emergencies occur: unless you were to have a ready stock of offcuts of British pipe and fittings, you'd be ill-prepared to deal with a deluge.

Copper pipe in France is frequently supplied in coils (*couronne cuivre*) in addition to straight lengths (*barre cuivre*). The advantage of the coil is that the copper is soft, i.e. annealed (*recuit*), and can be bent cold, whereas straight lengths are dead hard tempered (*écroui*) and therefore must be annealed (heated with a blowtorch)

Vive La Différence!

Typical French copper pipe sizes for various installations							
(all sizes: internal/external diameter in mm)							
	8/10	10/12	12/14	14/16	16/18	18/20	22/24
Washbasin		•	•				
Kitchen sink				•			
Bath					•	•	
Shower			•	•	•		
Bidet			•	•			
Washing machine/ dishwasher			•				
W/C	•	•					
Outside tap				•			
Hot water cylinder *							•
* in copper for 1m, if changing to plastic							

before bending. Coiled pipe is intended to be sheathed and flush fixed, i.e. not surface mounted.

In Britain, copper pipe is also measured nominally by its outside diameter in millimetres (pre-metrication in 1972, pipes were measured by the inside diameter in inches). Common pipe sizes are 6, 8, 10, 12, 15, 18, 22, 28, 35 and 42mm diameter, which you'll see equates roughly to the French, with some differences. The 8mm and 10mm sizes are mainly used for microbore central heating systems; the 12 and 15mm sizes for connections to taps and other appliances; and to maintain consistent water pressure

Vive La Différence!

and flow on longer runs, 22, 28 and 35mm sizes. In practice, the only problem you'd be likely to encounter is if you wanted to use a British 15mm connector with French 16mm pipe, or British 15mm pipe with a French 16mm connector. Although there are ways to get round this, the simplest solution is: just don't. Use native French fittings and avoid the problem in the first place.

Capillary fittings *Raccords à souder*
A capillary joint is made by melting a 'filler' metal such as solder at the edge of a slip fit so that it is drawn into the joint by capillary action and, on cooling, forms a tight bond. In the UK there are two main types of joint: pre-soldered 'Yorkshire' fittings, which incorporate an internal ring of solder in a channel formed in the socket, and plain end feed types that have no solder ring. Pre-soldered fittings are less robust than end feed types, but they are useful when working in confined spaces and where single-handed fitting is required.

In France, you'll find only the end feed type (*raccord cuivre à souder*). This is partly due to the fact that the French *plombieres* traditionally braze (*braser*) rather than solder (*souder*), using oxy-acetylene and phosphor-bronze filler rod; although the processes are broadly the same, the temperatures used in brazing to melt the filler metal are higher (300-400° C for cold water pipes; 450-500° C for hot water and heating). One reason for the preference to braze is that, because of the generally higher water pressure, pipes in France are of a thicker gauge than those in the UK. Older properties were plumbed straight from the mains, and brazing creates a much stronger joint that's less liable to leak.

It's true that many expat Brits re-plumb their French properties using the solder method – you can buy all you

> **CLEAN ACT**
> It's likely that leaky joints are the fault of the plumber's poor workmanship, rather than from the use of solder instead of brazing. Whichever method you opt for, remember that the job is all about being meticulous: cleanliness is paramount when soldering or brazing.

need for soldering in France – and don't experience leaks, while others have reported continual problems with leaky soldered joints. You may even come across native plumbers stooping to use soft solder on small jobs, but this is mainly for convenience: the oxy-acetylene bottles used for brazing are cumbersome to lug around just for one joint!

Compression fittings *Raccords sans souder bicône*
The easiest method of joining pipework is to use a mechanical fitting – either brass compression fittings with screw-threaded nuts and copper or PTFE sealing olives, or else a plastic push-fit system. The problem with mechanical fittings is that they're inherently impermanent, not as flexible or reliable as capillary types, and therefore more prone to leaking than soldered joints. Professional plumbers only use such fittings where future disconnection may be required for maintenance or replacement, such as between taps and water inlets.

In France you'll find standard brass compression fittings with copper olives, the same as you'll be familiar with in the UK, the *systeme americaine*, which replaces the olive with a metal grab ring and rubber washer, and 'automatic' fittings, which comprise a serrated grab ring and a spacer that connect to the body of the fitting with a screwed nut.

Surprisingly, the screwed threads of compression fittings are universal throughout Europe and the UK, conforming to the ¾in. and ½in. BSP (British Standard Pipe) threads!

Plastic pipe *Tuyau en plastique*
If you baulk at the very notion of brazing and soldering, you'll be relieved to know there's an easier option particularly suited to the do-it-yourselfer, in the form of bendy plastic pipe and push-fit or compression joints. The main types of plastic pipe you'll find widely available in France are:

- **Tuyau polyéthylène eau potable** MDPE polyethylene pipe.
- **Tube PER** Cross-linked polyethylene pipe.
- **Tube multicouche** multilayer pipe.

Vive La Différence!

Tuyau polyéthylène eau potable

MDPE polyethylene pipe, coloured black with four sky blue stripes down the length, is reserved for the incoming potable water main supply from the water company's meter to your home. It's available in 20, 25 and 32mm diameters (external dimension) in 10, 25, 50 and 100m coils. It's laid in ribbed blue plastic conduit (*gaine*) 50mm in diameter and buried to 60cm minimum depth. The pipe is connected using plastic or brass compression fittings.

You'll also find it used above ground in various situations: both of my barns, pre-conversion, featured a network of black pipework strung from joist to joist and down the walls to feed the little valve-operated *cuvettes* (bowls) that provided drinking water for the bovine occupants of the *étable* (cowshed).

Tube PER

Known in Great Britain as PEX, cross-linked polyethylene, PER (*polyéthylène réticulé*) pipework is used for internal water and central heating supplies. It comes bare (*nu*) or encased in ribbed plastic conduit (*prégainé*), in blue to carry cold water and red for hot (although, apart from colour, the pipes are identical). Sizes are (internal/external) 10/12, 13/16 and 16/20mm diameter in 5, 10, 15, 25 and 50m coils. PER pipe must be protected from UV, so it is run under floors, in roof spaces or within walls.

Special fittings are required to join lengths of pipe and to connect it to taps, valves and other accessories; metal formers are needed to support bends and prevent 'throating', where the pipe walls collapse when bent in a tight radius. Brass insert sockets are required to reinforce the ends of the pipe before being connected to a fitting.

There are basically three choices of PER fitting:

• Compression fittings (*raccords à visser métalliques*) in brass, comprising a notched ring (*bague crantée*) and screw-threaded locking nut, which

> **MEASURE TWICE CUT ONCE**
> Make sure you've measured the length of pipe correctly first time before making up a PER glissement joint, as you will not be able to remove the collar once it's been tightened.

requires only an adjustable spanner to fit. This type is the most expensive option.
• Slip fittings (*raccords à glissement*) consist of a brass collar (*collier simple de fixation PER*) that is slotted over the pipe, which is then flared (*évasée*) with a *pince à évasement* (flaring tool) and the fitting's ribbed spigot inserted; dedicated pliers, *pince à glissement*, are used to draw the collar over the pipe and spigot to form a watertight seal. Buying a set of tools for this system is well worth it if you're installing an entire plumbing system.
• Crimp connectors (*raccord à sertir*). Brass crimp connectors comprise a joint with a collar that is fitted onto the end of the pipe, which is then crimped tight using special pliers, *pince à sertir*.

> **BENDY BENEFIT**
> The joy of using plastic pipe for water and heating supplies is that it can generally be run around the house to fittings, radiators and so on with very few joints required: changes of direction are usually negotiated simply by bending the pipe around a former. Fewer joints mean a reduced risk of leaks.

Tube multicouche

Also for internal water and central heating supplies, *tube multicouche* comprises an inner and outer layer of cross-linked polyethylene sandwiching a thin central layer of aluminium flanked by two adhesive layers. The inner polyethylene layer is oxygen-impermeable, which prevents the ingress of air into the system, reducing the effect of corrosion on metal components. Because of its low thermal conductivity, when carrying hot water, multicouche pipe is cooler and therefore safer to touch; it also reduces the noise that can be associated with metal pipe.

It's flexible and easy to assemble using one of three methods:
• Compression fittings (*raccord à compression*). Brass compression joints are the same as used in the UK, incorporating a copper olive and screw-threaded nut that is tightened with a spanner.
• Push-fit fittings (*raccord automatique*). Brass push-fit joints incorporate a toothed washer that grips the pipe when inserted in the joint and the integral nut is tightened.
• Crimp connectors (*raccord à sertir*), as used for PER pipe.

Multicouche pipework does not need to be protected from UV, so the pipe can be fixed on skirtings, walls and other surfaces within the house, although it is also available pre-installed in ribbed plastic conduit (*gaine*), where it will be concealed within partition walls and beneath floors.

Available in 16, 20 and 26mm diameters (external), multicouche pipe comes in 1.5, 2, 2.5 and 3m lengths, in 10 or 25m coils, or pre-installed in *gaine* in 25 or 50m coils.

Electricity supply
Fourniture d'électricité

Electricity in France is supplied by EDF (*Électricité de France*), who provide a meter, fuses and main current-operated circuit breaker (*disjoncteur différentiel*). This remains the property of EDF and is sealed to prevent tampering (for which there is a fine). The consumer only has access to the outgoing terminals of the circuit breaker. EDF's circuit breaker has a sensitivity of 500 or 650ma, which is rated to suit your chosen tariff, and protects against faults on the inside and exterior of the property (but does not protect against earth faults: an additional 30 amp device will be needed at the consumer unit for this purpose).

> **VOLTAGE DROP**
> Electrical supplies in France, particularly those in rural areas, are apt to annoyingly fluctuate during the day, which can cause computers and other equipment that uses microprocessors to fail. It's essential that you fit surge protectors to such sensitive equipment to avoid problems associated with a sudden drop in voltage.

The standard domestic supply in France, for new builds and rewires, is single phase (*monophasé*) 230 volts (50Hz). It's not unusual to find three phase (*triphasé*) 380v supplies in larger or older properties, particularly farms or buildings with industrial use (see right).

The householder is able to stipulate the kilowattage of electricity supply required –

Vive La Différence!

from 3kVA to 36kVA, depending on the tariff they choose. (A kVA is simply 1,000 volt amps.) A single phase 9kVA (45 amp) supply is adequate for a modern two- to three-bedroom house. If you have full electric central heating, however, you'd need 12kVA (60 amps).

French houses are wired using a spur system, rather than the loop (ring main) that we use in the UK. A series of spurs run from a distribution box feeds sockets and fittings, although appliances such as washing machines, hot water tanks and dishwashers must have their own dedicated spur. Circuit breakers must be incorporated into the circuits to protect against power surges and faults.

> **FAZED BY PHASES?**
> Three-phase basically means that there are three live terminals and one neutral at EDF's meter. This would entail a higher standing charge for your electricity because each phase supplies 5kVA (i.e. 15kVA, or 25A). The current must be balanced on each phase to avoid overloading one phase and causing the system to continually trip. If you don't think you will need this rather beefy electrical set-up, speak to EDF: they operate an English-speaking helpline for each of their regions. Check out their website for details: www.edf.fr

The property must be properly connected to earth, but, unlike in the UK, the French authority does not provide this connection, which is the responsibility of the consumer. The usual connection is via an earth rod buried in the garden. All gas and water pipes must also be earthed using 2.5mm, 4mm or 6mm insulated cable. Exposed metal surfaces or equipment, particularly in kitchens and bathrooms, must also be bonded to avoid the risk of electric shock. Earth rods, pipe clamps and earthing plates can be obtained from electrical suppliers.

If your property has no electricity supply, you'll need to apply to EDF, or to be precise ERDF (*Électricité Réseau Distribution France*, the electricity supply distributor of EDF), for a *demande de raccordement*. If you're involved in renovating an old property, or transforming a barn into a house, for example, you can arrange

Vive La Différence!

for a temporary 'builder's supply' to be provided by EDF. This *alimentation de chantier* will be taken from the nearest electrical pylon. The householder is responsible for purchasing a meter box (*coffret de chantier*), obtainable from a builder's merchant. This type of supply is really only intended for a maximum of six months, but in reality the authority tend to allow a longer extension.

Electric cable & flex
Power and lighting cable and appliance flex in the UK comes with wire cores pre-installed in a protective PCV sheath, while in France cores are traditionally sold separately, intended for installation in ridged plastic conduit called *gaine*.

Available in-store by the metre on reels, or pre-packed in specified lengths, look for *fil de phase* (live); *fil de terre* (earth); or *fil de neutre* (neutral), encased in red, blue, and green/yellow striped PVC sheathing respectively. Other colour coded sheathing is also available for specific electrical circuitry. Individual cores are either *rigide* (rigid, as with UK cable) or *souple* (flexible, as with UK flex).

With some stockists, such as Castorama, the same sheathed flexible cores are described as *câble souple unifilaire*. More familiar to UK buyers, Castorama also sell PVC-sheathed flex and cable, with various combinations of two, three, four or more cores, colour-coded in PVC sheathing.

Apart from cores and conduit sold separately, you'll also find reels of conduit with pre-installed cables or cores, called *gaine pré-câblée* or *pré-filée* respectively. Conduits without cores or cables often come with a pre-installed pull-through to assist with fitting the wires. While *gaine* is intended to be concealed from view within floor voids, roof spaces and walls, surface-mounted conduit is, in France, called *moulure*, or mouldings.

> **PLUG FUSES**
> Fused plugs are not used in France, and this means that whatever is connected into an electrical socket outlet, is only protected at the consumer unit (unless there's a sub fuse within the appliance or power outlet).

Sanitation
Assainissement

Most urban properties in France are connected to mains drainage, but the majority of rural and village properties are not. Waste water and sewage from the kitchen, bathroom and toilet are dealt with on site by the *fosse septique*. Modern septic tank systems, *fosses septiques toutes eaux*, are designed to accept all wastewater and sewage from the household.

The system consists of a tank cast from concrete or moulded from tough polymer, buried in the ground about seven metres from the house. The volume of the tank is calculated according to the number of main rooms of the household: as a guide, allow 1000 litres per bedroom, with a minimum tank volume of 3000 litres.

Most tanks contain two linked chambers. The first chamber is the main holding vessel for the waste material. The second chamber takes the waste from the first, acting as a baffle to prevent solids from being washed into the outlet pipe. Waste material (influent), enters the tank through a pipe in the side wall, 1.1m from its base. Inside the chamber, it separates and the lighter solids – grease, fat and oil – rise to the surface, forming a floating crust of 'suspended solids'.

The heavier solids settle at the base as thick 'sludge', while water circulates between the layers. The sludge is digested by anaerobic bacteria (micro-organisms that don't need oxygen to live), while the suspended solids are digested by aerobic bacteria (that need oxygen to live). These are transformed into water, and methane and carbon dioxide gases. The gases are vented from the tank above the house roofline.

The waste is stored in the tank for about three days, during which about 30% of pollutants is removed. When the tank is full of liquid, fresh influent enters the inlet, driving out by displacement the remaining 70%, still containing germs and pathogens. This effluent enters a pipe positioned 1m from the base of the tank and, passing into a soakaway – a gravel-filled trench or pit – is purified and percolated to earth. The design of the soakaway depends on the number and function of the main rooms of the house, on the

Vive La Différence!

permeability of the soil, the maximum water table, and the slope of the land. There are three main types of soakaway:
- *Epandage*, for free draining soil, consists of gravel-filled drainage trenches.
- *Filtre à sable vertical non-drainé*, for free draining soil where there is no space for the *épandage*, comprises a sand filter, without the use of drain pipes.
- *Filtre à sable drainé*, for poorly draining soil, or where there's a well or water source nearby, is constructed from a sand filter that includes drain pipes.

If space is limited, and the septic tank must be positioned 10m or more from the house, you might be obliged to install a separate grease trap (*bac dègraisser*) to accept the waste from the kitchen and/or the bathroom.

It's necessary to apply for permission to install a septic tank, with a *demande d'installation d'un dispositif d'assainissement non-collectif* obtained from the Mairie responsible for your commune. Before the form can be completed, the property must be surveyed by a specialist contractor.

Plasterboarding
Plaque de plâtre

You would be forgiven for assuming that plasterboard is the same the world over, but not so. While standard sheets in the UK measure 2440 x 1200mm and 12.5mm thick, their French counterparts measure 2500 x 1200mm x 13mm thick. A small difference, although, in the grand scheme of things, this is largely irrelevant – the width of the panel is the most important measurement to be aware of, when you're setting out the centres for a stud partition wall, for example.

> **PLACOPLÂTRE**
> Plasterboard is widely known in France by this name, although Placoplâtre (commonly shortened to 'Placo') is actually the trade name of the French company Saint-Gobain for their extensive range of plaques de plâtre.

Roughcast/render
Crépi & enduit

Almost ubiquitous in France is *crépi*, the roughcast coating applied to exterior walls as both protection and decoration. It's applied by flinging or smearing it onto the wall with a trowel, or by using a hand-operated projector (or 'flicker gun'), the *machine à crépir*, or a pneumatic version with a pistol applicator. The finish can then be smoothed off with a trowel, left rough and rustic, or patterned by dabbing with a sponge, streaking with a brush, or using a textured roller. *Crépi* comes in a range of earthy (sometimes a trifle garish) tones, although, being acrylic, it can have a somewhat shiny polymer finish (although this does weather in time).

> **SAUSAGE FLICKER**
> Some French folk call the *crépi* projector a *crépinette*, but this is also the name for a small, flattened sausage made from minced or ground pork, turkey, veal, lamb or chicken and wrapped in caul fat. *Crépinette* originates from the word *crépine*, meaning 'pig's caul'. Although the *machine à crépir pneumatique* does resemble an old fashioned meat mincer, I'm sure this is coincidental.

Similar to *crépi*, and more natural-looking, is *enduit tyrolien* a cement-based material familiar in the UK as 'Tyrolean finish'. Reputedly based on alpine building methods, and intended to impart an attractive 'aged' finish, this Austrian import is applied to the wall by the same type of projector as *crépi*, and can be textured or patterned in a similar fashion.

There's also an interior version of *crépi*, which older readers may recognise as being scarily similar to Artex. This product was used with abandon in the UK during the 1970s to apply stippled and swirled patterns to cracked ceilings, and also to walls (where its rough finish could result in a nasty graze to unwary flesh). Artex proved to be a devil to remove and, up until the 1980s, was made with white asbestos to strengthen it (although harmless if left alone coated with emulsion). Since 2005, Artex has been owned by France's Saint-Gobain group.

Happily, tins of interior grade *crépi* typically bear the joyous word *décollable*, which means 'strippable', should you tire of the effect.

Vive La Différence!

Bricks
Briques

Mass-produced bricks, both in the UK and in France, are manufactured in numerous classes, types, materials, and sizes that vary with regions of the respective countries and the time period when they were first introduced. It's this and the resultant diversity of colours and textures that typify the character of specific regions.

Bricks are made either by extrusion (a long clay column is created and then cut into individual brick units), or by soft mud moulding (bricks are formed in mould boxes, by hand, by craftsmen producing one brick at a time, or by automation where large numbers of bricks can be produced at one time). Extruded bricks are typically perforated, and may be solid, but without frogs (the indentation in one or more bed surfaces). Moulded UK bricks are typically made with frogs, although some can be solid.

The bricks are then dried to reduce moisture, preventing them from bursting when they are fired. During firing, clay particles and impurities are fused together, producing a hard, weatherproof material. Unfired bricks are not weatherproof and are generally used for internal walls. In the UK, a modern stock facing brick measures 215 x 102.5 x 65mm (about 8⅝ x 4⅛ x 2⅝in.), which, with a nominal 10mm (⅜in.) mortar joint, forms a unit size of 225 x 112.5 x 75mm (9 x 4½ x 3in.).

Some stockists offer 50 or 73mm deep versions, but this is rare. French facing, or *façade*, bricks offer much greater variety. You may find a size that matches the UK standard, but also, widely available from stockists such as Leroy Merlin, Bricomarché, Mr. Bricolage and Castorama, come these impressive options:

> **ROLL A JOINT**
> A nifty gadget for producing perfectly formed mortar joints on terracotta bricks is the *rouleau applicateur pour joints minces* (roller applicator for thin joints). It comprises a handled tray with a roller at one end: the tray is filled with mortar and, as it is drawn along the top of the wall, feeds a thin bed of mortar under the roller and onto the masonry.

Vive La Différence!

- 210 x 100 x 50mm
- 210 x 100 x 65mm
- 215 x 100 x 65mm
- 215 x 102 x 65mm
- 220 x 105 x 54mm
- 220 x 105 x 60mm
- 220 x 105 x 65mm
- 220 x 220 x 65mm
- 495 x 100 x 38mm

Although French bricks do not incorporate the frog, they are invariably pierced with 10–12 holes.

A type of brick that you're unlikely to find in the UK is the hollow terracotta type, which is widely used in France. Some types are used for non-loadbearing interior partition walls (*brique de cloison*), while there are also versions that can be used to construct exterior structural walls (*brique terre cuite*). These large format bricks provide improved sound and thermal insulation. They're ridged on both sides to take a plaster or render coat, or can be clad in some other way.

Sizes of bricks for partitions range from around 250mm long x 60mm wide x 150mm high to about 500mm long x 115mm wide x 299mm high.

The structural type of brick is laid with mortar joints in the same way as conventional bricks. Common sizes include (L x W x H):

- 248 x 300 x 249
- 500 x 150 x 299
- 500 x 200 x 249
- 500 x 250 x 249
- 500 x 270 x 200

> **CLAMPING PEG**
> Another personal favourite, widely used by French brickies, but not used widely in the UK, at least by do-it-yourselfers, is a nifty clamping device, the *chevillette*. It's similar to a Dutch pin, or mason's clamp. Comprising a long metal chisel-shaped peg, with an adjustable clamp, it's hammered into a mortar joint, or the wall or floor alongside the workpiece, and the clamp slid into place and wedged on the shank to securely hold formwork or other temporary fixings in place, for example while concrete is curing.

Blocks
Blocs

The grey aerated concrete block – or breezeblock – familiar to us Brits, is also available in France, albeit in different sizes. Whereas the standard British version measures 440 x 215 x 100mm, the French equivalent measures 500 x 200 x 50mm.

French concrete blocks are also available hollow, in numerous sizes, such as:

- 500 x 200 x 150mm
- 500 x 200 x 200mm
- 500 x 250 x 250mm

A special shape block, the *parpaing d'angle* (pilaster block) is pierced with a circular hole to take a metal reinforcing rod; the *parpaing de chaînage* (reinforcing block) incorporates a channel to take reinforcement rods.

Another type of block commonly used in France as an infill for metal-framed interior partition walls is the *carreau de plâtre* (plaster tile). Measuring 660 x 500 x 50mm or 70mm, the blocks are solid or hollow, and may incorporate tongued-and-grooved side joints. Blocks for general use are white, while *hydrofugés* types are waterproof and suitable for using in bathrooms or steamy kitchens and utility rooms.

Sand, gravel & materials in bulk
Sable, gravier et matériaux en vrac

Sand and gravel are available pre-packed in various size bags, which is ideal for smaller jobs, but costly in the long run. Some suppliers will even sell sand by the spade full, tossed directly into a hatchback or car boot (line it first with polythene!), but beware of overloading the vehicle's suspension. Cement, plaster, and pre-mixed mortar, come in 35kg paper sacks, as in the UK.

For larger jobs, and where you have storage space, it's best to buy in bulk. All the major builder's merchants sell various grades of sand (*sable*) loose, and sand mixed with gravel for concrete (*gravier à béton*), and will deliver at a cost charged by mileage and weight.

Many people invest in a trailer (*remorque*) and collect the materials from the builder's merchant or local quarry; the trailer will pay for itself over the duration of a renovation and gives you the independence to get things when you need them. The materials are literally dumped in the trailer by a loader, and you must be careful not to overload it – and bear in mind you'll need to shovel it out on site!

> **LE BIG BAG**
> Sand and aggregate, and soil for the garden, is also available in the rather stuffily entitled Flexible Intermediate Bulk Containers (FIBCs), more commonly known as 'big bags'. FIBCs are made of thick woven polyethylene or polypropylene, and measure around 110cm in diameter and from 100–200cm high. Capacity is typically around 1000–1500kg. The bag has two or four loops at the top, used to hoick the container onto a pallet or into a trailer using a fork lift truck or loader. Some bags incorporate a spout at the base for discharge, although you can simply slice the disposable bag open and spill its contents onto the ground.

Vive La Différence!

Timber
Bois

Planed and rough-sawn timber comes in a wide range of sizes, as it does in the UK, but the two do not relate. If you're looking for a length of good old 'two by one' (or 50 x 25mm in metric), you won't find one. The nearest French equivalent would be 40 x 20mm. As for the trusty 'four by two' (100 x 50mm), your nearest match would be 95 x 45mm, a disparity of 5mm.

Your best option, at the end of the day, is just to forget the familiar British sizes and think French from the start.

As a guide, the chart (right) lists most commonly available sizes of French timber, gleaned from the big DIY retailers' and builder's merchants' catalogues (although I don't claim that it's exhaustive; you'll most likely find other variations). Most of the sizes shown come in a range of lengths, typically 3, 4, 5 and 6m.

When buying from the big sheds, you might be tempted by the apparent convenience of blister-wrapped packs of boards, but it's a costly way to create a floor or wall panelling. You may also see special offers of *déclassé* (downgraded) packs, but remember that they're dirt cheap precisely because they're likely to be split, oozing sticky resin, or overly knotty (and the knots are likely to pop out, leaving a sizeable hole you could easily poke your thumb into).

> **TIMBER SOURCE**
> While you can buy timber from timber merchants and large DIY stores, you can also purchase direct from the sawmill (*scierie*). Bear in mind that they may quote by volume rather than by lengths. There are also many specialist companies offering green oak, air- and kiln-dried oak and exotic wood. You can buy beams, sleepers and boules (logs sawn through and kept together).

Vive La Différence!

STANDARD TIMBER SIZES (mm)

mm	27	32	38	40	55	60	63	70	75	80	95	100	105	120	145	150	155	160	175	190	195	200	225
14	×												×										
15				×																		×	
18				×																			
20																							
21				×																×			
22																	×				×		
25	×															×						×	
27	×		×													×		×				×	
32		×					×									×							
34					×													×					
38				×					×	×					×								
40						×			×	×					×	×							
45						×					×												
50									×	×									×				
60								×											×				
63												×											
75						×				×								×					
80														×									
100																							
120																							×
200																						×	

ENGLISH
FRENCH

BUILDING
MAÇONNERIE

Building

Additives/treatments for mortar & concrete

Additifs/traitements pour mortier & béton

additive additif *m;* adjuvant *m*
additive, concrete anti-freeze adjuvant *m* pour bétonnage par temps froid
additive, mortar and concrete adjuvant *m* des mortiers
  ~ **cold temperature accelerator** adjuvant *m* accélérateur antigel
  ~ **plasticiser** adjuvant *m* plastifiant
additive, mortar and concrete reinforcing adjuvant *m* fibres synthétiques
additive, mortar and concrete water repellent adjuvant *m* hydrofuge
agent agent *m*
agent, concrete air entraining agent *m* entraîneur d'air
agent, concrete mould release décoffrant *m* démoulage
agent, setting fixateur *m*
agent, shuttering release agent *m* décoffrage décoffre
anti-moss masonry treatment, colourless traitement *m* incolore antimousse
bitumen bitume *m*
bituminous liquid revêtement *m* bitumineux
colourant colorant *m*

colourant, concrete and mortar colorant *m* béton et mortier
colourant, iron oxide colorant oxyde de fer
colourant, powder colorant *m* en poudre
concrete béton *m*
concrete repairer/restorer réparation *f* béton
concrete retarder retardateur *m* de prise pour béton
concrete set accelerator accélérateur *m* rapid
concrete surface hardener durcisseur *m* de surface fixateur
exterior masonry treatment traitement *m* façades, murs extérieurs
liquid waterproofer hydrofuge *m* liquide
pigment pigment *m*
pigment, natural pigment *m* naturelle
  ~ **sienna** ~ terre de sienne
  ~ **umber** ~ terre d'ombre
  ~ **yellow ochre** ~ ocre jaune
plasticiser plastifiant *m*
resin résine *f*
resin, latex-based résine *f* à base de latex
resin, protection/reinforcement of concrete slab résine *f* traitement liquide incolore à base de resins
resin binder résine *f* d'adjonction
waterproofing treatment
  ~ **for bases, colourless** imprégnation *f* incolore, pavés

Building

et dalles béton
~ **for cellars** traitement *m* caves et sous-sols/revêtement *m* d'imperméabilisation pour travaux de cuvelages
~ **for floors** traitement *m* sols
~ **for masonry, colourless** traitement *m* incolore d'imperméabilisant

Wood treatments
Traitements du bois

treatment, anti-termites traitement *m* anti-termites
treatment, insect, fungal attack and termites traitement *m* multi-usages: insecticide, fongicide et anti-termites
treatment, interior wood traitement *m* bois intérieurs
treatment, termites and woodboring beetles traitement *m* contre termites, vrillettes et capricornes
treatment, timber beams and frames traitement *m* poutre et charpente

Bricks & blocks
Briques & blocs

block bloc *m*
block, cellular terracotta insulating bloc *m* auto-isolante en terre cuite
block, concrete bloc *m* béton
~ **cellular insulating** ~ cellulaire
~ **hollow** creux en béton
block, foundation massif *m* de fondation
block, lintel bloc *m* linteau
block, perforated bloc *m* perforé
block, solid aggregate bloc *m* de granulats
block, solid concrete bloc *m* en béton
breezeblock bloc *m*; parpaing *m*
breezeblock, alleviated bloc *m* allégé
breezeblock, full size parpaing *m* plein
breezeblock, hollow parpaing *m* creux à bancher
breezeblock, pilaster, with hole for reinforcing rod parpaing *m* d'angle
breezeblock, reinforcing, with channel to take reinforcing rods parpaing *m* de chaînage
brick brique *f*
brick, arch brique *f* à couteau
brick, burnt brique *f* flammée
brick, engineering (no French equivalent)
brick, facing brique *f* de façade
brick, full size brique *f* pleine

Building

brick, glass brique f de verre
brick, hollow terracotta brique f creuse de terre cuite
brick, insulating brique f isolant
brick, paving brique f de pavage; carrelage m en briques
brick, perforated brique f perforée
brick, standard brique f de type courant
brick, terracotta brique f de terre cuite
brick, ventilation brique f de ventilation
concrete walling block, decorative muret m béton décoratif
facing brick/block plaquette f de parement
half-brick demi-brique f
half-width brick mulot m
pillar, walling pilier m
plaster tile/block carreau m de plâtre (for use in metal-framed partition walls)
  ~ **hollow** ~ creux
  ~ **honeycomb** ~ alvéolé
  ~ **solid** ~ plein
  ~ **waterproofed** ~ hydrofugé
reconstituted stone walling block muret m pierre reconstituée

Masonry & aggregates
Maçonnerie & granulats

aggregate/s agrégat/s m
aggregate, expanded clay agrégat m d'argile expansée
aggregates, decorative, in bulk agrégats m décoratifs en vrac
aggregate, polystyrene agrégat m polystyrène adjuvanté
ballast blocaille f; granulat m
building stone moellon m
cement ciment m
cement, all-purpose ciment m multi-usages
cement, dry-mixed ciment m prêt a l'emploi
cement, extra-white ciment m super blanc
cement, grey ciment m gris
cement, heat-resistant ciment m fondu
cement, high-performance ciment m haute performance
cement, masonry ciment m à maçonner
cement, quick-setting ciment m bâti prompt
cement, special-purpose ciment m spécial
cement, sulphate-resisting ciment m milieux agressifs
cement, tile-joint ciment m joint
cement, white ciment m blanc
concrete béton m
concrete, lightweight béton m allégé libre

Building

concrete, rapid-setting béton *m* à prise rapide
gravel gravier *m;* gravillon *m*
gravel, fine non-rolled gravier *m* mignonnette non-roulée
gravel, in bulk gravier *m* en vrac
gravel, rolled gravier *m* roulé
lime chaux *f*
lime, coloured chaux *f* colorée/teintée
lime, grey chaux *f* grise
lime, hydrated/slaked chaux *f* aérienne
lime, hydraulic chaux *f* hydraulique
lime, naturally formulated chaux *f* naturelle formulée
lime, natural white chaux *f* blanche naturelle
lime, St Astier chaux *f* de Saint Astier
lime, white chaux *f* blanc
marble marbre *m*
mortar; grout mortier *m*
mortar, coloured mortier *m* coloré
   ~ **brick red** ~ rouge brique
   ~ **dark beige** ~ beige foncé
   ~ **dark grey** ~ gris profond
   ~ **pink amber** ~ rose ambre
   ~ **white** ~ fin blanc
mortar, dry-mixed mortier *m* prêt à l'emploi
mortar, finishing and smoothing mortier *m* de ragréage et de lissage
mortar, grey mortier *m* gris
   ~ **ready-mixed pointing** ~ prêt mix jointoiement gris
mortar, heat-resistant/refractory mortier *m* réfractaire
mortar, lime; cement/lime mix mortier *m* bâtard
mortar, limestone mortier *m* pierre calcaire
mortar, pointing mortier *m* de jointoiement
mortar, quick-setting mortier *m* à prise rapide
mortar, repair mortier *m* de réparation
mortar, waterproofing mortier *m* d'imperméabilisation
pebbledash cailloutage *m*
rendering enduit *m*
rendering/roughcasting crépi *m;* crépissage *m*
sand sable *m*
sand, concreting sable *m* de mélange béton
sand, in bulk sable *m* en vrac
sand, masonry sable *m* à maçonner
sand, river sable *m* de rivière
sand, sharp sable *m* liant/mordant
sand, silver sable *m* argenté
sand, soft sable *m* doux
Tyrolean finish (spray-on render, using pneumatic or hand-operated projector) enduit *m* tyrolien

Building

Paving
Pavage

concrete decking lame *f* de terrasse en béton
edging bordurette *f*
edging block rive *f*
edging block, aged effect in concrete rive *f* vieilli en béton
'field' slab with moulded design (smaller slabs; separate pieces; woven effect) trame *f*
flagstone; cobblestone pavé *m*
interlocking concrete paver pavé *m* autobloquant en béton
paving, marble dallage *f* marbre
paving, rubber dalle *f* amortissante
paving, stone dalle *f* en pierre
  ~ **natural** ~ naturelle
  ~ **reconstituted** ~ reconstitutuée
paving block bloc *m*
paving block, aged effect in concrete bloc *m* vieilli en béton
paving sets, varying sizes/shapes (e.g. crazy paving) dallage *f* multi-formats
paving slab dalle *f;* dallage *f*
paving slab, brick pattern dalle *f* aspect brique de pavage
paving slab, clip-together system dalle *f* clipsable
paving slab, concrete dalle *f* en béton
  ~ **gravel surface** ~ aspect de surface: gravillonné
paving slab, grass-reinforcing, in polyethylene dalle *f* gazon en polyéthylène
paving slab, gravel-faced dalle *f* gravillons
paving slab, grit finish dalle *f* grainaillée
paving slab, slate dalle *f* en ardoise
pebble frieze frise *f* galet
slab, small dallette *f* pierre
slab, turf dalle *f* à engazonner
slab path unit dalle *f* de cheminement en béton
stepping stone, Japanese style pas *m* japonais
stone pebble galet *m* de pierre naturelle
tiling carrelage *m*
tiling, exterior carrelage *m* exérieur
tiling, stoneware carrelage *m* grès cérame émaillé
tiling, terrace/patio carrelage *m* terrasse

Plastering & filling
Plâtrage & de remplissage

angle bead bourrelet *m* d'étanchéité; éclisse *f* cornière; baguette *f* d'angle
expanding polyurethane foam filler mousse *f* expansive polyuréthane
filler; coating; rendering enduit *m*
filler, fine joint enduit *m* poudre de collage et finition

Building

filler, fine-surface enduit *m* de lissage
filler, finishing enduit *m* de finition
filler, high quality enduit *m* surfin
filler, joint enduit *m* à joint
  ~ **ready to use** ~ prêt à l'emploi
  ~ **slow-drying** ~ prise lente
filler, quick-setting enduit *m* à prise rapide
  ~ **powder form** ~ poudre à prise rapide
filler, repair enduit *m* de rebouchage
filler, waterproof enduit *m* d'étanchéité
gypsum gypse *m*
gypsum, fibre reinforced gypse *m* renforcé fibre
mortar; grout mortier *m*
putty pâte/mastic *m*
plaster plâtre *m*
plaster, alleviated plâtre *m* allégé
plaster, backing plâtre *m* manuel gros
plaster, board finish no French equivalent
plaster, casting plâtre *m* prestia
plaster, fine white plâtre *m* fin blanc
plaster, fire-resistant plâtre *m* incendie
plaster, hand-mixing plâtre *m* manuel
plaster, moulding plâtre *m* à modeler
plaster, multi-finish; universal plâtre *m* multi-usage
plaster, projection plâtre *m* à projecter
plaster bead, galvanized aluminium protège *m* angle galvanisé
plaster of Paris plâtre *m* de Paris
plaster powder plâtre *m* en poudre
pumice plaster plâtre *m* ponce

Plasterboarding
Plaque de plâtre

gypsum board plaque de gypse *f*
jointing tape bande *f* à joint
jointing tape, corner bande *f* renfort d'angle
plasterboard plaque de plâtre *f*
plasterboard, acoustic plaque de plâtre *f* acoustique
plasterboard, cellular core plaque de plâtre *f* paroi alvéolaire; ~ cartonnée
plasterboard, firecheck plaque de plâtre *f* feu
plasterboard, fireproofed plaque de plâtre *f* ignifugée
plasterboard, flooring plaque de plâtre *f* de sol
plasterboard, high density plaque de plâtre *f* haute densité
plasterboard, high resistance plaque de plâtre *f* haute résistance (for timber framed buildings)

Building

plasterboard, insulating panneau *m* de doublage plaque de plâtre
plasterboard, waterproofed plaque de plâtre *f* hydrofugée

Partition walls & ceilings
Cloisons & plafonds

Frames
Ossatures

angle frame, galvanized steel cornière *f* d'angle métallique
ceiling rail, U-shaped profil *m* en U pour plafond
channel, metal, to hold plasterboard montant *m*
connector plate for frames raccord *m* eclisse
cork strip, resilient, to avoid cracks bande *f* résiliente en liège
door lining, profiled wooden elargisseur *f* de cloison pour bloc porte
frame armature *f* de cloison
frame bracket (to attach frame to support wall) cavalier *m*
furring strip, galvanized metal fourrure *f* métallique
furring strip connector connecteur *m* assemblage fourrure
jointing peg, wooden, for panels (cellular partition) clavette *f* bois

nosing nez *m* de cloison
nosing, round-edged, pine nez *m* sapin angles arrondis
rail rail *m*
rail, horizontal rail *m* horizontal
rail, top, wooden rail *m* haut en bois
rail, U-shaped channel rail *m* U
sill lisse *f* basse en bois
sole plate, chipboard semelle *f* bois (aggloméré)
suspension bracket (suspended ceiling) suspente *f*
~ **articulated** ~ articulée
trap door/hatch trappe *f* de visite
universal fastener (wall and ceiling rails) attache *f* universelle

Tools for assembly of partitions
Outils pour l'assemblage des cloisons

metal snips cisaille *f* à tôle universelle
nibblers, for cutting frame pieces grignoteuse *f*
plasterboard screws vis *f* plaque de plâtre
pliers pince *f*
pliers, crimping pince *f* à sertir
pliers, stapling pince *f* à agrafer (system Placostil)
telescopic prop etai *m* télescopique

Sheet materials
Matériaux en feuille

polystyrene polystyrène *m*
polystyrene, expanded
　polystyrène *m* expansé
polystyrene, extruded
　polystyrène *m* extrudé
　~ **groove-edged** ~ bord rainuré
　~ **square-edged** ~ bord droit
roof panel, corrugated plaque *f* ondulée

Beams & supports
Les poutres & les supports

beam poutre *f*; poutrelle *f*
beam, ceramic poutrelle *f* céramique
beam, prestressed concrete poutre *f* récontrainte; ~ béton
beam, prestressed concrete (to take ceramic flooring/ceiling blocks between) poutrelle *f* béton entrevous céramique
girder; RSJ (rolled steel joist) poutre *f* en fer; poutrelle *f*
hip rafter arêtier *m*
joist solive *f*
joist hangar sabot *f* de poutre
lath latte *f*; volige *f*
lintel linteau (*pl* -x) *m*
lintel, concrete prelinteau *m* précontraint
purlin panne *f*
purlin, eaves panne *f* sablière
purlin, ridge panne *f* faîtière
rafter chevron *m*
ridge bar longeron *f* de faîtage

Insulation, ventilation & damp-proofing
Isolation, la ventilation & l'imperméabilisation

air grille grille *f* d'aeration
aluminium foil reflective insulation mince alu *m* réfléchissant
damp-proof course couche *f* isolant
damp-proof membrane pare-vapeur *m*; ~ kraft; protection *f* soubassement
double glazing double vitrage *m*
extractor fan ventilateur *m* extracteur
flashing strip bande *f* de étanchéité
flashing strip; flaunching bande *f* de solin
flashing strip, self-adhesive tear-resistant bande *f* de étanchéité indéchirable autocollante
glass wool laine *f* de verre
glass wool roll rouleau *m* de laine de verre
hemp laine *f* de chanvre
insulating mastic (doors and windows) mastic *m* isolation portes-fenêtres

Building

insulating material isolant *m*
insulation film, exterior aluminium layer isolation *m* extérieur réflecteur alu
insulation, sound isolation *m* acoustique; ~ phonique
~ **for damp floors** ~ phonique pour sol humide
~ **soundproof membrane for floors** ~ phonique pour sols
insulation, thermal/heat isolation *m* thermique
insulation film, intermediate layer isolation *m* réflecteur intermédiaire
insulation film, tear-resistant reflective membrane isolation *m* armé réflecteurs résistants à la déchirure
insulation film (aluminium) with air bubble layer isolation *m* à bulle d'air sec
insulation roll, reflective, roof rouleau *m* multi réflecteur
radiator reflector foil plaque *m* isolante et réfléchissante
rockwool laine *f* de roche
rockwool, flakes in bulk flocons *f* de laine de roche, en vrac
rockwool, panel panneau *m* laine de roche
~ **unsurfaced panel** ~ non revêtue
rockwool, roll rouleau *m* laine de roche
suspension clip, insulation suspente *f* pour laine de verre

thermal/sound insulating tile dalle *f* isolante/phonique
underlay sous-couche *f*
underlay, cork insulating sous-couche *f* liège isol
~ **for fitted carpet** ~ moquette
~ **phonique** ~ soundproofing, floors
~ **for tiles** ~ carrelage
ventilation grille cour *f* anglaise
ventilator fan ventilateur *m*
ventilator fan, electric ventilateur *m* électrique
vermiculite vermiculite *f*
vermiculite, bitumen-coated vermiculite *f* enrobée de bitume
vermiculite, granulated vermiculite *f* granulé isolant

Adhesives
Adhésifs

adhesive colle *f*
adhesive, for insulating materials colle *f* matériaux d'isolation
adhesive, neoprene colle *f* néoprène
adhesive, plaster block colle *f* à carreau de plâtre
adhesive, tile ciment *m* colle
adhesive, waterproof colle *f* hydro

Building

Rainwater drainage
Evacuation des eaux pluviales

downpipe tuyau *m* de descente
drainage channel caniveau (*pl* -x) *m*
drainage channel, concrete caniveau *m* en béton
drainage channel, glass fibre reinforced caniveau *m* polyester renforcé de fibre de verre
gutter gouttière *f*
rainwater gully regard *m* de branchement pour eaux pluviales
waterspout gargouille *f*

Sanitation
Assainissement

cesspool fosse *f* d'aisances
drain *m* drain
drain clearing kit kit *m* de débouchage
drainage system système *m* de drainage
drainpipe tube *m* de assainissement; ~ de drainage
galvanized steel mesh grating grille *f* caillebotis en acier galvanisé
grease trap bac *m* dégraisseur
inspection chamber; manhole regard *m*; ~ de drainage; ~ d'assainissement; trappe *m* de visite
inspection chamber, concrete regard *m* béton
inspection chamber cover couvercle *m*; plaque *f* d'égout
land drainpipe drain *m* agricole; drain *m* routier
septic tank fosse *f* septique
septic tank, 'all water' fosse *f* septique 'toutes eaux'
sewage system systeme *m* du tout à l'égout
waste outlet system systeme *m* de vidange

Roofing
Toiture

pantile; roman tile tuile *f* canal
roof shingle bardeau (*pl* -x) *m*
roof shingle, bituminous felt bardeau *m* verrier bitumen
roof truss armature *f* à toit; ferme *f* de charpente
roof underfelt écran *m* de sous-toiture
roofing slate ardoise *f*
roofing slate, fibre cement ardoise *f* fibres-ciment
slate fixing hook crochet *m* ardoise
tile tuile *f*
tile, gutter tuile *f* creuse
tile, interlocking tuile *f* à emboîtement
tile, interlocking, large mould, shallow curve tuile *f* grande moule faiblement galbée

Building

tile, interlocking, ribbed tuile *f* à côtes
tile, interlocking roman (large mould, deep curve) tuile *f* grande moule fortement albée
tile, interlocking, shallow curved tuile *f* à onde douce
tile, interlocking, small mould, shallow curve tuile *f* petit moule faiblement galbée
tile, plain tuile *f* plate
tile, plain half-round tuile *f* romaine
tile, plain interlocking tuile *f* à emboîtement; ~ à pureau plate
tile, ridge tuile *f* faîtière
tile, transparent tuile *f* en verre transparente
tile, ventilator tuile *f* à chatière grillagée; ~ à douille
tile, verge tuile *f* de rive
tiling batten liteau *m* couverture

Tools & equipment
Outils & équipement

Hand tools
Outils à main

awl alêne *f*
axe hache *f*
bolt cutters coupe-boulons *f*
caulker couteau (*pl* -x) *f* à enduire
clamp agrafe *f*; bride *f*
clamp serre-joint *m*
clamp, formwork serre-joint *m* de cimentier
clamp, mason's serre-joint *m* de maçon
clamping peg chevillette *f*
file lime *f*
fork, digging fourche *f* bêche
laser level niveau *m* laser
mattock pioche *f* de cantonnier
pick pioche *f*
pick axe pioche *f* de terrassier; ~ hache *f*
plane rabot *m*
screwdriver tournevis *m*
shovel pelle *f*
shovel, round pelle *f* ronde
shovel, square pelle *f* carrée
spade bêche *f*
spirit level niveau *m* à bulle
staple gun agrafeuse *f*

Roofer's tools
Outils de couvreur

anvil, roofer's enclume *f* de couvrer
batten remover (and parquet floor lever) arrache *m* liteaux (et lames de parquet)
guillotine, batten guillotine *f* à liteaux
hammer marteau (*pl* -x) *m*
hammer, garnishing marteau *m* à garnier
hammer, roofer's marteau *m* de couvreur
lead beater batte *f* à plomb

Building

pliers, zinc-bending pince *f* à border
slate cutter guillotine *f* ardoise
slate cutting pliers pince *f* à ardoise
slate/sheet metal roofing punch poinçonneuse *f* ardoise et tôle
slater's ripper arrache-clou *m*

Saws & blades
Scies & lames

saw scie *f*
hacksaw scie *f* à métaux
hole saw scie-cloche *f*
saw blade lame *f* de scie

Trowels & floats
Truelles & taloches

brick jointer (flat/half-round) fer *m* à joint plat/demi-ronde
float platoir *m*
float, plasterer's taloche *f*
float, plastic taloche *f* plastique
float, polystyrene foam taloche *f* polystyrène
float, stainless steel platoir *m* inoxidable
float, wooden taloche *f* bois
hawk taloche *f*
trowel truelle *f*
trowel, bricklaying truelle *f* à brique; ~ briqueteuse
trowel, bucket (square edged) truelle *f* carrée; ~ italienne carrée
trowel, builder's truelle *f* à maçonner
trowel, cement; finishing; flooring platoir *m* à enduire
trowel, corner truelle *f* d'angle
trowel, notched platoir *m* denté
trowel, plaster mixing gâche *f*
trowel, pointing truelle *f* langue du chat (UK: pointed tip; French: rounded tip). Nearest UK equivalent: gauging trowel.
trowel, roofer's truelle *f* de couvreur
trowel, round tip truelle *f* italienne ronde
trowel, rounded tip truelle *f* ronde
trowel, smoothing truelle *f* de plâtrier à degrossir

Projectors of cement & thick coatings
Projecteurs de ciment & d'enduits épais

projector, roughcast/render machine *f* à crépir
projector, roughcast/render, pneumatic, with pistol machine *f* à crépir pneumatique avec pistolet
projector, Tyrolean finish machine *f* à crépir tyrolienne

Building

Measuring & marking
De mesure & de marquage

adjustable/sliding/combination bevel fausse équerre *f*; sauterelle *f*
builder's string cordeau *m* de maçon
measure mesure *f*
measure, laser télémètre *m* laser
measure, retractable tape mesure *f* roulante
plumbline fil *f* à plomb maçon
rule (darby) règle *f* de maçon
rule, folding mesure *f* pliante

Hammers & hatchets
Marteaux & hachettes

hammer marteau (*pl* -x) *m*
hammer, brick marteau *m* à briques
hammer, claw marteau *m* arrache-clou
hammer, club/lump marteau *m* de maçon; massette
hammer, garnishing marteau *m* à garnir
hammer, lath/drywall hachette *f* de plâtrier
hammer, packer's/claw marteau *m* de coffreur; ~ d'emballeur
hammer, roofer's marteau *m* de couvreur
hammer, sculptor's marteau *m* à boucharder (for dressing concrete, marble, granite)
hammer, small (e.g. **slater's**) martelette *f*
hatchet hatchette *f*
pick, small hand-held décintroir *m* à pic. Not widely available in UK
poleaxe merlin *m*
sledgehammer masse *f* couple

Masonry chisels
Ciseaux de maçon

chisel ciseau (*pl* -x) *m*
chisel, bolster ciseau *m* à brique; ~ à pierre
chisel, bull point broche *f*; pointerolle *f* de maçon
chisel, chasing chasse *f* à pierre
chisel, cold burin *m*; ~ de maçon
  ~ **flat blade** ~ plat
  ~ **pointed** ~ pointu
chisel, masonry broche *f*; pointerolle *f*
chisel, plaster-cutting ciseau *m* à rainurer
chisel, plugging no French equivalent
chisel, stone ciseau *m* à pierre
chisel, tiler's brochette *f* de carreleur
mushroom hand shield/grip for chisel pare coupe *f*; poignée *f* pare-coup; riflard *m* de maçon

Building

Crowbars
Pieds de biches

box/crate opener ouvre-caisse *f* plat
claw bar pince *f* à talon
crowbar pied-de-biche *m*
formwork prise pince *f* à décoffrer
pliers pince *f*
pry bar griffe *f* à cintrer
pry bar, straight barre *f* à mine

Equipment, powered
Équipement motorisé

air compressor compresseur *m* d'air
cement mixer bétonneuse *f*; bétonnière *f*
generator groupe électrogène *m*
high pressure cleaner nettoyeur *m* haute pression
material lift monte-matériaux *f*
mixer (paste, plaster, mortar) malaxeur *m*
plate compactor plaque *m* vibrante
sandblaster sableuse *f*
vacuum cleaner, water and dust aspirateur *m*, eau et poussières

Power tools & accessories
Outils électriques & accessoires

Drills & screwdrivers
Perceuses & visseuses

drill perceuse *f*
drill, demolition hammer démolisseur *m*; piqueur *m*
drill, hammer perforateur *m*
drill, percussion, corded perceuse *f* à percussion filaire
drill, percussion, cordless perceuse *f* à percussion sans fil
drill, pneumatic hammer perforateur *m* électropneumatique
drill, screwdriver visseuse *f*
screwdriver, electric visseuse *f*

Drill bits
Forets/mèches

drill bit foret *m*; mèche *f*
drill bit, auger mèche *f* à spiral unique
drill bit, expansive wood mèche *f* à bois extensible
drill bit, flat wood mèche *f* à bois plate
drill bit, glass/ceramic/porcelain mèche *f* ~ à ogive; ~ carbure; ~ de tungstene

Building

drill bit, twist mèche *f* hélicoïdal
drill bit, masonry foret *m* à beton
drill bit, metal foret *m* à métaux
drill bit, wood mèche *f* à bois
drill bits, set coffret *m* de forets/
 mèches

Files & grinders
Limes & meuleuses

angle grinder meuleuse *f*
 électrique d'angle
filer, electric lime *f* électrique
grinder meuleuse *f* électrique

Saws
Scies

bandsaw scie *f* à ruban
chainsaw tronçonneuse *f*
jigsaw scie *f* sauteuse
saw scie *f*
saw, circular scie *f* circulaire
saw, sabre scie *f* sabre

Planes & routers
Rabots & defonceuses

plane rabot *m*
router défonceuse *f*
wall chaser attachment
 rainureuse *f*

Sanders
Ponceuses

sander ponceuse *f*
sander, belt ponceuse *f* à bande
sander, delta ponceuse *f* delta
sander, disc ponceuse *f*
 excentrique
sander, orbital ponceuse *f*
 vibrantes

Scaffolding, ladders & steps
Échafaudage, échelles & escabeaux

ladder échelle *m*
scaffold board planche *f* de
 échafaudage
scaffolding échafaudage *m*
step/hop-up marchepied *m*
stepladder escabeau (*pl* -x) *m*
support prop (Acrow) étai *m*
support prop, adjustable étai *m*
 reglable *m*
trestle trétau *m*

Building

Equipment & accessories
Équipement & accessoires

broom balai *m*
bucket seau (*pl* -x) *m*
bucket, builder's seau *m* de maçon
log-splitting wedge coin *m*
mixing attachment (for drill) malaxeur *m* portif
mixing trough auge *f*
motorised hoist palin *m* électrique
sieve tamis *m*
tarpaulin bâche *m*
toolbelt ceinture *f* porte-outils
toolbox boîte *f* à outils; porte-outils *m*
rubble chute, reinforced polypropylene goulotte *f* à gravats en polypropylène renforcée
skip benne *f*
skip, tilting, two-wheeled conteneur *m* deux roues à basculement
slab lifter pose-dalle *f*
wheelbarrow brouette *f*
workbench établi *m*

Manual construction equipment
Matériel chantier manuel

chain hoist palin *m* à chain
FIBC (Flexible Intermediate Bulk Container) for bulk delivery of flowable products (sand, gravel etc) 'big bag' *m*
formwork coffrage *m*
hopper (for rubble shoot) trémie *f* de chargement
lever winch treuil *m* à levier
plasterboard lifter lève *f* plaque de plâtre
rubbish bin, plastic poubelle *f* plastique

Appendix

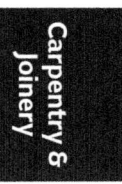

CARPENTRY & JOINERY
MENUISERIE

Carpentry tools
Outils de menuiserie

Carpenter's hammers
Marteaux de charpentier

hammer marteau *m*
hammer, carpenter's hachette *f* de charpentier; marteau *m* à menuisier
hammer, claw marteau *m* arrache-clou; ~ de coffreur
hammer, packer's marteau *m* d'emballeur
mallet maillet *m*
mallet, cabinet maker's maillet *m* d'ébéniste (round head)
mallet, woodwork maillet *m* de menuisier (square head)

Wood chisels & gouges
Ciseaux à bois & gouges

adze herminette *f*
axe hache *f*
chisel ciseau (*pl* -x) *m*
chisel, bevel-edged ciseau *m* de menuisier; ~ de sculpteur
chisel, firmer ciseau *m* de charpentier
chisel, mortise bédane *m* de menuisier; bédane *m* (woodturning)
chisel, parting ciseau *m* à grain d'orge (woodturning)
chisel, straight-edged ciseau *m* droit (woodturning)
chisel, wood ciseau *m* à bois
gouge gouge *f* (woodturning)
gouge, bowl gouge *f* à creuser (woodturning)
gouge, roughing-out gouge *f* à dégrossir (woodturning)
gouge, spindle gouge *f* à profiler (woodturning)
scraper ciseau *m* à racler arrondis (woodturning)

Measuring & marking
Mesure & traçage

adjustable/sliding/combination bevel fausse équerre *f*
auger vrille *f* (for pilot holes)
bradawl/gimlet tarière *f* à gouge
caliper gauge compas *m* d'épaisseur (woodturning)
marking/mortise gauge trusquin *m*; troussequin *m*
rule règle *f*
rule, flexible steel réglet *f* inox flexible
rule, folding mètre *m* pliant

Clamps
Serre-jointes

clamp serre-joint *m*; presse *m*; pince *f*
clamp, bar/speed serre-joint *m* automatique

Carpentry & Joinery

clamp, F-type gripper serre-joint *m* à pompe; serre-joint *m*; presse *m* mâchoire
clamp, G presse *f* de mécanicien
clamp, handy pince *f* de serrage
clamp, ratchet étau *m* à cliquet
clamp, sash grand serre-joint *m*
clamp, spring pince *f* à ressort

Saws
Scies

bandsaw scie *f* à ruban
chainsaw tronçonneuse *f*
handsaw égoïne *f*; scie *f* à main
handsaw, for constructional timber égoïne *f* à denture américaine; ~ grosse coupe
handsaw, for mouldings, panelling égoïne *f* coupe fin
jigsaw scie *f* sauteuse
padsaw; keyhole saw scie *f* à guichet
saw scie *f*; égoïne *f*
saw, all-purpose égoïne *f* universelle
saw, carpenter's scie *f* de charpentier
saw, coping/fret scie *f* à chantourner (see also: **scroll saw, electric**)
saw, cross-cut égoïne *f* pour coupe transversal
saw, frame scie *f* à monture de menuisier
saw, gent's/back scie *f* à araser
saw, mitre scie *f* à onglets
saw, panel scie *f* à panneaux
saw, rip égoïne *f* pour coupe longitudinal
saw, scroll (electric) scie *f* à défilement (see also: **coping/fret saw**)
saw, tenon scie *f* à dos
saw, veneer scie *f* à placage

Planes, rasps & scrapers
Rabots, râpes & grattoirs

draw knife rabot *m* de charron
file lime *f*
plane rabot *m*
plane, bench rabot *m* établi
plane, block rabot *m* en fonte
plane, cabinetmaker's rabot *m* d'ébéniste
plane, cast iron rabot *m* en fonte
plane, hand/jack rabot *m* à main; ~ manuel
plane, jointer/try varlope *f*
plane, moulding rabot *m* moulure
plane, pocket rabot *m* de poche
plane, rebate/shoulder/bullnose guillaume *m*
plane, sheet steel rabot *m* en tôle
plane, smoothing rabot *m* métallique
plane, wooden rabot *m* en bois
planer file (Surform) Surform *m*
rasp râpe *f*
riffler rifloir *m* riflard *m*

Carpentry & Joinery

scraper ciseau *m* à racler arrondis (woodturning); racloir *m* de finition
spokeshave racloir *m* acier; vastringue (or wastringue) *f*

Drills
Perceuses

brace vilebrequin *f*
drill perceuse *f*
drill, hand chignole *f*

Carpentry equipment & accessories
Matériel de menuiserie et accessoires

bench, carpenter's établi *m* de bois/de menuisier
dowel/pin cheville *f*; tourillon *m*; repère *m* de tourillon
glasspaper/sandpaper papier *m* de verre
metal clip for T&G panelling clip *m* à frisette; crochet *m* à lambris
mitre box boîte *f* à onglets
nail punch chasse-clou *m*; chasse pointe *m*
pencil, carpenter's crayon *f* charpente
sandpaper block/wedge cale *f*
shooting board planche *f* à dresser
vice étau *m*
workbench-vice, portable établi étau *m*
workbench-vice, portable, folding and adjustable pliante et reglable

Lathes & accessories
Tours & accessoires

copy turning attachment, for lathe copieur *m* universel
lathe tour *m* à bois
lathe bed banc *m*
lathe faceplate plateau *m* de tournage
lathe headstock poupée *f* fixe
lathe motor block bloc-moteur *m*
lathe spindle broche *f*
lathe tailstock poupée *f* mobile
lathe tool rest éventail *m*

Wood
Bois

board; plank; flooring batten planche *f*
hardwood dur *m*
lath latte *f*
matchboard planche *f* bouvetée
softwood bois *m* tendre
timber bois *m* de charpente; ~ de menuiserie
weatherboarding planche *f* de recouvrement
wood bois *m*

Carpentry & Joinery

wood, roofing bois *m* de couverture
wood, length of tasseau (*pl* -x)
wood, planed bois *m* raboté
wood, untreated bois *m* brut

Sheet materials
Panneaux de bois

blockboard panneau (*pl* -x) *m* lattés
chipboard panneau (*pl* -x) *m* d'aggloméré; ~ de particules
chipboard, melamine-faced panneau *m* d'aggloméré mélaminé
chipboard, waterproof panneau *m* d'aggloméré hydrofuge
floor panel (chipboard or OSB) dalle *f* de plancher
hardboard isorel *m*; fibres *fpl* dures
MDF (medium density fibreboard) MDF *m*
oriented strand board panneau (*pl* -x) *m* OSB
plywood contreplaqué *m*; contrecollé *m*
plywood, hardwood contreplaqué *m* bois exotique

Construction timber
Bois de charpente

beam poutre *f*
beam, large madrier *m*
beam, small poutrelle *f*
floor batten; wall plate lambourde *f*
joist solive *f*
lath; strip of cladding volige *f*
plank bastaing *m*
rafter chevron *m*
roofing batten liteau *m*
timber, framing bois *m* d'ossature

Woodstrip flooring, floorboards & panelling
Parquet, plancher & lambris

board; plank planche *m*
floor panel (chipboard or OSB) dalle *f* de plancher
floor panel (chipboard or OSB), insulated dalle *f* de plancher isolantes
parquet flooring parquet *m*
parquet flooring, solid parquet massif *m*
tongued-and-grooved flooring, 'seconds' quality plancher *m* déclassé
tongued, grooved and v-jointed (TGV) panelling lambris *m* (avec languettes et rainures)
tongued, grooved and v-jointed

Carpentry & Joinery

(TGV) panelling, unplaned lambris *m* (avec languettes et rainures) aspect brut
tongued, grooved and v-jointed (TGV) panelling, planed lambris *m* (avec languettes et rainures) raboté
woodstrip flooring parquet *m* plancher
woodstrip flooring, laminated parquet *m* plancher contrecollé ~ stratifié

Mouldings & beadings
Moulures & baguettes

beading/casing baguette *f*
cover strip, two rounded edges champlat *m*; chant plat *m*
dowel tourillon *m*; cheville *f*
dowel, fluted tourillon *m* cannelé
dowel, smooth tourillon *m* lisse
frieze, decorative frise *f* décorative
glazing bead pareclose *f*
moulding moulure *f*
moulding, cornice corniche *f*
moulding, half-round moulure *f* demi-rond
moulding, ogee encadrement *m* doucine
moulding, quarter-round moulure *f* quart de rond
moulding, right-angle baguette *f* d'angle
moulding, window frame chambranle *m*
nosing bord *m* arrondi; nez *m*
nosing, partition nez *m* de cloison
nosing, staircase nez *m* de marche
skirting board plinthe *f*
water bar (window casement or door) jet *m* d'eau

Wood varieties
Variétiés de bois

acacia acacia *m*
alder aune *m*; aulne *m*
ash frêne *f*
bamboo bambou *m*
beech hêtre *m*
birch bouleau *m*
cherry wood merisier *m*
chestnut, horse marronnier *m*
chestnut, sweet châtaigner *m*
cypress cyprès *m*
deal bois *m* blanc; ~ de sapin
Douglas fir sapin *m* de douglas
ebony ébène *f*
elm orme *m*
exotic wood bois *m* exotique
fir sapin *m*
hornbeam charme *m*
iroko iroko *m*
larch mélèze *m*
lime/linden tilleul *m*
mahogany acajou *m*
maple érable *m*
meranti méranti *m*
oak chêne *m*
pine pin *m*

Carpentry & Joinery

pitch pine pitchpin *m*
plane (tree) platane *m*
ramin ramin *m*
redwood séquoia *m*
rosewood palissandre *m*
scots pine pin *m* sylvestre
spruce épicéa *m*
sycamore sycomore *m*
teak teck *m*
thuja thuya *m*
unseasoned/green wood bois *m* vert
walnut noyer *m*
western red cedar thuya *m* (see also: **thuja**)
willow saule *m*
yew if *m*

Stairs & stair parts
Escaliers & balustrades

baluster balustre *f*
balustrade balustrade *f*
child safety barrier barrière *f* de sécurité enfant
handrail main *m* courant
ladder échelle *f*
ladder, loft échelle *f* de grenier
ladder, 'miller's' (open tread, with single handrail) échelle *f* de meunier
ladder, retractable échelle *f* escamotable
landing palier *m*
newel post pilastre *m*; poteau *m*
rail rampe *f*
railing rambarde *f*
riser contremarche *m*
staircase escalier *m*
staircase, mezzanine escalier *m* de mezzanine
staircase, modular escalier *m* modulaire
staircase, quarter turn escalier *m* quart tournant
  ~ **at base** ~ bas
  ~ **at centre** ~ milieu
  ~ **at top** ~ haut
staircase, with risers escalier *m* avec contremarche
staircase, space-saving escalier *m* gain de place
staircase, spiral escalier *m* en colimaçon; ~ hélicoïdal
  ~ **round** ~ rond
  ~ **square** ~ en colimaçon carré
staircase, straight escalier *m* droite
step pas *m*
step, offset pas *m* décalés; ~ japonais
trapdoor, insulated, for retractable loft ladder trappe *f* isolée pour échelle escamotable
tread marche *f*

Appendix

DECORATING
DÉCORATION

Decorating tools
Outils de décoration

Paintbrushes
Pinceux & brosses

brush brosse *f*; pinceau *m*
brush, acrylic paint brosse *f* spécial acrylique; pinceau acrylique
brush, all paint types pinceau *m* toute peinture
brush, badger hair brosse *f* en poils de blaireau
brush, ceiling brosse *f* à plafond
brush, cleaning/washing brosse *f* à lessiver
brush, 'codfish tail' queue *f* de morue (for varnish, lacquer and smoothing without loss of hairs)
brush, colourwashing brosse *f* pour effet badigeon
brush, dragging brosse *f* pour effet moucheté (for flecked/dappled effect)
brush, 'English tail' brush queue *f* anglaise (for large areas and products containing solvents Nearest UK equivalent: wall brush)
brush, flat brosse *f* plat; pinceau *m* plat
~ **extra-thick brush** ~ plate extra-épaisse
~ **flat, lacquer** ~ plate à lacquer
~ **matt/satin finishes** pinceau *m* mate/satinée
~ **nylon bristles** pinceau *m* nylon plat
brush, oil-based paint brosse *f* spécial glycerol; pinceau *m* glycéro
brush, pointed, for delicate work/mouldings brosse *f* à rechampir
brush, radiator brosse *f*; pinceau *m* radiateur
~ **forward-angled** ~ coudée sur le plat
~ **side-angled** ~ coudée sur le chant
brush, rectangular brosse *f* rectangulaire
brush, retouching brosse *f* à raccords
brush, round stock brosse *f* rond
brush, round stock, for delicate work/mouldings brosse *f* de pouce; brosse *f* pouce à rechampir; pinceau *m* à rechampir)
brush, sash brosse *f* de pouce (round stock; round end to bristles)
brush, small flat/round brosse *f* à tableau plate/ronde (for retouching/detailed artistic work)
brush, soft, for paint effects brosse *f* douce
~ **with synthetic bristles** ~ synthetique
brush, stain/wood treatment brosse *f* lasure, traitement bois

Decorating

brush, stencil pinceau *m* à pochoir
brush, stippling brosse *f* à pocher
brush, tightly packed bristles brosse *f* hermétique
brush, universal use pinceau *m* universel
  ~ **flat** ~ plat
  ~ **round (thumb)** ~ pouce
brush, varnish brosse *f* vernis; pinceau *m* bois/verni
brush, whitewash/emulsion brosse *f* à badigeon
brush, whitewash/emulsion/paste brosse *f* ronde (round stock, large, squared end to bristles)
paintbrush pinceau *(pl -x) m*
paintbrush, artist's pinceau *m* de artiste
paintbrush, glaze pinceau *m* à glacis
paintbrush, pointed, for delicate work pinceau *m* à rechampir
paintbrush, sealing pinceau *m* à vitrifier; ~ vitrificateur
paintbrush, watercolour pinceau *m* aquarelle rond
spalter spalter *f* for smoothing lacquer and varnish

Rollers, paint pads & sprayguns

Rouleaux, tampons de peinture & pistolets à peinture

paint pad tampon *m* à peindre
painting mitt, lambswool gant *m* à peindre en peau de mouton
roller rouleau *(pl -x) m*
roller, angled rouleau *m* d'angle à peindre
  ~ **ribbed** ~ nervuré
roller, canvas effect rouleau *m* effet toile
roller, disposable rouleau *m* jetable
roller, exterior rouleau *m* façade
roller, fibre rouleau *m* fibre
  ~ **long** ~ longue
  ~ **short** ~ court
roller, fine finish foam rouleau *m* mousse fin
roller, flocked foam rouleau *m* mousse floquée
roller frame monture *f* rouleau
roller, gloss finish rouleau *m* finition brilliante
roller handle, telescopic, for frame perche *f* télescopique; ralonge *f* télescopique
roller, honeycomb foam rouleau *m* mousse alvéolée
roller, laquer rouleau *m* lacqueur
roller, matt finish rouleau *m* finition mate
roller, mini rouleau *m* mini
roller, mohair rouleau *m* en mohair

Decorating

roller, lambswool, natural rouleau *m* mouton laine naturel
roller, lined rouleau *m* rayé
roller, non-drip rouleau *m* anti-gouttes
roller, one-coat rouleau *m* monocouche
roller, polyamide rouleau *m* d'une polyamide tissée
roller, radiator rouleau *m* à radiateur
roller, rubber rouleau *m* en caoutchouc
roller, satin finish rouleau *m* finition satinée
roller, small roulette *f*
roller, sponged/wiped effect rouleau *m* essuyé
roller, stain (and other fluids) rouleau *m* lasure
roller, stencil rouleau *m* pochoir
roller, synthetic foam rouleau *m* de mousse sythétique expansée; mousse
roller, texturing rouleau *m* à effet crépi
  ~ **coarse grain** ~ gross grain
  ~ **fine grain** ~ grain fin
roller, varnish rouleau *m* à vitrifier; ~ vernis
roller, wall and ceiling rouleau *m* mur et plafond
roller, for wood rouleau *m* pour les bois
roller sleeve manchon *m*
  ~ **replacement** recharge *f* rouleau

roller tray bac *m* à peinture pour rouleaux; bac *m* spécial à reservoir; égouttoir *m*
spraygun pistolet *m* à peinture

Paperhanging tools & equipment
Outillage du tapissier

adhesive comb couteau *m* à colle
brush brosse *f*
brush, dusting brosse *f* époussette
brush, paperhanging brosse *f* à tapisser/tapissier
brush, wallpaper pasting brosse *f* à encoller; ~ à mouiller; balai *m* de colleur; pinceau *m* de tapissier
glue syringe seringue *f* à colle
knife couteau (*pl* -x) *m*
knife, extendable blade couteau *m* automatique
knife, fixed-blade couteau *m* lame fixe
palette/spatula, smoothing palette *f* à maroufler; spatule *f* à maroufler; ~ rigid rigide; ~ flexible souple
paste bucket seau *m* à colle
pasting table table *f* à tapisser
plumb bob and line plomb *m* de tapissier
roller rouleau *m*
roller, paperhanger's roulette *f* de tappisier
roller, paste rouleau *m* à colle
roller, seam roulette

Decorating

~ conical ~ angle conique
~ ribbed ~ angle nervurée
roller, spiked rouleau *m* à pointes (for perforating wallpaper prior to stripping); rouleau *m* débulleur (for removing bubbles)
rule règle *f*
rule, cutting couteau *m* à emarger
rule, cutting; metal straightedge règle *f* de coup
rule, stainless steel règle *f* de colleur inox
scissors, paperhanger's ciseaux *f* de colleur
soaking tray bac *m* de trempage
steam stripper décolleuse *f* à papier peint; décolleuse *f* à vapeur
trimming wheel lame *f* d'arasement; roulette *f* d'arasement
wallpaper pasting trough encolleuse *f* à papier peint

Tiling tools
Outillage du carreleur

adhesive comb peigne *m* à colle
contour gauge jauge *f* de contour
cutters/pincers, ceramic tile pince *f* coupe carreaux; ~ coupe carrelage
  ~ for delicate work ~ de céramiste
  ~ for mosaics/small tiles ~ mosaïste double molette

~ jaw offset, for delicate work ~ mosaïste à machoire déportée
cutting wheel, replacement molette *f* de rechange
drill bit, extensible mèche *f* à percer
file, ceramic tile grille *f* a poncer; râpe *f* à céramique
file, double-sided lame *f* abrasive double face
float (for pressing down tiles) batte *f*
float, expanded polystyrene (for smoothing large areas of mortar) taloche *f* polystyrène expanse
glue spatula spatule *f* à colle
grinding stone, double-faced pierre *f* à greser double face
hole saws, tungsten, set of kit *m* trepan carbure de tungstène
joint brush brosse *f* à joints
joint smoother lisseur *m* de joints
lifter, suction pad ventouse *f* de préhension
mallet, rubber (for bedding tiles) maillet *m* caoutchouc
nibblers, ceramic tile pince *f* à bec perroquet
pliers, tile-cutting tenaille *f* de carreleur
saw, ceramic tile scie *f* de carreleur
saw, ceramic tile, cranked scie *f* vilebrequin
saw blade, replacement lame *f* de scie ronde
scorer pointe *f* à tracer
  ~ with tile-breaker ~ avec système de casse

Decorating

squeegee raclette *f* de carreleur
tile-cutting disc, diamond disque *f* diamant carrelage
tile-cutting jig carrelette *f*
 ~ **electric** électrique

Tiles
Carreaux

tile carreau (*pl* -x) *m*; dalle *f*; plaquette *f*
tile, antique marble carreau *m* mural en marbre antique
tile, carpet dalle *f* moquette
tile, ceiling dalle *f* de plafond
tile, ceramic carreau *m* céramique
tile, ceramic wall muraux *m* en faïence
tile, cork carreau *m* liège; plaque *f* de liège
tile, cork wall dalle *f* de liège murale
tile, floor dalle *f*
tile, floor, PVC carreau *m* de sol en PVC
tile, plaster wall cladding (interior) plaquette *f* de parement
tile, reconstituted stone carreau *m* pierre reconstituée
tile, stoneware wall carreau *m* mural en grès cérame
tile, terracotta carreau *m* de terre cuite
tile, vinyl carreau *m* vinyle
tile, wall plaquette *f*

Tiling materials
Matériaux de carrelage

ceramic tile spacer croisillon *m*
grout ciment *m* joint; enduit *m*
spacing wedges cales *f* d'épaisseur
tile joint sealant joint *m* en pâte
tile sheen patine *f* carreaux

Preparation for walls & ceilings
Préparation des murs & plafonds

cleaner, brush/painting equipment nettoyant *m* outils peinture
cleaner, tile nettoyant *m* carreaux
degreaser dégraissant *m*
filler/coating enduit *m*
filler, polyester resin enduit *m* résine armée
filler, ready-to-use enduit *m* de rebouchage
 ~ **fine paste** ~ de lissage pâte, prêt à l'emploi
joint mastic (in a tube) mastique *m* fixation cartouche
paint-drying accelerator accélérateur *m* de séchage
paint stripper, chemical décolleuse *f* de peint
paint stripper, gel décapant *m* gel
 ~ **all surfaces** ~ universel
 ~ **biological, for stain** ~ spécial

Decorating

tâche de organiques
~ **cement stain** ~ voile et laitance ciment carrelage non émaillé (unglazed tiles)
~ **dry** ~ sec confort
~ **grease stain, for tiles** ~ carrelage spécial tâches de graisse
~ **iron surfaces** ~ fer
~ **multi surfaces** ~ multi supports
~ **non-scratching, for metal surfaces** ~ métal sans grattage
~ **for wood surfaces** ~ bois
paint thinner diluant *m*
paint thinner, cellulose diluant *m* cellulosique
paint thinner, synthetic diluant *m* synthétique
polish/shine remover décirant *f*
primer, metal antirouille *m* primaire protecteur
putty mastic *m* de vitrier
rust inhibitor antirouille *m*
sheen remover délaqueur *m*
solvent dissolvant *m*
stabilizer/hardener (friable surfaces) fixateur *m* de fonds
stain remover détachant *m*
tile waterproofer imperméabilisant *m* carreaux
tile wax/polish cire *f* carrelage
turpentine térébenthine *f*
wallpaper stripper, chemical décolleuse *f* de papiers peints
white-spirit white spirit *m*
~ **odourless** ~ inodore

Primers & undercoats
Apprêts et sous-couches

hardener durcisseur *m*
primer apprêt *m*; avant-peinture *m*
primer, stabilizing durcisseur *m* pour plâtre
undercoat sous-couche *f*
undercoat, absorbent/unstable surfaces sous-couche *f* grands travaux
undercoat, acrylic sous-couche *f* acrylique
undercoat, all-surface sous-couche *f* universelle
undercoat, anti-rust sous-couche *f* anti-rouille
undercoat, blockwork and concrete sous-couche *f* parpaing/béton
undercoat, condensation resistant, anti-mould (kitchens, bathrooms, plasterboard) sous-couche *f* cuisines et bains, plaque de plâtre
undercoat, exotic hardwoods sous-couche *f* bois exotiques
undercoat, interior and exterior woodwork sous-couche *f* bois intérieur et extérieur
undercoat, oil-based sous-couche *f* glycéro
undercoat, plaster and cement sous-couche *f* plâtre et ciment
undercoat, plasterboard sous-couche *f* plaques de plâtre

Decorating

undercoat, porous surfaces sous-couche *f* supports poreux
undercoat, pre-tiling sous-couche *f* avant carrelage
undercoat, PVC and galvanized aluminium sous-couche *f* PVC alu galva
undercoat, smooth surfaces sous-couche *f* carrelage/stratifié/PVC/alu/galva
undercoat, wood and metal sous-couche *f* bois et fer
undercoat, wood, exterior sous-couche *f* pour bois extérieurs

Paint
Peinture

aerosol spray paint bombe *f* de peinture
colourwash badigeon *m* effet douceur blanc à colorer
interior wall coat, fine granular finish enduit *m* grain fin
limewash badigeon *m* de chaux
paint peinture *f*
paint, acrylic peinture *f* acrylique
paint, aerosol radiator peinture *f* aérosol radiateur
paint, anti-condensation peinture *f* anti-condensation
paint, anti-graffiti peinture *f* anti graffitis finition
paint, anti-humidity peinture *f* traitement anti-humidité
paint, basement/small walls peinture *f* soubassement et murets
paint, bottle of (for stencils) peinture *f* en flacon
paint, ceiling peinture *f* plafond
paint, cracked/stuccoed walls peinture *f* murs fissurés ou crépis
paint, emulsion peinture *f* émulsion
paint, fluorescent peinture *f* fluo
paint, gloss peinture *f* brilliante
paint, hammered metal finish, aerosol peinture *f* martelée en aérosol
paint, high temperature (for ferrous metal and copper) peinture *f* haute température
paint, interior/exterior bases peinture *f* sol intérieur extérieur
paint, interior wood peinture *f* boiseries intérieures
paint, lacquer peinture *f* laquée
paint, masonry peinture *f* façade
paint, matt peinture *f* mate
paint, metallic peinture *f* métallisée
paint, metalwork peinture *f* spécial fer
paint, microporous peinture *f* microporeuse
paint, non-drip peinture *f* antigoutte
paint, odourless peinture *f* inodore
paint, oil-based peinture *f* glycéro
paint, one-coat peinture *f* monocouche

Decorating

paint, radiator peinture *f* spécial radiateurs
paint, satin peinture *f* satinée
paint, spray peinture *f* en aérosol
paint, tube of (for stencils) peinture *f* en tube
paint, two-coat peinture *f* bicouche
paint, walls/ceilings peinture *f* murs et plafonds
paint, walls/woodwork peinture *f* murs et boiseries
paint, window sill peinture *f* appui de fenêtre
stucco finish crépi *m*
stucco finish, exterior crépi *m* de façade
stucco finish, peelable crépi *m* décollable
stucco finish, peelable interior crépi *m* intérieur décollable
whitewash badigeon *m*

Paint for decorative effects
Peintures décoratives

finishing glaze, semi-transparent patine *f* de finition
gel, crackle finish gel *m* à craqueler
gilding dorure *f*
glaze glacis *m*
glaze, acrylic glacis *m* acrylique
glaze, crackle glacis *m* à craqueler
glaze, oil glacis *m* à huile
glaze, wax glacis *m* à la cire
paint peinture *f*
paint, aged patina peinture *f* à vieillir
paint, blackboard peinture *f* tableau
paint, glaze effect peinture *f* effet glacis
paint, limewash effect peinture *f* effet de chaux
paint, pearl finish peinture *f* effet nacrée
paint, 'white lead' effect céruse *f* murale
wax coating cirer *f* murale; enduit *m* à cirer

Stain, varnish, oil & wax
Lasure, vernis, huile & cire

grate polish crème *m* ferronerie-font
oil huile *f*
oil, for worktops huile *f* pour plan de travail
oil, teak huile *f* de teck
stain lasure *f*; teinte *f*
stain, semi-opaque, for bleached/aged wood effect lasure *f* badigeon
stain, furniture teinte *f* pour meuble
stain, interior wood lasure *f* bois

Decorating

  intérieur
  ~ **opaque** ~ opaque
  ~ **satin** ~ satiné
  ~ **transparent** ~ transparente
stain, wood teinte *f* à bois
varnish vernis *m*
varnish, cement vernis *m* ciment
varnish, clear vernis *m* clair
varnish, coloured vernis *m* coloré
varnish, exterior vernis *m* extérieur
varnish, for furniture/objects vernis *m* pour meuble et objets
varnish, gloss vernis *m* brillant
varnish, interior vernis *m* intérieur
  ~ **moisture-resistant** (for kitchens/bathrooms) vernis *m* cuisines et bains
varnish, matt vernis *m* mat
varnish, satin vernis *m* satiné
varnish, stone vernis *m* pierre
varnish, yacht/marine vernis *m* marin
wax cire *f*
wax, bleached effect cire *f* effet blanchi
wax, tinted, for furniture cire *f* teintée pour meuble
wood grain filler bouche-pores *m*

Wallpapers & wallcoverings
Papier peints & revêtements muraux

frieze frise *f*
frieze, adhesive backed frise *f* adhésive
frieze, wall frise *f* murale
glass cloth toile *f* de verre
wallcovering revêtement *m* mural
wallcovering, cork liège *m* mural
wallcovering, for painting revêtement *m* mural à peindre
wallcovering, glass fibre revêtement *m* mural fibre de verre; voile *m* de verre
  ~ **anti-crack** ~ anti-fissure
  ~ **reinforcing** voile *m* de renfort
wallcovering, glass fibre, fine revêtement *m* mural fibre de verre mini-maille
wallcovering, glass fibre mesh revêtement *m* mural fibre de verre maille
wallcovering, glass fibre, non-inflammable revêtement *m* mural fibre de verre non-inflammable
wallcovering, glass fibre, pre-painted revêtement *m* mural fibre de verre prépeinte
wallcovering, non-woven textured (for painting) structure *f* à peindre sur intissé maille
wallcovering, for smoothing

Decorating

rough surfaces revêtement *m* de lissage; revêtement *m* de rénovation
wallpaper papier peint *m*
wallpaper, ceramic effect papier peint *m* en grès cérame
wallpaper, dappled effect, for painting papier peint *m* effet pommelé
wallpaper, embossed papier peint *m* gaufré
wallpaper, expanded vinyl, paper-backed papier peint *m* expansé sur papier
wallpaper, mural papier peint *m* mur d'image
wallpaper, non-woven papier peint *m* intissé
wallpaper, for painting papier peint *m* à peindre
wallpaper, pre-pasted papier peint *m* préencollé
wallpaper, textile effect papier peint *m* motif textile
wallpaper, vinyl papier peint *m* vinyle
  ~ **expanded** ~ expansé
  ~ **heavy, non-woven back** ~ vinyl lourd sur intissé
  ~ **sur intissé** ~ non-woven
wallpaper, washable papier peint *m* lavable
wallpaper, woodchip papier peint *m* motif naturel (incrustation de copeaux de bois)
wallpaper, woven effect papier peint *m* effet tissé

Decorating tools & materials
Outils et matériaux de décoration

Masking tape
Masquage

insulating tape, electrical adhésif *m* de protection électrique
masking tape masquage *m*; adhésif *m* de protection
masking tape, fabric toile *f* adhésive de protection
masking tape, kraft paper, solvent free adhésif *m* écologique kraft
masking tape, for wood masquage *m* bois
masking tape, non-slip adhésif *m* de protection antidérapant
masking tape, painting adhésif *m* de protection peinture
masking tape, painting curves adhésif *m* de protection peinture spécial courbes
masking tape, painting straight lines adhésif *m* de protection peinture lignes droites; masquage *m* lignes droites
masking tape, painting, heavy duty for large areas (e.g. walls) adhésif *m* de protection peinture gros oeuvre murs/façades
parcel tape, adhesive adhésif *m* emballage kraft

Decorating

Dust sheets & protective accessories

Bâches & accessoires de protection

dust sheet adhésif *m* de protection
dust sheet, floors/windows adhésif *m* de protection sols & fenêtres
dust sheet, hallways adhésif *m* de protection couloirs & passages
dust sheet, roll bobine *f* de protection
dust sheet, with zip closer (masking/sealing doorways) adhésif *m* de protection avec fermeture
prop, extendable, to secure dust sheet to walls support *m* extensible pour bâche
protective overalls, one-piece (including hood!) combinaison *f* de bricolage
rubble bags, tough plastic sacs *m* à gravats
tarpaulin bâche *f*

Decorating tools & accessories

Outils & accessoires de décoration

glass cutter coupe-verre *f*
hawk; flat trowel taloche *f*
hot air gun pistolet *m* décapeur à air chaud
knee pads genouillères *f*
metal rule règle *f* à émarger
mitre box boîte *f* à coupe
paint colour chart nuancier *m* chromatique
paint mixer malaxer *m* de peinture
paint shield spatule *f* à maroufler
paint stirrer mélangeur *m* à peinture
palette knife sabre *m* de tapissier
rubber gloves gants *m* de caoutchouc
sanding block cale *m* à poncer
scissors ciseaux *fpl*
scraper grattoir *m* racloir *m*
scratching blade grattoir *m* à lame
shavehook, triangular grattoir *m* à fissures triangulaire
smoothing knife (for filler) couteau *m* à enduire
spatula spatule *f*
spatula, notched spatule *f* crantée
sponge éponge *f*
sponge, natural éponge *f* naturelle
sponge, synthetic éponge *f* synthetique
squeegee raclette *m*
squeegee, rubber-bladed raclette *m* à emmancher; ~ à joint
stripping knife couteau *m* de peintre
wire brush brosse *m* à la main métallique
wire brush, rotary (for power drill) à decaper
wirecutters cisailles *fpl*
wire wool laine *f* d'acier

Decorating

Tools for special paint effects

Outils pour les effets spéciaux de peinture

comb peigne *m*
comb, rubber (combed effect) peigne *m* en caoutchoc
corrugated card (combed effect) peigne *m* en carton
wood graining roller boisette *m*
wood graining veiner outil *m* à veiner effet bois

Wallpaper paste

Colle à papier peint

glue; paste colle *f*; pâte *f*
glue, all-purpose colle *f* tous papiers peints
glue, border/frieze colle *f* frise
glue, cork colle *f* murale liège; ~ pour liège
glue, cornices and roses colle *f* corniche et rosace
glue, glass cloth colle *f* toile de verre
glue, polystyrene tile colle *f* pour dalles polystyrène
glue, reinforced colle *f* renforcée
  ~ **for border/frieze** ~ frise
  ~ **for touch-up** ~ raccord
glue, textile colle *f* revêtement textiles muraux
glue gun pistolet *m* à colle
glue syringe seringue *f* à colle

paste, wallpaper colle *f* papier peint
paste, wallpaper, joins colle *f* papier peint raccords
paste, wallpaper, non-woven colle *f* papier peint intissé
paste, wallpaper, vinyl colle *f* papier peint vinyle

Carpet & vinyl floorcoverings

Moquette & sol vinyle

carpet moquette *f*
carpet, Berber moquette *f* berbère
carpet, cocoa fibre moquette *f* fibres do coco
carpet, cut pile moquette *f* à la coupe
carpet, looped moquette *f* bouclée
carpet, needle pile moquette *f* aiguilletée
carpet, printed moquette *f* imprimée
carpet, raised pile moquette *f* à relief
carpet, raised wool moquette *f* laine
carpet, velvet pile moquette *f* velours
carpet, woven moquette *f* tressée
carpet tile dalle *f* de moquette

Decorating

floorcovering, PVC revêtement *f* de sol PVC
floorcovering, rush rabane *f* jonc de montagne
floorcovering, seagrass rabane *f* jonc de mer
floorcovering, sisal revêtement *f* de sol sisal
floorcovering, strip, PVC lame *f* PVC
  ~ **adhesive-backed** ~ auto-adhesive
floorcovering, vinyl roll revêtement *f* de sol en vinyle rouleaux
floor tile, PVC dalle *f* PVC
floor tile, vinyl, adhesive-backed dalle *f* vinyle auto-adhesive
rafia matting rabane *f* jonc

Decorating

Appendix

ELECTRICITY
ÉLECTRICITÉ

Electricity

Electrical sheathing & accessories
Gaines & accessoires électriques

cable pull through, nylon tire-fil *f* en nylon
lubricant, for feeding cores and cables through sheathing lubrifiant *m* pour tirage de fils
sheath bracket, screw-in fixation *m* pour gaines; stop gaine *m*
~ **double** ~ double
~ **single** ~ simple
sheathing, with cable pull through gaine *f* avec tire-fil
sheathing, electric (polypropylene corrugated, flexible) gaine *f* électrique; ~ de protection
sheathing, empty gaine *f* vide
sheathing, pre-installed with ADSL telephone cable, green gaine *f* préfilée téléphone ADSL vert
sheathing, pre-installed with cable cores gaine *f* préfilée
sheathing, pre-installed with circuit cable gaine *f* précâblée
sheathing, pre-installed with TV coaxial cable, green gaine *f* préfilée TV coaxial vert
sheathing, rigid plastic gaine *f* plastique rigide
sheathing connector, clip-on manchon *m* ouvrable

Mouldings & trunking
Moulures & goulottes

cable conduit tube *m;* baguette *f* de distribution
cable conduit, flared end (for connection to adjoining length) tube *m* tulipé
cable conduit, floor-mounted passage *f* de plancher; baguette *f* de distribution sol
cable conduit, self-adhesive cache-câble *f* en PVC, auto-adhésif
moulding, angled (corner fixing) moulure *f* angle
moulding, ceiling moulure *f* plafond
moulding, PVC moulure *f* PVC
moulding fixing bracket clou *m* spécial moulure
skirting board, decorative plinthe *f* décor
skirting junction box boîte *f* de dérivation plinthe
trunking, PVC goulotte *f*
trunking, PVC, surface-fixed (with clip-on cover) goulotte *f* pour installation en saillie

Electricity

Accessories: mouldings & trunking
Accessoires: moulures & goulottes

Trunking
Goulottes

ceiling duct, conical cornet *m* de plafond
electric socket mount support *m* de prise électrique
end piece, push-in embout *m*

Mouldings
Moulures

adapter (switch/socket installation) adaptateur *m* pour moulure
junction box for ceiling light boîte *f* pour point lumineux
junction box for moulding boîte *f* de dérivation pour moulure
junction cover jonction *f* couvercle
moulding, angle moulure *f* angle
moulding, end piece embout *m* pour moulure
moulding, exterior angle connector moulure *f* angle extérieur
moulding, flat right-angle joint moulure *f* plat
moulding, interior angle connector moulure *f* angle intérieur
moulding, partitioned moulure *f* avec séparation
moulding, tee-connector moulure *f* en té
tee junction box té *m* de dérivation pour moulure

Skirting boards
Plinthes

joint clip, decorative agrafe *f* décorative
junction, decorative (skirting and moulding) chambranle *f* décorative

Conduit
Tubes

bracket, clip-in clip *m*
bracket, screw-in fixation *m* pour tube
connector, curved courbe *m*
connector, elbow coude *m* équerre
connector, tee té *m*
sleeve, connecting lengths manchon *f*
sleeve, snap-on, hinged manchon *f* ouvrable

Electricity

Cable & wire
Câble & fil d'installation

cable, electric câble *m* électrique
cable, electric, by the length câble *m* électrique à la coupe
cable, electric, by the metre câble *m* électrique au mètre
cable, mains câble *m* électrique de distribution
cable, multi-core câble *m* électrique multifilaire
cable, reel of câble *m* électrique en couronne
cable, rigid câble *m* d'alimentation rigide
cable, silicone-sheathed (use in hot atmospheres) câble *m* électrique silicone
cable core conducteur *m*
earth cable câblette *m* de terre
earth wire, bare copper câble *m* de terre, cuivre nu
wire; filament fil *m*
wire; filament, bare fil *m* nu

Flex & power cords
Câble souple & cordon d'alimentation

cable, coaxial terrestrial and satellite TV câble *m* coaxial tv hertzien et satellite
cable, multimedia câble *m* multimédia
cable, multimedia, hi-fi câble *m* multimédia hi-fi
cable, multimedia, telephone câble *m* multimédia téléphone
cable, multimedia telephone, internet and computer câble *m* multimédia téléphone, internet et informatique
cable, multimedia, telephone, for meter connection, EDF-installed câble *m* téléreport armé
flex câble *m* souple
flex, PVC-sheathed câble *m* souple
  ~ by the metre ~ au mètre
  ~ in a reel ~ en bobine
flex core, PVC-sheathed (not available in UK) câble *m* unifilaire souple
hi-fi cable, twin-core sheathed, flat câble *m* haut parleur, translucide, méplat

Conduit & cable fixings
Fixation des gaines & câbles

cable clip, nail fixing attache-fil *m*
cable clip, screw fixing serre-câble *m* à cheville
cable tie (use with: embasse) collier *m* de fixation; collier *m* de serrage
clip, head piece (use with: collier) embasse *f*

Electricity

clip, head piece, nail fixing
  embasse *f* à frapper
clip, head piece, screw fixing
  embasse *f* à visser; ~ à cheville
clip, twin (for parallel cables) clip *m* double

Junction boxes
Boîtes de dérivation

branch box; connection box boîte *f* de distribution; boîte *f* de jonction en saillie
grommet entrée *f* étanche en saillie
junction box boîte *f* de dérivation; coffret *m* de dérivation
junction box, cover couvercle *m* de finition
  ~ **clip-on** ~ à clipser
  ~ **screw-on** ~ à visser
junction box, drywall recessed boîte *f* de dérivation cloison sèche à encastrer
junction box, for masonry boîte *f* de dérivation maçonnerie à encastrer
junction box, recessed boîte *f* de dérivation à encastrer
junction box, sealed (in masonry) boîte *f* de dérivation à sceller
junction box, surface-mounted boîte *f* de dérivation en saillie
junction box, waterproof boîte *f* de dérivation étanche

Mounting boxes
Boîtes d'encastrement

blanking plate plaque *f* d'obturation
mounting box boîte *f*
mounting box, ceiling boîte *f* plafond
mounting box, door/window frame boîte *f* avec patte de chambranle
mounting box, flush boîte *f* d'encastrement
mounting box, flush, all materials boîte *f* d'encastrement multi-matériaux; ~ tout type de matériaux
mounting box, flush, for ceiling boîte *f* d'encastrement point de centre pour plafond
mounting box, flush, double boîte *f* d'encastrement deux postes
mounting box, flush, for hollow walls boîte *f* d'encastrement pour mur creux
mounting box, flush, for plasterboard wall boîte *f* d'encastrement plaque de plâtre
mounting box, flush, quadruple boîte *f* d'encastrement quatre postes
mounting box, flush, recessed, sealed boîte *f* d'encastrement à sceller
mounting box, flush, for solid wall boîte *f* d'encastrement pour mur plein

Electricity

mounting box, flush, triple boîte *f* d'encastrement trois postes
mounting box, surface-fixed boîte *f* appliquée
mounting box, surface-fixed, partition wall boîte *f* appliquée cloison sèche

Switches & sockets
Interrupteurs & prises

cable outlet sortie *f* de câbles
cover plate plaque *f* simple
dimmer switch variateur *m* interrupteur
faceplate, junction box obturateur *m*
faceplate, socket outlet cache *f* pour prise
faceplate, switch cache *f* pour interrupteur
push button/switch poussoir *m*
push button/switch, luminous poussoir *m* à voyant, témoin ou lumineux
push button/switch, recessed poussoir *m* à encastrer
push button/switch, waterproof poussoir *m* étanche
socket outlet prise *f* électrique
socket outlet, double prise *f* électrique double
  ~ **earthed** ~ avec terre
  ~ **two-pole** ~ deux pôles
socket outlet, earthed prise *f* électrique avec terre
~ **recessed** ~ automatique à encastrer
socket outlet, programmable prise *f* électrique programmable
  ~ **time switch, digital** ~ digital
  ~ **time switch, mechanical** ~ mécanique
socket outlet, recessed prise *f* électrique à encastrer
socket outlet, recessed, skirting board prise *f* électrique plinthe
socket outlet, remote control prise *f* électrique à distance
socket outlet, surface-mounted prise *f* électrique en appliqué
socket outlet, telephone prise *f* téléphone
socket outlet, telephone/computer prise *f* informatique
socket outlet, television/stereo/satellite prise *f* TV/FM/SAT
socket outlet, three-pole, plus earth prise *f* électrique trois P+T
socket outlet, two-pole, with earth pin prise *f* électrique deux pôles and terre (P+T)
socket outlet, two-pole, without earth prise *f* électrique sans terre
socket outlet, wall fixed prise *f* électrique murale
switch interrupteur *m*
switch, consumer unit main interrupteur *m* différentiel
switch, control interrupteur *m* de contrôle
switch, foot-operated interrupteur *m* à pied

Electricity

switch, recessed interrupteur *m* à encastrer
switch, remote control interrupteur *m* à distance
switch, surface-mounted interrupteur *m* combiné pac saillie
switch, two-pole interrupteur *m* bipolaire
switch, two-way interrupteur *m* va-et-vient
switch, two-way, waterproof exterior interrupteur *m* étanche
toggle switch poussoir *m* à bascule

Plugs & lampholders
Fiches électriques & douilles

lampholder douille *f*
lampholder, bayonet fitting douille *f* à baïonnette
lampholder, brass finish douille *f* acier laitonné
lampholder, one retaining ring douille *f* simple bague
lampholder, screw fitting douille *f* à vis
lampholder, two retaining rings douille *f* double bague
lampholder, waterproof douille *f* étanche
plug fiche *f* électrique
plug, caravan fiche *f* électrique caravanne

plug, female fiche *f* électrique femelle
  ~ **2-slot** ~ 2 pôles
  ~ **2-slot plus earth pin** ~ 2 pôles + terre
plug, male fiche *f* électrique mâle
  ~ **2-pin** ~ 2 pôles
  ~ **2-pin plus earth** ~ 2 pôles + terre
  ~ **3-pin plus earth** ~ 3 pôles + terre
plug, rubber fiche *f* électrique caoutchouc

Consumer units
Tableaux électriques

blanking plate obturateur *m* coffret
box, 'builder's', temporary site consumer unit coffret *m* de chantier
box, to distribute TV/multimedia systems, computer network and telephone coffret *m* de communication; ~ multimedia
consumer unit tableau *m* électrique; ~ de protection; ~ de répartition
consumer unit, empty casing tableau *m* électrique nu
consumer unit, partition cloison *f* de séparation
consumer unit, pre-installed and pre-cabled tableau *m* électrique prééquipé et précâblé

Electricity

consumer unit, for water heater tableau *m* électrique chauffe-eau câblé
consumer unit, waterproof tableau *m* électrique étanche
consumer unit, for workshop tableau *m* électrique d'atelier
support bar for terminal cover support barrette *f* pour cache borne
switch board, main tableau *m* de commande principal
terminal borne *f*; bornier *f*
terminal, consumer unit borne *f* de raccordement
terminal, phase/neutral borne *f* d'alimentation
terminal, principal consumer unit borne *f* d'arrivée
terminal block strip peigne *f*
~ **horizontal reversible** ~ horizontal reversible
~ **vertical** ~ vertical

Circuit breakers
Disjoncteurs

circuit breaker disjoncteur *m*
circuit breaker, fused coupe-circuit *m*
circuit breaker, miniature disjoncteur *m* divisionnaire différentiel
circuit breaker, switched interrupteur *m* différentiel
lightning surge protector parafoudre *m*; ~ modulaire; ~ de secteur
lightning surge protector, replacement cartridge (after many triggers) recharge parafoudre *m*
residual current device (RCD) disjoncteur *m* différentiel

Light bulbs & tubes
Ampoules & tubes

bayonet cap culot *m* B bayonnette
E-type (Edison screw) cap culot *m* E
G-type bi-pin cap culot *m* G
light bulb ampoule *f*; lampe *f*
light bulb, 'candle in the wind' ampoule *f* flamme coup de vent
light bulb, cap culot *m*
light bulb, clear ampoule *f* clair
light bulb, energy efficient ampoule *f* économie d'énergie (éco)
light bulb, flame effect ampoule *f* flamme
light bulb, frosted ampoule *f* dépoli
light bulb, globe ampoule *f* globe
light bulb, half-silvered standard ampoule *f* demi argentée
light bulb, halogen ampoule *f* halogène
~ **spotlight** ~ spot
light bulb, incandescent ampoule *f* incandescent
light bulb, LED (light-emitting

Electricity

diode) ampoule *f* LED
light bulb, lotus-shaped ampoule *f* lotus
light bulb, low voltage ampoule *f* halogène TBTS (très basse tension)
light bulb, reflector ampoule *f* réflecteur
light bulb, Soft Tone ampoule *f* Soft Tone
light bulb, spherical ampoule *f* sphérique
light bulb, spiral ampoule *f* spirale
light bulb, spotlight ampoule *f* spot
light bulb, standard ampoule *f* standard
tube, fluorescent tube *m* fluorescent
  ~ **white** ~ blanc
tube, halogen tube *m* halogène
  ~ **energy-efficient** ~ éco
tube, incandescent tube *m* incandescent
  ~ **frosted** ~ dépoli
  ~ **opal** ~ opale

Fuses
Fusibles

fuse fusible *m*
fuse, cartridge fusible *m* à cartouche; coupe-circuit *m* á broche
fuse, ceramic fusible *m* céramique
  ~ **with indicator** ~ avec voyant
  ~ **without indicator** ~ sans voyant
fuse, glass fusible *m* verre
fuse adapter (porcelain fuseholder) adaptateur *m* porte-fusible à broches
fuse holder porte-fusible *m*
fuse wire fil *m* fusible plomb

Electrical accessories
Accessoires électriques

battery pile *f*
battery, alkaline pile *f* alcaline
battery, button pile *f* bouton
battery, lithium pile *f* lithium
battery, rechargeable pile *f* rechargeable
battery charger chargeur *m* de piles
cable connector câble *m* connecteur
cable reel câble *m* enrouler
connector block dés *m* de raccordement (domino)
crimp connector cosse *f*
crimp connector, female cosse *f* clip femelle
crimp connector, flat cosse *f* clip plat mâle
crimp connector, forked cosse *f* fourche
crimp connector, male, flat cosse *f* fiche mâle
detector, carbon monoxide détecteur *m* de monoxide de

Electricity

carbone
detector, electrical current cut détecteur *m* de coupure de courant
detector, flood détecteur *m* d'inondation
detector, frost détecteur *m* de gel
detector, smoke détecteur *m* de fumée
earth spike piquet *m* de terre
extension lead rallonge *m* électrique
~ **long** prolongateur *m* électrique
extension reel enrouleur *m*
freezer alarm détecteur *m* de panne de congélateur
generator, electrical générateur *m*; groupe électrogène *m*
insulating tape ruban *m* adhésif; ruban *m* isolant
multiple socket extension lead bloc *m* multiprise
~ **with lightning protection** ~ parafoudre
plug adapter fiche *f* multiprise
surge/lightning protector parafoudre *m* de secteur
surge/lightning protector, socket-mounted prise *f* parasurtenseur
surge/lightning protector, for telecommunications equipment parafoudre *m* pour ligne téléphonique
terminal borne *f*

terminal, automatic push-in core connector borne *f* automatique
terminal, cable embout *m* de câble
terminal, cable socket borne *f* de câble
terminal, junction box borne *f* de jonction
terminal block strip barrette *f* de connexion; peigne *f* d'alimentation
terminal nut écrou *f*
trailing socket bloc *m* ménager
wire connector, self-stripping raccord *m* auto-dénudant

Electrician's tools
Outils d'électricien

ammeter ampèremètre *m*
cable cutter coupe-câble *m*
cable stripper dénundeur *m* de câble
~ **coaxial cable** ~ coaxial
cartridge fuse tester testeur *m* de cartouche fusible
circuit tester multimètre *f* digital
crocodile clip pince *f* crocodile
hammer, electrician's marteau *m* d'électricien
knife, electrician's couteau *m* d'électricien
detector, cable détecteur *m* de câbles
detector, metal détecteur *m*

Electricity

de metaux
detector, phase détecteur *m* de phase
ohmmeter ohmmètre *m*
pliers; pincers pince *f*
pliers, cable tie pince *f* de serrage pour collier
pliers, crimp connector pince *f* à cosses; ~ à sertir
pliers, cutting pince *f* coupante
screwdriver, electrician's tournevis *m* électricien
  ~ **flat blade** ~ plat électricien
  ~ **Phillips pattern** ~ Phillips
  ~ **Posidriv pattern** ~ Pozidriv
  ~ **slotted screws** ~ pour vis à fente
sheathing cutter couteau *m* à degainer
tester, current testeur *m* de courant
tester, voltage testeur *m* de tension
voltmeter voltmètre *m*
wattmeter wattmètre *m*
wirecutters pince *f* à dénuder et coupe-fil
wirecutters, adjustable pince *f* à dénuder et coupe-fil reglable
wirecutters, automatic pince *f* à dénuder et coupe-fil automatique
wirecutters, side-cutting pince *f* à dénuder et coupe-fil à becs
wirestrippers pince *f* à dénuder

Appendix

IRONMONGERY & HARDWARE
QUINCAILLERIE & VISSERIE

Ironmongery & Hardware

Adhesives
Adhésifs

adhesive colle *f*; adhésif *m*
adhesive, cold bituminous colle *f* à froid bitumineuse
adhesive, contact, interior colle *f* contact intérieur
adhesive, cornice and ceiling rose colle *f* corniche et rosace
adhesive, elastic, for parquet flooring colle *f* parquet
adhesive, elastic, for thin laminate flooring/mosaics colle *f* contrecolles mince/et mosaïques
adhesive, epoxy resin colle *f* résine époxydique
adhesive, fibreglass fabric colle *f* pour toile de verre
adhesive, flexible, for plaster tiles, cement, terracotta tiles liant colle *m*
adhesive, gap-filling colle *f* de blocage
adhesive, for insulation roll colle *f* rouleaux isolants
adhesive, interior wall colle *f* murale universelle
adhesive, for laminate/floating floors colle *f* stratifié et flottant
adhesive, mastic colle *f* mastic
  ~ **neoprene** ~ de fixation néoprène
  ~ **solvent-free** ~ sans solvant
adhesive foam pad fixer *m* mousse double face
adhesive, multi-purpose flooring colle *f* sol polyvalente
adhesive, multi-purpose neoprene gel colle *f* néoprène gel multi-usages
adhesive, neoprene colle *f* néoprène
  ~ **liquid** ~ liquide
adhesive, neoprene, for pipe lagging colle *f* manchon d'isolation
adhesive, for plaster slabs colle *f* carreaux de plâtre (not available in UK)
adhesive, plastic colle *f* plastique
adhesive, polystyrene colle *f* polystyrène, for ceilings and panelling
  ~ **soundproofing** phonicolle (in France; other brands in UK)
adhesive, polystyrene tiles dalles *f* polystyréne
adhesive, PVC joint and guttering colle *f* PVC raccords et gouttières rigide
adhesive, refractory colle *f* réfractaire
adhesive, for rigid plastic colle *f* plastique rigide
adhesive, rubber colle *f* caoutchouc
adhesive, stair nosing colle *f* nez de marche
adhesive, tile colle *f* carrelage
adhesive, tile, dust-free colle *f* carrelage rénovation sans poussière

Ironmongery & Hardware

adhesive, tile, interior and exterior floor tile colle *f* sol intérieur/extérieur
adhesive, tile, interior floor and wall tile colle *f* sol et mur intérieur
adhesive, tile, for terraces colle *f* à carrelage spéciale terrasse
adhesive, wallboard colle *f* plaquettes et parement
adhesive, wallcovering colle *f* revêtement
adhesive, wallcovering, non-woven colle *f* muraux sur intissés
adhesive, wallcovering, special colle *f* muraux spéciaux
adhesive, wooden shingle colle *f* bardeau
adhesive mortar mortier *f* colle
adhesive mortar, for cellular concrete mortier *f* colle béton cellulaire
adhesive mortar, grey mortier *f* colle gris, for floor tiles
adhesive mortar, for plasterboard mortier *f* adhésif pour plaque de plâtre et doublage
adhesive mortar, vinyl mortier *f* colle vinylique
  ~ **exterior wood** ~ bois exteriéur
  ~ **interior wood** ~ bois interiéur
  ~ **paper and cardboard** ~ papier et carton
fire cement joint *m* foyers et inserts
glue colle *f*; adhésif *m*

glue, acrylic (cork, rubber, leather, paper, metal, laminate, chipboard, hard plastic) colle *f* acrylique
glue, acrylic, for underlay colle *f* acrylique sous couche
glue, acrylic resin, for insulating materials colle *f* acrylique l'insonorisation
glue, carpet colle *f* moquette
glue, carpet and natural fibre floorcoverings colle *f* moquette et fibre naturelle
glue, carpet and plastic/PVC floorcoverings (tile or roll) colle *f* moquette et plastique/PVC
glue, ceiling tile colle *f* dalles de plafond
glue, cork colle *f* liège
glue, cyanoacrylate colle *f* cyanoacrylate
glue, cyanoacrylate, for plastics colle *f* plastique
glue, cyanoacrylate, for porcelain and earthenware colle *f* porcelaine et faïence
glue, decorative friezes colle *f* frises décoratives
glue, epoxy colle *f* époxy
glue, epoxy, glass colle *f* époxy verre
glue, epoxy, metal colle *f* époxy métal
glue, epoxy, rapid-setting colle *f* époxy rapide
glue, epoxy, universal colle *f* époxy universelle

Ironmongery & Hardware

glue, epoxy, wood colle *f* époxy bois
glue, expanded polystyrene insulation colle *f* isolants minces polystyrène expansé
glue, fabric colle *f* tissu
glue, fibreglass wallcovering colle *f* fibre de verre
glue, glass colle *f* spéciale verre
glue, heavy objects inside/outside colle *f* objets lourds intérieur/extérieur
glue, hot melt colle *f* thermofusible
glue, hot melt, low temperature, for delicate materials colle *f* basse température (matériaux délicats)
glue, inside/outside, sheltered colle *f* intérieur/extérieur sous abris
glue, items subject to vibration and high temperatures (e.g. washing machine/oven) colle *f* vibrations et hautes températures
glue, latex, for special fabrics colle *f* spéciale tissus
glue, leather colle *f* cuir
glue, metal colle *f* métaux
glue, mirror colle *f* miroir
glue, modelmaker's colle *f* maquette
glue, natural fibre floorcoverings colle *f* sol, fibres naturelles
glue, natural latex, for fabrics latex colle *f* naturel pour tissu
glue, 'no nail, no screw' colle *f* Ni Clou Ni Vis; Fixer sans Percer *f*
~ removable ~ démontable
glue, penetrating (wood fibres) colle *f* spéciale blocage pour bois
glue, plastic, PVC and vinyl floorcoverings colle *f* sols plastiques, PVC, vinyles
glue, polymer colle *f* polymère universelle
glue, polystyrene (ceilings and panelling) colle *f* polystyrène
glue, PVC colle *f* PVC
glue, PVC pipes colle *f* spéciale tuyaux PVC
glue, reinforced, for friezes colle *f* renforcée frise
glue, repositionable colle *f* repositionnable
~ for stencil ~spécial pochoir
glue, silicone colle *f* silicone
glue, soft plastic items colle *f* spéciale plastique souple
glue, solvent-free colle *f* sans solvant
glue stick bâton *m* de colle
glue stick, hot-melt (for glue gun) bâton *m* de colle à chaud
glue, synthetic rubber colle *f* élastomères synthétiques
glue, textile colle *f* textile
glue, textile, wall colle *f* muraux
glue, transparent drying colle *f* transparente après séchage
glue, ultra-violet, for glass, crystal, transparent plastics colle *f* UV matériaux transparent
glue, vinyl wood, outdoor, moderate humidity colle *f*

Ironmongery & Hardware

milieu humide
glue, wallpaper colle *f* papiers peints
glue, wallpaper, all types colle *f* tous papiers peints
glue, wallpaper, non-woven colle *f* papiers peints intissé
glue, wallpaper, thick colle *f* papiers peints épais
glue, wallpaper joints colle *f* raccords tous papiers peints
glue, wood colle *f* à bois
  ~ **exterior** ~ extérieur
  ~ **in a baby's bottle!** ~ en biberon
  ~ **in a pot** ~ en boîte
  ~ **polyurethane** ~ polyuréthane
  ~ **quick-setting** ~ prise rapide
  ~ **vinyl** ~ rapide vinylique
glue and joint for showers and swimming pools colle *f* et joint spéciale douche à l'italienne et piscine
glue cartridge cartouche *f* de colle
glue cartridge, for sealing and caulking cartouche *f* de colle fixation étanchéité
glue paste colle *f* en pâte
glue paste, for cork walls/ceilings colle *f* en pâte spéciale liège murs/plafonds
glue paste, for interior wall tiling colle *f* en pâte mur intérieur
mastic adhesive mastic *m* colle
mastic adhesive, auto/marine mastic *m* colle auto/marine

mastic adhesive, glass and window (cartridge) mastic *m* colle verre-vitrage cartouche
polyester putty/glue/sealer, for slight indentations mastic *m* colle polyester standard
resin and hardener (fixing, patching, reshaping, repairing) pâte *f* à coller
self-adhesive pads pastilles *f* adhésives
superglue, instant all-purpose colle *f* universelle instantanée
wallpaper paste colle *f* papier peint
  ~ **high bond** ~ adhérence élevée

Adhesive tapes
Ruban adhésifs

adhesive tape ruban *m* adhésif
adhesive tape, all-purpose ruban *m* adhésif multi-usages
adhesive tape, aluminium, for chimney hoods and flues ruban *m* adhésif alu/aluminium
adhesive tape, anti-slip ruban *m* adhésif anti-dérapant
adhesive tape, canvas-backed repair/reinforcing ruban *m* adhésif toilé
adhesive tape, double sided ruban *m* adhésif double face
  ~ **exterior grade** ~ extérieur
  ~ **extra strong** ~ extra fort
  ~ **mirror-fixing** ~ miroirs

Ironmongery & Hardware

~ **multi-purpose** ~ multi-usages
~ **skirting boards** ~ plinthe
adhesive tape, fine (indoor/outdoor use) ruban *m* adhésif fin intérieur/extérieur
adhesive tape, insulating ruban *m* adhésif isolant
adhesive tape, leak repair ruban *m* adhésif anti-fuites
adhesive tape, for mineral fibre and glass fibre insulation ruban *m* adhésif laine de verre
adhesive tape, for mineral fibre insulation ruban *m* adhésif laine de roche
adhesive tape, non-perforated, for sealing polycarbonate roof panels ruban *m* adhésif pour plaque
adhesive tape, perforated, for sealing polycarbonate roof panels ruban *m* adhésif perforé pour plaque
adhesive tape, plasterboard jointing ruban *m* adhésif raccord plaques de plâtre
adhesive tape, PVC exterior grade ruban *m* adhésif PVC spécial extérieur
adhesive tape, PVC rigid ruban *m* adhésif rigid PVC
adhesive tape, repairing and reinforcing ruban *m* adhésif réparer/renforcer
adhesive tape, self-adhesive ruban *m* adhésif auto-grippant
adhesive tape, supple PVC ruban *m* adhésif PVC souple
adhesive tape, translucent ruban *m* adhésif translucide
adhesive tape, for underlay ruban *m* adhésif pour sous-couche
masking tape ruban *m* adhésif de masquage
masking tape, for corners and curves ruban *m* adhésif de masquage courbe protection
masking tape, crepe ruban *m* adhésif de masquage crêpe
masking tape, for glass and tiles ruban *m* adhésif de masquage vitres/carrelages
masking tape, for all paintwork (wood, walls, paints) ruban *m* adhésif de masquage protection toutes peintures
masking tape, smooth, for flat surfaces ruban *m* adhésif de masquage lisse
masking tape, for straight edges ruban *m* adhésif de masquage droit protection
masking tape, woodwork, walls ruban *m* adhésif de masquage bois/murs/peints
packing tape, heavy duty glass fibre ruban *m* adhésif spécial emballage *m* lourds

Ironmongery & Hardware

Adhesive tools & equipment
Outils pour adhésifs

applicator, notched couteau *m* de colle
glue comb peigne *f* à colle
glue gun pistolet *m* à colle
~ **cordless** ~ sans fil
~ **high temperature** ~ haute température
~ **low temperature** ~ à basse température
~ **nozzle** ~ buse pour pistolet à colle
~ **variable temperature** ~ avec sélecteur de température
glue roller rouleau *m* à colle
glue spatula spatule *f* à colle
glue syringe seringue *m* à colle
paste bucket seau *m* à colle

Abrasives
Abrasifs

abrasive cloth toile *f* abrasive
abrasive pad patin *m* abrasive
abrasive pad, Scotchbrite patin *m* abrasive scotchbrite
abrasive paper papier *m* abrasif
abrasive paper, anti-clogging papier *m* abrasif anti-encrassant
abrasive paper, coarse grain papier *m* abrasif gros grain
abrasive paper, fine grain papier *m* abrasif fin grain
abrasive paper, flint papier *m* abrasif silex
abrasive paper, medium grain papier *m* abrasif moyen grain
abrasive paper, perforated (for dust extraction) papier *m* abrasif perforé
abrasive paper, sheet of feuille *f* abrasive
~ **finishing** ~ de finition
~ **paintwork** ~ décapage peinture
~ **rough surfaces** ~ préparation surfaces brutes
~ **varnish/paintwork** ~ abrasive vernis/peintures
~ **wood** ~ bois
abrasive paper, silicon carbide papier *m* abrasif carbure de silicium
abrasive paper band, for belt sander bande *f* abrasif
abrasive sponge éponge *f* abrasive
~ **waterproof** ~ perméable
corundum paper papier *m* abrasif corindon
emery cloth toile *f* émeri
garnet paper garniture *f* papier abrasive
~ **for plasterwork** ~ à plâtre
sanding block cale *f*; cale *f* à poncer; bloc *m* à poncer
sanding block, with abrasive grill cale *f* et grille abrasive
sanding block, for plasterwork cale *f* à poncer de plâtre

Ironmongery & Hardware

sanding disc, Velcro-backed, for power sander disque *m* abrasive autogrippant
steel wool paille *m* de fer
~ **synthetic** ~ synthétique

Fixings
Fixations

Nails
Clous

band, for regular alignment of upholstery tacks bande *f* pré-clouée plastique
brad clou *m* à tête perdue
corrugated fastener clou *m* ondulé
glazing sprig clou *m* de vitrier
nail; tack clou *m*; pointe *f*
nail, brass head clou *m* doré
nail, brass round head pointe *f* tête ronde laiton
nail, clout clou *m* à tête diamant
~ **extra large head** ~ à tête plate, extra large
nail, copper, flat head clou *m* à tête plate en cuivre
nail, countersunk head, galvanized pointe *f* tête fraisée acier galvanisé
nail, cut clou *m* découpé;
~ étampé
nail, diamond head clou *m* à tête diamant

nail, domed head clou *m* à tête bombeé
nail, flat head pointe *f* tête plate
~ **stainless steel** ~ inox
~ **steel** ~ acier brut
nail, flooring clou *m* à bateaux
nail, glazing, zinc-plated steel pointe *f* vitrier acier zingué
nail, headless clou *m* étêté
nail, large head galvanized pointe *f* tête plate large galvanisée
nail, large head zinc-plated wire clou *m* à tête plate large en acier zingué
nail, lost head clou *m* à tête perdue (see also: **brad**)
nail, masonry clou *m* à béton
nail, masonry, steel clou *m* maçon acier brut
nail, masonry, steel, ribbed, zinc-plated pointe *f* striée béton acier zingué
nail, oval wire clou *m* à tête d'homme
~ **brass-plated steel** ~ en acier laitonné
~ **polished steel** ~ en acier poli
~ **stainless steel** ~ en acier inoxydable
~ **tempered steel** ~ en acier trempé
~ **zinc-plated steel** ~ en acier zingué
nail, plasterboard (not available in France)
nail, round head clou *m* à tête ronde

nail, round head, polished steel for skirting/panelling clou *m* de plinthes/lambris en acier poli, tête homme
nail, round head, tempered steel pointe *f* tête ronde béton acier trempé
nail, round wire clou *m* à tête plate
~ **polished steel** ~ en acier poli
nail, steel oval pointe *f* tête homme acier brut
nail, steel round head, zinc-plated pointe *f* tête ronde acier zingué
nail, twisted shank clou *m* torsadé
nail, twisted shank steel pointe *f* torsadée acier brut
~ **zinc-plated steel** ~ acier zingué
nail, wire clou *m* de Paris
nail, zinc-plated steel, for roof shingles clou *m* pour shingles, acier zingué
nail, zinc-plated steel, headless pointe *f* à placage acier zingué
moulding pin pointe *f* moulures
screw head cover, hammer-on clou *m* cache vis tête martelée
slate peg pointe *f* à ardoise
staple crampillon *m*; *conduit m*
staple, galvanized steel crampillon *m* en acier galvanisé
staple, zinc-plated steel conduit *m* acier zingué
tack clou *m* de bouche; ~ de soufflet; petit clou *m*; semence *f*
tack, cobbler's/upholsterer's, bichromate steel semence *f* chaussure acier bichromaté
tack, thumb punaise *f*
tack, upholstery semence *f* de tapisser
~ **copper** ~ cuivre
~ **tempered steel** ~ acier bleui
upholstery pin clou *m* tapissier
~ **aged bronze** ~ bronze vieilli
~ **brass** ~ laitonné
~ **bronze, with rosette head** ~ rosace bronze
~ **nickel** ~ nickelé
upholstery pin, dome headed pointe *f* décorative à tête bombée

Screws
Vis

coach screw; lag screw tire-fond *f*
~ **plated steel** ~ acier bichromaté
~ **galvanized steel** ~ acier zingué
machine screw (Allen pattern) vis *f* à métaux cylindrique pans creux
screw vis *f*
screw, batten-fixing vis *f* pour tasseau
screw, brass slotted countersunk head vis *f* tête fraisée fendue laiton
screw, chipboard vis *f* à bois et aggloméré; ~ agglo
~ **countersunk head (Posidriv)**

Ironmongery & Hardware

~ tête fraisée pozi
~ **cylindrical head (Posidriv)**
~ tête cylindrique pozi
screw, countersunk head Posidriv plated steel vis *f* pozi acier bichromaté tête fraisée
screw, countersunk head, slotted vis *f* plate, fraisée et fendue
screw, cross-headed Phillips vis *f* empreinte cruciforme (Phillips)
screw, flanged, for sheet metal vis *f* à tôle tête hexagonale à collerette
screw, galvanized steel round headed vis *f* tête ronde acier zingué
screw, non-removable vis *f* indesserrable
screw, plasterboard vis *f* plaque de plâtre
~ **steel, phosphate** ~ acier phosphaté
screw, Posidriv vis *f* empreinte cruciforme (Posidriv)
screw, round topped vis *f* fraisée bombée
screw, self-drilling, self-tapping (for sheet metal) vis *f* à tôle autoperceuse
~ **countersunk head** ~ tête fraisée
~ **cylindrical head** ~ tête cylindrique
~ **dome-headed stainless steel countersunk Posidriv** ~ tête fraisée bombée pozi inox
~ **pan head Posidriv** ~ tête cylindrique pozi
~ **stainless steel countersunk head** ~ tête fraisée bombée inox
~ **trumpet-head** ~ tête trompette
screw, slot-headed vis *f* à tête fendue
~ **domed** ~ ronde fendue
screw, steel star-pattern, black (for hinges on shutters, gates etc) vis *f* penture empreinte étoile acier noir
screw, TORX vis *f* empreinte cruciforme (TORX)
woodscrew vis *f* à bois

Plugs
Chevilles

anchor fixing, metal cheville *f* métallique
anchor fixing, metal, hollow wall cheville *f* métallique à expansion
anchor fixing, metal, small hammer-in cheville *f* métallique mini
anchor fixing, metal, with screw cheville *f* métallique et vis
anchor stud, expanding goujon *m* d'ancrage à expansion
cavity fixing, expanding locking steel, for plasterboard cheville *f* à ancrage et verrouillage de forme
chemical anchor scellement *f* chimique

Ironmongery & Hardware

chemical anchor, cartridge of cartouche *f* de scellement chimique
chemical anchor, sleeve tamis *f* avec centreur pour scellement chimique
chemical anchor, threaded rod tige *f* filetée pour scellement chimique
chemical anchor, threaded sleeve douille *f* filetée pour scellement chimique
chemical anchor cartridge, mixing tip embout *m* mélangeur pour cartouche de scellement chimique
expansion bolt boulon *m* à expansion
frame fixing, long, with coach screw cheville *f* rallongée à tire fond
frame fixing, long, with screw cheville *f* traversante, expansion au vissage
plasterboard fixing, light to medium loads (no pre-drilling) cheville *f* à écartement
plug, nylon cheville *f* nylon
  ~ **for breezeblocks** ~ spécial
  ~ **expanding** ~ à expansion
  ~ **expanding, spreading** ~ à ancrage et écartement
  ~ **frame-fixing, doors and windows** ~ fendue pour encadrement de portes et fenêtres
  ~ **hammer-in** ~ à clouer
  ~ **screw-in auger bolt (for plasterboard)** ~ à visser
  ~ **split, expanding** ~ fendue
  ~ **with screw** ~ avec vis
  ~ **without screw** ~ sans vis béton cellulaire
spring toggle, steel cheville *f* en acier à ressort
  ~ **with eye** ~ avec piton
  ~ **with hook** ~ avec crochet
  ~ **with screw** ~ avec vis
spring toggle, suspended light fitting cheville *f* à bascule appui sur support
  ~ **with screw, eye or hook** ~ avec vis, piton ou crochet
wallplug; anchor; pin cheville *f*
wallplug, basic cheville *f* universelle
wallplug, brass corrosion-resistant cheville *f* en laiton
wallplug, cast iron heavy duty cheville *f* en fonte
wallplug, expanding, thin walls cheville *f* parois minces
wallplug, expanding brass, for suspended ceiling cheville *f* fendue pour plafond suspendu
wallplug, hammer-in plug/screw cheville *f* à frapper
wallplug, plasterboard cheville *f* plaque de plâtre
wallplug, polypropylene cheville *f* polypropylène
wallplug, screw and cover, fixing WC cistern to wall cheville *f* pour WC

Ironmongery & Hardware

wallplug, self-drilling cheville *f* auto-foreuse/auto-perceuses
wallplug, self-drilling, for plasterboard (medium load) cheville *f* auto-foreuse/auto perceuses à ancrage
wallplug, self-drilling steel cheville *f* auto-foreuse/auto-perceuses en acier à visser
wallplug, self-drilling toggle, plasterboard cheville *f* auto foreuse/auto-perceuses à bascule

Accessories for plugs
Accessoires pour des chevilles

gun for chemical fixing cartridge pistolet *m* pour cartouche de scellement chimique
hinge pin, right-angle, for spring toggle fixings gond *m*
hook for spring toggle fixings, with flange crochet *m* à collerette à boulonner
screw eye for spring toggle fixings, with flange piton *m* à collerette à boulonner
suspension eye suspension *f* Speedy-Fix (proprietary screw eye for suspending chain, wire, hooks and carabiners)
threaded stud, for pipe collar patte *f* à vis

Nuts & bolts
Boulonnerie

bolt boulon *m*
bolt, anchor boulon *m* d'ancrage
bolt, cotter boulon *m* à clavette
bolt, countersunk head boulon *m* fraisée
bolt, cylindrical-headed boulon *m* cylindrique
bolt, fastener boulon *m* d'assemblage
bolt, foundation boulon *m* de fondation
bolt, galvanized steel boulon *m* acier zingué
bolt, hexagonal-headed boulon *m* hexagonale
bolt, hook boulon *m* à croc
bolt, nylon boulon *m* en nylon
bolt, retaining boulon *m* de retenue
bolt, round-headed boulon *m* ronde
~ **with square collar** ~ collet carré
bolt, square-headed boulon *m* à tête carrée
bolt, stainless steel boulon *m* inox
bolt, tap boulon *m* poêlier acier zingué
circlip/snap ring circlip *m* extérieur
cotter pin, galvanized steel goupille *f* fendue acier zingué
cup washer, nickel-plated cuvette *m* laiton nickelé

Ironmongery & Hardware

locknut écrou *m* autobloquant; ~ contre-écrous; ~ indesserrable de blocage
nut écrou *m*
nut, blind écrou *m* borgne
nut, flange écrou *m* à embase
nut, hexagonal écrou *m* à six pans
nut, square écrou *m* carré
nut, standard écrou *m* ordinaire
nut, wing écrou *m* à oreilles
nut cover, hammer-in cache écrou *f* à pointe
rod, threaded tige *f* filetée
screw, headless threaded, for use with Allen key vis *f* de pression
screwbolt boulon *m* à écrou
sleeve, plated steel, for connecting threaded rod manchon *f* acier bichromaté
washer rondelle *f*
washer, felt rondelle *f* en feutre
washer, flat rondelle *f* plate
  ~ **large** ~ *f* plate large
  ~ **thin** ~ plate étroite
  ~ **thin nylon** ~ plate étroite nylon
washer, insulation rondelle *f* isolation
washer, large rondelle *f* carroissier
washer, for plasterboard screw rondelle *f* pour vis plaque de plâtre
washer, serrated rondelle *f* à denture/dentelée
washer, spring/split rondelle *f* à ressort/frein à ressort
washer, very large! rondelle *f* trés large

Screw hooks, pegs & eyes

Crochets, pitons & gonds de fixation

connecting strip, screw threaded vis *f* patte de jonction à visser
hinge gond *m*
hinge, brass gond *m* en laiton
hinge, galvanized steel gond *m* en acier zingué
hinge, stainless steel gond *m* en acier inoxydable
hinge, with white/black epoxy coating gond *m* en epoxy blanc/noir
hinge pin, screw-in gond *m* à visser
hook crochet *m*
hook, picture crochet *m* à tableau
hook, screw crochet *m* à visser
  ~ **brass** ~ en laiton
  ~ **galvanized steel** ~ en acier zingué
  ~ **stainless steel** ~ en acier inoxydable
  ~ **with white/black epoxy coating** ~ en epoxy blanc/noir
ring nut, screw-on anneau-écrou *m* à visser
screw eye piton *m* à visser
  ~ **brass** ~ en laiton
  ~ **galvanized steel** ~ en acier zingué

Ironmongery & Hardware

~ **stainless steel** ~ en acier inoxydable
~ **with white/black epoxy coating** ~ en epoxy blanc/noir

Fixing & assembly
Fixation & assemblage

bracket, angle équerre *f*
bracket, corner, triangular metal; flange bracket coin *m* métallique
bracket, corner plate équerre *f* d'angle
bracket, flat plate équerre *f* d'assemblage; ~ de chassis
  ~ **elbow** ~ coudée
bracket, half-round équerre *f* demi ronde
bracket, for post platine *f* pour poteau
bracket, right-angled chair équerre *f* de chaise
bracket, right-angled reinforcement équerre *f* de renfort
  ~ **plastic-coated** ~ acier plastifié
plate, flat rectangular patte *f* d'assemblage forte
  ~ **plastic** ~ plastique
  ~ **reinforced** ~ tronquée

Riveting & stapling
Rivetage & agrafage

blind nut, steel écrou *m* aveugle acier
extractor (nails, tacks, staples) extracteur *m* (clous, punaises, agrafes)
pliers, blind nut crimping pince *f* à écrou
pliers, crimping pince *f* à sertir
pliers, riveting pince *f* à riveter
  ~ **pivoting-head** ~ tête pivotante
rivet rivet *m*
rivet, blind rivet *m* aveugle
  ~ **aluminium/steel** ~ alu/acier
  ~ **corrugated aluminium/steel** ~ cannelé alu/acier
  ~ **plastic/aluminium** ~ plastique/alu
  ~ **stainless steel** ~ inox
  ~ **steel** ~ acier
  ~ **waterproof** ~ étanche
rivet, for attaching car number plate rivet *m* spécial plaque d'immatriculation
rivet, round-headed rivet *m* à tête ronde
rivet, tubular male/female rivet *m* tubulaire mâle et femelle
staple agrafe *f*
staple, galvanized steel agrafe *f* galvanisée
staple, green for wire mesh fence agrafe *f* grillage verte; ~ plastifiée verte
staple, narrow agrafe *f* étroite

Ironmongery & Hardware

staple, oval agrafe *f* cavalier
staple, single point pointe *f*
staple, small agrafe *f* bébé
staple gun agrafeuse *f*
staple remover dégrafeur *f*
stapler/nailer agrafeuse-cloueuse *f*
  ~ **cordless** ~ sans fil
  ~ **electric** ~ électrique
  ~ **manual** ~ manuelle
  ~ **pneumatic** ~ pneumatique

Security
Sécurité

latch, automatic verrou *m* automatique
bar, anti-panic, for door barre *f* antipanique pour porte
bar, lock reinforcement bride *f* de renfort
bar, security, for louvre shutter barre *f* de sécurité pour persienne
bar, security, reinforced barre *f* de sécurité renforcée
bar, security, for shutter barre *f* de sécurité pour volet
bolt/lock pêne *f*; targette *f*; verrou *m*
bolt, button-operated verrou *m* à bouton
  ~ **night latch with cylinder** ~ avec cylindre
  ~ **night latch with sliding bar** ~ sûreté à bouton
  ~ **night latch without exterior key entry** ~ sans entrée de clé extérieur
bolt, face-fixed verrou *f* en applique
bolt, flat latch targette *f* à pêne plat
bolt, locking, for window verrou *m* de condamnation pour menuiserie
bolt, round targette *f* à pêne ronde
bolt, sliding, vertical verrou *m* vertical
bolt, stable verrou *m* d'écurie
bolt, WC door verrou *m* de cabine
cable lock, key-operated câble *m* antivol à clé
chain lock, key-operated chaîne *f* antivol à clé
cupboard door stay (child safe) bloque-poignée *f* de placard
cylinder lock cylindre *f* de serrure
cylinder lock, for anti-panic bar, crutch-handled béquille *f* à cylindre pour barre antipanique
cylinder lock, disengaging cylindre *f* de serrure débrayable (allows key operation from outside even if a key is inserted on the inside)
cylinder lock, pressed steel, button-operated verrou *m* embouti bouton cylindre
cylinder plate, reinforcing plaque *f* de renfort à cylindre
  ~ **for profiled cylinder** ~ profilée
cylinder rim lock verrou *m* cylindre

Ironmongery & Hardware

cylinder rim lock, button-operated verrou *m* cambré bouton cylindre
cylinder rim lock, deadbolt verrrou *m* à pêne dormant
cylinder rim lock, double, with reversible keys verrou *m* double cylindre clés réversibles
cylinder rim lock and plate, key operated verrou *m* cylindre clés protégées et plaque
door chain entrebâilleur *m* à chaîne
door closer ferme-porte *f*
door closer, rack and pinion ferme-porte *f* à pignon et crémaillère
door closer, spring ferme-porte *f* à ressort
door lock, base serrure *f* bas de porte
door lock, entry crémone *f* serrure
door lock, top serrure *f* haut de porte
door viewer judas *m*
French window, top lock for crémone *f* à têtière
garage door, double lock combine *f* double verrouillage pour porte de garage
gate latch, key-operated loquet *m* de portail à clé
handle; doorknob poignée *f*
hasp and staple porte-cadenas *m*
keep plate gâche *f*
keep plate, electrically-operated door lock gâche *f* électrique
keep plate, recessed gâche *f* universelle à encastrer
keep plate, for roller shutter gâche *f* rouleaux
lock serrure *f*
lock, barrel, for French window crémone *f* (porte-fenêtre) à barillet
lock, cylinder serrure *f* à cylindre
 ~ **vertical** ~ verticale
lock, electrically-operated serrure *f* électrique
lock, mechanical, code-operated verrou *m* à code méchanique
lock, mortise serrure *f* à encastrer
 ~ **key-operated** ~ à clé
 ~ **WC or bathroom** ~ à condamnation
 ~ **with cylinder** ~ à cylindre
lock, multiple point serrure *f* multipoint (i.e. with connecting bars to secure top and bottom of door)
 ~ **face-fixed** ~ à appliquer
 ~ **recessed** ~ à encastrer
lock, rim serrure *f* en applique
 ~ **horizontal** ~ horizontale
 ~ **vertical** ~ verticale
lock, single point serrure *f* monopoint
 ~ **face-fixed** ~ à appliquer
 ~ **recessed** ~ à encastrer
lock, tubular, button-operated, with locking nib (WC or bathroom) serrure *f* tubulaire bec-à-cane à condamnation

Ironmongery & Hardware

lock tumbler gorge *f*
locking bar, multi-point serrure *f* à bandeau
padlock cadenas *m*
padlock, closed shackle cadenas *m* anse protégée
padlock, combination cadenas *m* à combinaison
padlock, key-operated cadenas *m* à clé
padlock, long shackle cadenas *m* anse haute
pin (in cylinder lock) goupille *f*
rim lock, button-operated, with separate cylinder verrou *m* médial à bouton avec cylindre
rim lock, double entry verrou *m* double entrée
rosette trim for cylinder hole rosace *f* de finition à trou de cylindre
~ **for profiled cylinder** ~ profilé
stay, for door entrebâilleur *m* fixe
stay, for shutters entrebâilleur de sécurité pour volets
stay, for window entrebâilleur fenêtre
~ **serpentine** ~ serpentin
window grille grille *f* de hublot
window handle, locking poignée *f* à condamnation par barrillet
~ **button-operated** ~ à bouton
~ **key-operated** ~ à clé
window hinge protector protège *f* gonds de fenêtre
~ **side hung or pivoting**
~ battante ou oscillo-battante

window latch crémone *f*
window latch, for fire door, with rotating handle crémone *f* pompier à poignée rotative
window latch, mortise crémone *f* à larder
window latch, recessed, without square bolt crémone *f* à encastrer sans pêne carré
window lock verrou *m* de fenêtre
window lock, swinging/pivoting verrou *m* pour fenêtre oscillant battante
window lock, swinging/sliding verrou *m* de fenêtre battante ou baie coulissante

Hinges
Charnières & paumelles

brass spacers for lift-off hinges bagues *f* pour paumelles en laiton
hinge charnière *f*
hinge, bed charnière *f* de lit (not a UK category, but similar to a butt or backflap hinge)
hinge, bichromate finish charnière *f* bichromate
hinge, box/chest charnière *f* de caisse d'étui; ~ de coffre
hinge, brass charnière *f* en laiton
hinge, concealed clip-on charnière *f* invisible
hinge, cranked charnière *f* contre coudée

Ironmongery & Hardware

hinge, demountable (loose pin backflap) charnière *f* démontable
hinge, door charnière *f* pour porte
hinge, double action charnière *f* double action
hinge, flap charnière *f* à congé
hinge, flush charnière *f* à lamelles
 ~ **furniture** ~ de meubles
 ~ **for door** ~ pour porte
hinge, galvanized steel charnière *f* en acier zinguée
hinge, glass door charnière *f* pour porte en verre
hinge, lift-off paumelle *f*
hinge, lift-off, with decorative pin paumelle *f* à vase
hinge, lift-off, for door paumelle *f* pour porte
 ~ **inset** ~ rentrante
 ~ **lightweight door** ~ légère
 ~ **two-way** ~ va-et-vient
hinge, piano charnière *f* piano
hinge, pivot charnière *f* pivot
hinge, removable charnière *f* amovible
hinge, round end paumelle *f* à bout rond
hinge, scallop-edged decorative charnière *f* festonnée
hinge, screen/windbreak charnière *f* paravent
hinge, spring charnière *f* à ressort
 ~ **double action** ~ double action
 ~ **screw-on spring furniture hinge, door** ~ à visser avec ressort pour porte de meuble

hinge, stainless steel charnière *f* en inox
hinge, steel charnière *f* en acier
hinge, table paumelle *f* de table
hinge, table, drop leaf charnière *f* de table
hinge, universal paumelle *f* universelle
hinge, universal (butt and flap) charnière *f* universelle
screw hinge fiche *f* à visser; gond *m*
 ~ **with swivel pin** ~ à tourillon à visser
strap hinge penture *f*
strap hinge, English pattern penture *f* anglaise
strap hinge, fishtail pattern penture *f* queue de carpe
strap hinge for shutter penture *f* droite bout carré

Shutter accessories
Accessoires pour volets

bolt verrou *m*
bolt, adjustable verrou *m* à tige réglable cadenas
bolt, bayonet verrou *m* baïonnette
bolt, foot verrou *m* de pied
bolt, for roller shutter verrou *m* de serrage pour volet roulant
bolt, stable verrou *m* d'écurie
espagnolette lock serrure *f* de crémone
gimbal for roller shutter crank

Ironmongery & Hardware

cardan *m* de manivelle
hasp and staple entrebâilleur *m* de sécurité pour volets
hinge gond *m*
hinge bracket for solid wall fixing gond *m* à sceller double feuille
  ~ **chemical adhesive** ~ chimique
  ~ **plate fixing, vertical** ~ à platine verticale
  ~ **screw-in** ~ à vis bois
hook crochet *m*
hook and brace crochet *m* de contrevent
latch fermeture *f* de volet à loquet
lock set espagnolette *f* complète
nail, diamond-headed clou *m* tête diamant
pull ring anneau (*pl* -x) de tirage
retainer, automatic arrêt *m* volet automatique
retainer, base butée *f* surmoulée
retainer, pivoting portail *m* à bascule; tourniquet *m* à visser
retainer, pivoting, Marseille pattern (leaf motif) arrêt *m* marseillais à tourniquet
retainer, pivoting, with stop handle arrêt *m* de volet à poignée
retainer, shepherdess figure, coach screw fixing arrêt *m* tête de bergère à tire-fond
retaining bracket/hook crémaillère *f*
roller shutter crank manivelle *f* métal pour volet roulant
roller shutter guide guide *f* de sangle
roller shutter slat lame *f* à volet roulant
roller shutter strap sangle *f* pour volet
security bar barre *f* de sécurité
shutter catch poignée *f* de fleau
shutter lock ferrure *f* de volet
strap hinge penture *f* droite bout carré
T-shaped bracket (slots onto hinge) té droit/paire d'équerres

Door accessories
Accessoires de porte

chime; doorbell carillon *m*
chime, plug-in carillon *m* enfichable
chime, wired carillon *m* filaire
chime, wireless carillon *m* sans fil
door closer ferme-porte *f*
  ~ **automatic** ~ automatique
  ~ **spring** ~ à ressort
doorbell pushbutton bouton *m* de sonnette
  ~ **wired** ~ filaire
  ~ **wireless** ~ sans fil
doorknob bouton *m* de porte
  ~ **for entrance door** ~ d'entrée
doorstop arrêt *m* de porte; butée *f* de porte; butoir *m*
  ~ **recessed** ~ fixe à encastrer
escutcheon rosace *f*

Ironmongery & Hardware

escutcheon, for cylinder lock rosace *f* à cylindre; ~ de protection; ~ de sécurité
escutcheon, keyhole rosace *f* de porte à clé
escutcheon, for lock rosace *f* à serrure
escutcheon, lockable (for use inside WC or bathroom) rosace *f* de porte à condamnation
escutcheon, unlockable with screwdriver from outside (should occupant of WC or bathroom become trapped) rosace *f* de porte à décondamnation
finger latch cuvette *f* doigt têtière
handle; doorknob poignée *f*
handle, bowl lock poignée *f* de cuvette serrure
handle, crutch béquille *f*
handle, non-locking poignée *f* de porte sur plaque sans condamnation
handle, reversible for right- or left-hand fixing poignée *f* béquille réversible
handle and cylinder plate assembly poignée *f* de porte sur plaque à cylindre
handle and keyhole plate assembly poignée *f* de porte sur plaque à clé
handle and rosette assembly poignée *f* sur rosace
handle set ensemble *m* de porte
intercom interphone *m*

~ **audio** ~ audio
~ **video** ~ vidéo
knob; button bouton *m*
knocker marteau *m* de porte
pull handle barre *f* de tirage
push button poussoir *m*
rosette escutcheon rosace *f*
spindle, door handle carré *m* de poignée

Window accessories
Accessoires de fenêtre

French window catch espagnolette *f* crémone
metal rod for operating espagnolette tringle *f* pour crémone
window handle, lockable poignée *f* de sécurité
window latch crémone *f*
~ **handle** (to connect **tringle**) boîtier *m* crémone
~ **lockable** ~ serrure

Mosquito nets
Moustiquaires

mosquito net moustiquaire *f*
mosquito net, aluminium moustiquaire *f* alu
mosquito net, for bed moustiquaire *f* pour lit
mosquito net, for door/window, Velcro fixing moustiquaire *f*

Ironmongery & Hardware

pour porte/fenêtre avec fixation velcro
mosquito net, door curtain moustiquaire *f* porte-rideau
mosquito net, fixed, for window moustiquaire *f* cadre fixe pour fenêtre
mosquito net, folding moustiquaire *f* plissée
mosquito net, for French window moustiquaire *f* pour porte-fenêtre
mosquito net, for hinged doors moustiquaire *f* battante
mosquito net, for roof window moustiquaire *f* de toit
mosquito net, side-rolling, for door moustiquaire *f* à enroulement latéral
mosquito net, for sliding window and door moustiquaire *f* fenêtre et baie coulissante
mosquito net, for window moustiquaire *f* pour fenêtre
mosquito net, for window, vertical roller moustiquaire *f* à enroulement
mosquito net kit kit *m* de liaison moustiquaire
net, white glass fibre fibre *m* de verre blanc
net replacement toile *f* de remplacement pour moustiquaire
roller blind screen store *m* moustiquaire enroulable

Rope, webbing, chain & cable

Corde, sangle, sandow, chaîne & câble

belt strap sangle *f*
belt strap, for luggage rack sangle *f* bagagère
belt strap, for roller shutter sangle *f* pour volet roulant
belt strap, for stowage sangle *f* d'arrimage
  ~ with cam buckle ~ avec came à griffes
  ~ with moulded buckle ~ boucle surmoulée
belt strap, with ratchet sangle *f* à cliquet
belt strap, with self locking clamp sangle *f* pince autobloquante
bungee cord sandow *m*
bungee cord, with hooks sandow *m* à crochet
bungee cord, multicoloured sandow *m* multicolore
cable câble *f*
cable, galvanized steel câble *f* acier galvanisé
cable, lifting; traction; leverage câble *f* qualité levage
cable, sheathed câble *f* gainé
cable, steel lifting câble *f* levage acier
chain chaîne *f*
chain, chandelier chaîne *f* de lustrerie

Ironmongery & Hardware

chain, long link chaîne *f* maillons longs
chain, short link chaîne *f* maillons courts
chain, signalling chaîne *f* de signalisation
  ~ **plastic** ~ en plastique
chain, straight welded chaîne *f* droite soudée
chain, twisted chaîne *f* torsadée
halyard, polypropylene drisse *f* en polypropylène
rope cordage *f*
rope; string; cord corde *f*
rope, braided corde *f* tressée
rope, hemp cordage *f* chanvre
  ~ **natural** ~ naturel
  ~ **twisted** ~ torsadée
rope, knot of carotte *f* de drisse
rope, polypropylene cordage *f* polypropylène
rope, sisal cordage *f* sisal
string ficelle *m*
string, ball of pelote *f* de ficelle
string, plumbline, ball of pelote *f* de cordeau
stringline, mason's cordeau *m* de maçon
washing line corde *f* à linge
wire fil *m*
wire, brass fil *m* laiton
wire, copper fil *m* cuivre
wire, galvanized steel fil *m* galvanisé
wire, plastic-coated fil *m* plastifié
wire, reel of fil *m* en bottillon

Accessories for rope, webbing, chain & cable

Accessoires pour corde, sangle, sandow, chaîne & câble

buckle, quick release (for webbing) boucle *f* à ouverture rapide
butcher's hook esse *f* de boucher
cable clamp serre-câble *f*
cable clamp, flat serre-câble *f* plat
cable clamp, stirrup serre-câble *f* étrier
cable loop support cosse-coeur *f*
cable tightener tendeur *m* à cage
carabiner (quick link) maillon *m* rapide
cleat (for blind) arrêt *f* de cordon pour store
cotter pin goupille *f*
D-shackle manille *f* droite
eye-bolt boulon *m* oeil
fixing collar bride *f* de fixation
hook crochet *m*
hook, for bungee cord crochet *m* pour sandow
hook and eye, lifting, with safety latch crochet *m* de levage à oeil et linguet de sécurité
link maillon *m*
link, connecting maillon *m* de jonction
metal ring anneau *m*
metal ring, for rope handrail anneau *m* de corde à rampe
metal split ring anneau *m* brisé
pulley poulie *f*

Ironmongery & Hardware

pulley, with suspension hook poulie *f* à crochet
pulley, with suspension screw poulie *f* à visser
S-hook esse *f*; ~ égale
snap clasp; carbine hook mousqueton *m*; ~ à linguet
snap clasp, 'firefighter's' mousqueton *m* pompier
snap clasp, screwed mousqueton *m* à vis
snap clasp, with swivel mousqueton *m* pompe à touret
swivel rings, twin touret *m* double

Storage & transport: tools & materials

Stockage & transport: les outils & les matériaux

barrow diable *m*
barrow, sack diable *m* porte sac
case, with foam insert with tool profile cutout malette *f* mousse de protection
furniture lifter, with roller lève meuble *f*
roller support, pivoting support *m* roulant pivotant
shelf unit étagère *f*
storage case, with drawers for screws, nails etc. module *f* de rangement
suction lifter, double ventouse *f* double
tool basket panier *m* porte-outils
tool belt ceinture *f* porte-outil
tool board wall panel panneau *m* mural alvéolé
toolbox boîte *f* à outils; coffre *m* à outils; caisse *f* à outils; coffre *m* de chantier fixe
toolbox, wheeled boîte *f* à outils sur roulettes
toolbox, wheeled suitcase-type servante *f* à outils
toolchest, reinforced cantine *f* renforcée
tool holder, wall mounted or portable, magnetic porte-outils *m* magnétique
tool rack ratelier *m* pour outils
tool rack, magnetic barette *f* porte-outils magnétique
tool roll trousse *f*
tool storage rangement *m* des outils
tool storage cupboard, metal armoire *f* de rangement métal
tray, pivoting with divided compartments organisateur *m* à plateau
trolley chariot *m*; ~ de transport
trolley, folding chariot *m* pliant
wall bracket, with locking tool clips support support *m* mural avec crochets autobloquants

Ladders & stepladders
Escabeaux & marchepieds

hop-up, elephant foot pied *m* d'éléphant
ladder, telescopic échelle *f* télescopique
scaffolding échafaudage *m*
scaffolding, interior use échafaudage *m* d'intérieur
step; hop-up marchepied *m*
stepladder escabeau *m*

Workbenches & accessories
Etablis & accessoires

clamping wedge cale *f* de serrage
roller stand servante *f* à rouleau
trestle support tréteau-support *m*
vice jaws mâchoires *f* d'étau
vice jaws, aluminium mâchoires *f* d'étau en aluminium
vice jaws, plastic mâchoires *f* d'étau en plastique
workbench établi *m*
worbench, folding établi *m* pliant
workbench, mechanic's établi *m* de mécanicien
workbench-vice, portable établi-étau *m*

Draughtproofing; weatherseal
Calfeutrage

draught excluder, under-door dessous *m* de porte
draught strip, foam bourrelet *m*
excluder strip, brush bas *m* de porte brosse
~ **soft** ~ souple
excluder strip, door (draught/rain/sound) bas *m* de porte
~ **adhesive** ~ eau/air/bruit adhésif
excluder strip, flap bas *m* de porte à bavette
~ **for large gap** ~ gros espace
excluder strip, garage bas *m* de porte de garage
~ **brush** ~ grande brosse
~ **small brush seal** ~ petite bavette
~ **thermoplastic flap** ~ grande bavette
excluder strip, lipped bas *m* de porte à lèvres
excluder strip, pin on bas *m* de porte à clouer
excluder strip, pivoting bas *m* de porte pivotant
excluder strip, screw on bas *m* de porte à visser
excluder strip, bronze heavy-duty, brush bas *m* de porte bronze, brosse dure
excluder strip, silver heavy-duty, brush bas *m* de porte argent,

Ironmongery & Hardware

brosse dure
foam insulation, adhesive mousse *f* adhésive d'isolation
loft hatch insulation isolant *m* trappe de visite
weatherstrip joint *m* de calfeutrage
weatherstrip, adhesive joint *m* adhésif
  ~ long lasting foam ~ longue durée combles
  ~ rubber E-profile ~ caoutchouc profil E
  ~ rubber P-profile ~ caoutchouc profil P
weatherstrip, for doors, windows and sliding closet doors joint *m* adhésif de porte, fenêtre et placard coulissants
weatherstrip, foam joint *m* adhésif mousse universel
weatherstrip, grooved (windows) joint *m* adhésif fenêtre petites rainures
weatherstrip, PVC (doors and windows) joint *m* adhésif portes et fenêtres PVC

Wheels & castors
Roues & roulettes

castor roulette *f*
castor, slot-on roulette *f* à œil
castor, twin-wheeled, furniture roulette *f* d'ameublement double galet
castor, with mounting plate roulette *f* platine
  ~ pivoting, braked ~ pivotante et frein
  ~ with fixed plate ~ fixe
  ~ with pivoting plate ~ pivotante
castor, with smooth shank roulette *f* à tige lisse
castor, with threaded shank roulette *f* à tige filetée carénée
roller wheel roulette *f* galet
wheel roue *f*
wheel, flexible handling on all surfaces roue *f* manutention très souple sur tous sols
  ~ light loads ~ légere
  ~ medium loads ~ moyenne
wheel, inflatable roue *f* gonflable
wheel, jockey, telescopic roue *f* jockey télescopique
wheel, lawnmower roue *f* tondeuse
wheel, plastic roue *f* plastique
wheel, pushchair roue *f* de poussette
wheel, rubber roue *f* caoutchouc
wheel, wheelbarrow roue *f* de brouette

Furniture fittings
Ferrures de meubles

anti-slip/anti-vibration pad patin *m* anti-dérapant et anti-vibration
bracket, metal, square, with threaded hole équerre *f* carrée métal, trou taraudé
catch, two-part, metal, for cassettes or boxes verrou *m* en métal pour cassettes et caisses
drawer slide coulisse *f* de tiroir
end piece, plastic embout *m* plastique
~ **push-in cap for hollow leg** ~ entrant
~ **push-on cap for solid leg** ~ enveloppant
felt self-adhesive pad patin *m* feutre adhésif/auto collant
filing cabinet, label holder porte-étiquette *f* classeur
foam pad patin *m* alvéolaire
foam/rubber pads, noise cushioning pastille *f* mousse/caoutchouc anti-bruit adhésive
foot plate, pivoting/adjustable vérin *m*
foot/leg pied *m*
~ **plastic** ~ de meuble plastique
~ **with threaded shank** ~ avec vis filetée
~ **with threaded socket** ~ avec embout taraudé
foot/leg, for bed pied *m* de lit
foot/leg, for table pied *m* de table

~ **adjustable** ~ de table réglable
~ **folding** ~ rabattable
handle, finger-pull poignée *f* à patte
handle, furniture poignée *f* de meuble; ~ d'ameublement
handle, pendant poignée *f* pendant
handle, recessed poignée *f* à encastrer
handle, shell-shaped pull poignée *f* coquille
hook, metal, for cassettes or boxes crochet *m* en métal pour cassettes et caisses
knob/button bouton *m* de meuble
knob/button, drawer bouton *m* de tiroir
latch loquet *m*
latch, door, plastic loquet *m* en plastique
pin-on pad, plastic patin *m* à clouer plastique
ring pull handle anneau *m* rond
roller catch, metal loquet *m* à bille en métal
slider/furniture glide patin *m* glisseur lisse

Ironmongery & Hardware

Appendix

METALWORK
FERRONNERIE

… Metalwork

Metal
Métal

Types of metal
Types de métal

aluminium aluminium *m*
brass laiton *m*; cuivre *m* jaune
bronze bronze *m*
chromium chrome *m*
copper cuivre *m*
copper, annealed cuivre *m* recuit
iron fer *m*
iron, cast fer *m* de fonte
iron, galvanized fer *m* galvanisé
gold or *m*
lead plomb *m*
metal, ferrous métal *m* ferreux
metal, non-ferrous métal *m* non ferreux
nickel nickel *m*
nickel-plated steel acier *m* nickelé
nickel-silver nickel-argent *m*
platinum platine *m*
silver argent *m*
stainless steel inox *m*
steel acier *m*
steel, galvanized acier *m* galvanisé
steel, laminated acier *m* laminé
steel, zinc-coated acier *m* zinguée
tin étain *m*
tungsten tungstène *m*
zinc zinc *m*
zinc, electroplated electrozinguée

Metal sections
Sections métalliques

angle iron cornière *f*; fer *f* d'angle
angle iron, equal sides cornière *f* égale
angle iron, unequal sides cornière *f* inégale
bar, flat metal barre *f* plat métal
bar, metal barre *f* en métal
bar, round metal barre *f* ronde serrurier
iron, square section fer *f* carré
sheet metal tôle *f*
  ~ **electroplated** ~ electrozinguée
  ~ **galvanized** ~ galvanisée
  ~ **perforated** ~ perforée
steel, cold-rolled section acier *m* laminé à froid
steel, hot-rolled section acier *m* laminé à chaud
tube tube *m*
tube, rectangular hollow section tube *m* métal rectangulaire
tube, round tube *m* rond
tube, square hollow section tube *m* carré
U-shaped metal channel U *m* à conge
wire fil *m*
wire, solid fil *m* massif

Metalwork hand tools
Outils à main ferronnerie

bolt cutters coupe-boulons *mpl*
calliper pied *m* à coulisse
calliper, digital vernier pied *m* à coulisse digital
calliper, outside spring pied *m* à coulisse compas d'épaisseur
calliper, vernier pied *m* à coulisse vernier
centre punch pointeau *m*; ~ de précision
cold chisel burin *m* de mécanicien
compasses compas *m*
feeler gauge calibre *m* d'epaisseur
file lime *f*
file, flat lime *f* plate à main
file, half-round lime *f* mi-ronde
file, mini lime *f* de precision
file, needle lime *f* aiguille
file, round lime *f* ronde
file, saw lime *f* tiers point
file, square lime *f* carrée
hacksaw scie *f* à métaux
hacksaw, junior scie *f* à métaux junior
hacksaw, mini porte-lame *f*
hacksaw frame monture *f* scie à métaux
hammer marteau *m*
hammer, blacksmith's marteau *m* de forgeron
hammer, chipping marteau *m* à piquer les soudures
hammer, English/American pattern ball pein marteau *m* boule 'anglais'/'americain'
hammer, mechanic's marteau *m* de mécanicien
hammer, riveting marteau *m* rivoir
keyhole saw ergoscie *f*
mallet maillet *m*; masse *f*; massette *f*
mallet, copper-headed maillet *m* cuivre
mallet, plastic-headed maillet *m* à tête plastique
monkey wrench; adjustable clé *f* à molette
panel beater batte *f* de tôlier-carrossier
pincers tenaille *f*
pipe wrench, adjustable pince *f* reglable
pliers pince *f*
pliers, bent-nosed pince *f* à becs coudes effilés
pliers, cutting pince *f* coupante
   ~ **diagonal** ~ diagonale
   ~ **front** ~ de devant
   ~ **mechanic's** ~ mécanicien
   ~ **side-** ~ de coté
pliers, flat long-nosed pince *f* à becs plats
pliers, general purpose pince *f* universelle
pliers, locking pince-étaus *f*
   ~ **long-nosed** ~ bec longs
   ~ **short-nosed** ~ bec courts
pliers, long-nosed pince *f* à bec demi-rond de longueur
pliers, multi-purpose pince *f* multifonctions

Metalwork

pliers, round-nosed pince *f* à becs ronds
pliers, water pump pince *f* multiprise de longueur
protractor rapporteur *m* d'angle échancré
screwdriver, magnetic tip tournevis *m* lame magnétique
scriber point *m* à tracer
socket spanner douille *f*
spanner clé *f*
spanner, box/socket clé *f* à pipe
  ~ through ~ débouchée
spanner, combination clé *f* mixte
speed wrench clé *f* cliquet
spring divider compas *m* à pointes sèches
star key clé *f* étoile
tap and die set coffret *m* de tarauds et filières

Accessories for metalwork hand tools

Accessoires pour outillage à main ferronnerie

rule réglet *m*
rule, flexible stainless steel réglet *m* inox flexible
rule, stainless steel réglet *m* semi-rigides inox
saw blade lame *f* de scie
set square équerre *f*
  ~ aluminium ~ alu
  ~ steel ~ acier
set square, 90° square équerre *f* simple à 90°
tape measure mètre *m* ruban
toolbox, mechanic's caisse *f* mécanicien
vice étau *m*

Metalwork power tools

Outils électriques ferronnerie

angle grinder meuleuse *f* d'angle
angle grinder backing pad plateau *m* pour disques
bench grinder touret *m* à meuler
bench grinder, with wire wheel touret *m* à meuler mixte
drill perceuse *f*
drill, bench perceuse *f* d'établi
drill, manual perceuse *f* manuelle
drill press perceuse *f* sur colonne
filer, electric lime *f* électrique
grinding disk/wheel meule *f*
  ~ fine grain ~ grain fin
jigsaw scie *f* sauteuse
jigsaw, laser scie *f* sauteuse laser
jigsaw, pendular scie *f* sauteuse pendulaire
milling machine fraiseuse *f*
pedestal stand grinder socle *m* pour touret
saw scie *f*
saw, cut-off tronçonneuse *f* metal
saw, metal-cutting band scie *f* à ruban metal
saw, metal-cutting circular scie *f*

Metalwork

circulaire métal
saw, sabre scie *f* sabre
soldering gun, electric pistolet *m* à souder
soldering iron, electric fer *m* à souder électronique
whetstone meule *f* à eau

Accessories for metalwork power tools

Accessoires pour outils électriques ferronnerie

angle grinder cutting stand support *m* tronçonnage de meuleuse
bench support *m* touret a meuler
blade, band saw lame *f* pour scie à ruban métal
blade, cut-off saw lame *f* pour tronçonneuse métal
die head for thread cutting on lathe tête *f* de filière
disk, cutting disque *m* à tronçonner
disk, flap disque *m* à lamelles
disk, sisal polishing disque *m* sisal
drill stand support *m* de perçage
lathe cutting tools outils *m* à pastilles carbure démontables

Metalwork accessories
Accessoires ferronnerie

cleaning rag tampon *m* de nettoyage
drill bit foret *m*
drill bit, high speed steel (HSS) foret *m* HSS
drill bit, metal foret *m* métaux
 ~ **hexagonal shank** ~ queue hexag
 ~ **reduced shank** ~ queue réduite
ear defenders casque *m* antibruits
ear plugs bouchons *mpl* d'oreille
epoxy resin mastic mastic *m* soudre à froid universel
gas economiser économiseur *m* de gaz
gas flow meter débilitre *m* à colonne
letters and numbers punch set lettres *f* et chiffres à frapper
oil huile *f*
oil, hydraulic huile *f* hydraulique
oil, soluble huile *f* soluble
polishing paste pâte *f* à polir
propane propane *m*

Metalwork

Soldering, welding & brazing
Soudage & de brasage

ammonia stone for cleaning soldering iron pierre *f* ammoniacale
blowtorch lampe *f* à souder
brazing rod baguette *f*
brazing rod, aluminium baguette *f* d'aluminium enrobé
brazing rod, aluminium, low temperature brasure *f* aluminium basse temperature
brazing rod, copper, phosphorous silver baguette *f* de brasage, cuivre/phosphor argent
brazing rod, phosphorus copper baguette *f* en cuivre phosphore
burner brûleur *m*
burner, enveloping brûleur *m* à flamme enveloppante
burner, extra-fine point brûleur *m* à pointe super fine
burner, flat beak brûleur *m* à bec plat
burner, large flame brûleur *m* grande flamme
desoldering pump pompe *f* à dessouder
flame arrestor, oxygen, non return anti-retour *f* pare-flamme oxygène
flux décapant *m*
flux paste pâte *f* décapante
gas bottle, disposable cartouche *f* gaz jetable
gas bottle, refillable bouteille *f* gaz rechargeable
gas welding/soldering/cutting torch chalumeau *m*
 ~ **gas** ~ monogaz
 ~ **heating** ~ chauffeur
 ~ **lever-operated** ~ avec levier
 ~ **welding** ~ soudure
goggles lunettes *f* de soudage; ~de protection
headshield, arc/MIG welding masque *m* de soudure, arc/MIG
hose, acetylene tuyau *m* acetylène
hose, butane/propane tuyau *m* butane/propane
hose, oxygen tuyau *m* oxygène
liquid flux eau *f* à souder
oxyacetylene welder poste *f* à souder oxyacétylénique
oxygen oxygène *m*
oxygen canister cartouche *f* oxygène
regulating tap robinet *m* relais
regulator détendeur *m*
soldering gun pistolet *m* à souder
soldering iron fer *f* à souder
soldering iron, electric fer *f* à souder électrique
soldering iron, gas fer *f* à souder autonome à gaz
soldering lance lance *f* de soudage
tin solder, bobbin of soudure *m* étain en bobine
welding blanket pare-flamme *f*
welding nozzle buse *f* de soudage
welding ring bague *f* de soudage

Metalwork

welding rod baguette *f* de métal d'apport et étain
welding table table *f* de soudage
wire brush brosse *f* métallique

Arc welding
Soudure à l'arc

apron, protective tablier *m* de protection pour soudure à l'arc
arc welder poste *m* de souder à l'arc
brazing rod baguette *f* de souder arc
DC inverter redresseur *m* à courant continu DC
earth clamp prise *f* de masse
electrode électrode *f*
electrode, fluxed électrode *f* enrobée
electrode holder pince *f* porte électrode
gauntlets, welding gants *m* spécial pour soudure à l'arc
hammer, welder's marteau *m* pique soudure
magnetic welding positioner positionneur *m* aimant spécial soudure
rectifier générateur *m*
welding wire fil *f* fourré acier

MIG welding
Soudure MIG

anti-spatter spray spray *m* anti-adhérent
contact tube tube *m* contact vissé
electrode électrode *f*
gasless MIG wire fil *m* fourré acier sans gaz
pliers pince *f* MIG
torch torche *f* MIG
welder poste *m* à soudage MIG
welder, gasless poste *m* de soudage à l'arc sans gaz
welding nozzle buse *f* de souder
welding wire, bobbin of bobine *f* fourré
   ~ **gasless MIG** ~ pour poste sans gaz
wire adapter adaptateur *m* de fil MIG

Gas welding
Soudure à gaz

acetylene acétylène *m*
anti-thermic screen écran *m* thermique
cup lighter allume-brûleur *m*
cutting torch chalumeau *m* coupeur
cylinder trolley chariot *m*
dual gas welder (brazing & gas welding) poste *m* à souder bi-gaz
flashback arrestor anti-retour *m* pare-flamme

heat gel gel *m* thermique anti-chaleur
pencil flame torch stylo *m* soudure gaz
quick-fit connector raccord *m* rapide
reamer head tête *f* à aleser
two gases welding kit chalumeau *m* bi-gaz
welding torch chalumeau *m*

Metalwork abrasives
Abrasifs ferronnerie

abrasive abrasif *m*
abrasive sheet feuille *f* abrasive
corundum paper corindon *m*
emery paper papier *m* émeri
garnet paper garniture *f*
silicon carbide paper carbure *m* de silicium

Metalwork

Appendix

PLUMBING & HEATING
PLOMBERIE & CHAUFFAGE

Plumbing & Heating

Pipe & tube
Tuyaux & tubes

copper pipe, coil, annealed couronne *f* cuivre recuit
  ~ **carbon free** ~ sans carbone
  ~ **sheathed** ~ revêtu (or gainé)
garden hose tuyau *m* d'arrosage
pipe tuyau *m*
pipe, copper tuyau *m* cuivre
pipe, copper, length of barre *f* cuivre
pipe, feed tube *m* d'alimentation
pipe, feed, multilayer plastic tube *m* d'alimentation multicouche
  ~ **bar** ~ en barre
  ~ **coil** ~ en couronne
pipe, feed, polyethylene tube *m* d'alimentation en polyéthylène
pipe, feed, sheathed PER pipe tube *m* d'alimentation gainé en PER
pipe, flexible flexible *f*
pipe, flexible braided stainless steel (sanitary use) flexible *f* sanitaire tressé en acier inoxydable
  ~ **one female; one compression fitting** ~ femelle/jonction cuivre sans soudure
  ~ **one male, one female connector** ~ mâle/femelle
  ~ **two female connectors** ~ femelle/femelle
pipe, flexible, for natural gas tuyau *m* flexible pour gaz naturel
pipe, gas tuyau *m* à gaz
pipe, hand-bendable tuyau *m* flexible d'alimentation souple
pipe, length of multilayer plastic barre *f* multicouche
pipe, MDPE blue water tuyau *m* polyéthylène eau potable
pipe, overflow tuyau *m* de trop plein
pipe, PVC (polyvinylchloride) tuyau *m* PVC
sheath gaine *f*
sheath, ivory, for plastic/copper pipe gaine *f* sanitaire ivoire
sheath, translucent gaine *f* translucide
tap connector, flexible tuyau *m* pour robinetterie sanitaire
tube tube *m*
tube, copper tube *m* de cuivre
tube, copper, annealed tube *m* en cuivre recuit
tube, copper, hard tube *m* écroui
tube, CPVC tube *m* en PVC-C

Plumbing connectors
Raccords d'alimentation

Solder fittings
Raccords à souder

brass 'cocked hat' fitting for bypassing another pipe (female joints) chapeau *m* de gendarme à souder en laiton pour cuivre, femelle/femelle

Plumbing & Heating

capillary socket/threaded captive nut douille *f* cuivre avec emboîture à braser écrou prisonnier taraudé
connector, straight manchon *m*
   ~ without lip ~ sans lèvre
curve, 90° courbe *f* 90°
elbow, soldered coude *m* à souder
elbow, soldered, brass, for copper pipe 45°/90° coude *m* à souder en laiton pour cuivre, 45°/90°
   ~ female/female ~ femelle/femelle
   ~ male/female ~ mâle/femelle
end cap bouchon *m*
end cap, brass bouchon *m* à souder en laiton pour cuivre
end cap, female bouchon *m* femelle à souder
end cap, male bouchon *m* mâle à souder
gate valve té *m* purgeur droit à souder
joint raccord *m*
joint, angle, soldered raccord *m* courbe cuivre à souder
joint, copper capillary raccord *m* cuivre à souder
joint, elbow, soldered raccord *m* coude cuivre à souder
joint, straight, with captive compression nut raccord *m* droit à souder à écrou prisonnier
S-shaped brass fitting for bypassing another pipe clarinette *f* à souder en laiton pour cuivre, mâle/femelle
tee té *m*
tee, equal té *m* cuivre à souder égal
tee, female reducing té *m* femelle réduit
tee, reducing té *m* cuivre à souder réduction
tee, soldered copper té *m* cuivre à souder
tee, swept té *m* pied biche

Plastic fittings
Raccords en plastique

elbow coude *f*
elbow, plastic coude *f* de jonction polyéthylène plastique
joint raccord *m*
joint, polyethylene, screwed raccord *m* polyéthylène à visser
~ female ~ femelle
~ male ~ mâle
tee connector, plastic té *m* de jonction polyéthylène plastique

Compression fittings
Raccords sans souder bicône

compression fitting raccord *m* en laiton à visser
connector, male, hand-tightening union *m* mâle sans outil
elbow coude *f*

Plumbing & Heating

elbow, iron/copper coude *f* fer/cuivre femelle
elbow, male/female coude *f* mâle/femelle
elbow, male sockets coude *f* mâle
elbow, wall plate coudé *f* applique
elbow, with olives coude *f* bicône
joint raccord *m*
joint, brass compression, with olive raccord *m* à olive
joint, copper/PER raccord *m* à joint mixte mâle
joint, straight, with olives raccord *m* union bicône
~ **equal** ~ égal
~ **female** ~ femelle
~ **male** ~ mâle
~ **reducing** ~ réduit
locknut contre-écrou *m* à plateau
manifold, four male outlets nourrice *f* entrée quatre départs mâles
nipple mamelon *f*
nipple, double male reducing mamelon *f* double mâle réduit
nipple, equal mamelon *f* égal
~ **female** ~ femelle
~ **male** ~ mâle
~ **male/female** ~ mâle/femelle
nut and olive écrou *m* et olive bicône
olive bague *f* bicône; olive *f* bicône
pipe stop end bouchon *m*
PTFE joint sealing tape ruban *m* Téflon d'étanchéité
reduction connector, male/female réduction *m* mâle/femelle
straight connector, iron to copper manchon *f* fer/cuivre
~ **female** ~ femelle
~ **male** ~ mâle
tank connector (not available in France)
tap connector raccord *m* tournant bicône
tee, copper/PER té *m* joint mixte
~ **female** ~ femelle
~ **male** ~ mâle
tee, with olives té *m* bicône
tee connector té *m*

American system fittings

Raccords sans souder américains

American pattern, or instant joint raccord *m* instantané ou américain
~ **elbow, brass** ~ coudé en laiton rapide
~ **reducing connector** ~ réduit rapide U.S.
American pattern, proprietary fitting raccord *m* <<gripp>>
American pattern, quick joint joint *m*; jonction *f*; raccord *m* rapide U.S.
American pattern, straight brass connector manchon *m* en laiton rapide
American pattern, tee fitting, brass té *m* en laiton rapide

Plumbing & Heating

Automatic push-fit fittings
Raccords sans souder automatique

automatic joint (push-fit) raccord *m*; jonction *f*; ~ automatique
 ~ **brass** ~ en laiton
automatic joints, elbow/nipple/sleeve/straight/tee raccord *m* coude/mamelon/manchon/droit/té automatique
pipe insert, reinforcing douille *f* de renfort automatique
stop end, push-fit bouchon *m* automatique

Connections for washing machine & dishwasher
Raccordements pour machine à laver & lave-vaisselle

drain hose tuyau *m* de vidange
pipe/hose tuyau *m*
pipe/hose, supply tuyau *m* d'alimentation
steam outlet, dual, for washing machine and dishwasher entonnoir *m* d'évacuation double pour machine à laver et lave-vaisselle
tap robinet *m*
tap, self-cutting, for copper pipe robinet *m* de machine à laver auto-perceur pour tube cuivre
tap, washing machine robinet *m* pour machine à laver
trap and upstand, for washing machine siphon *m* pour machine à laver
waste connector, self-cutting bride *f* de vidange coudée auto perceuse
Y-junction feed pipe connector raccord *m* de jonction en Y pour tuyau d'alimentation

Valves & stop taps
Vannes & robinets d'arrêt

anti-pollution valve clapet *m* anti-pollution
ballvalve vanne *f* à sphere/boisseau sphérique
ballvalve, with compression connections vanne *f* à sphere raccord bicône
ballvalve, with drain vanne *f* à sphere avec purge
ballvalve, with hose connector vanne *f* à sphere puisage
stoptap; stopcock robinet *m* d'arrêt; ~ à boisseau
stoptap, with drain valve robinet *m* d'arrêt avec purge
stoptap, with hose connector robinet *m* d'arrêt de puisage
stoptap, without drain valve robinet *m* d'arrêt à raccord

Plumbing & Heating

sans purge
stopvalve vanne *f* d'arrêt
tap, garden robinet *m* de jardin
tap, outside robinet *m* extérieur
tap, push robinet *m* poussoir
tap, self-cutting robinet *m* autoperceur
tap head tête *m* de robinet; ~ à potence
valve vanne *f*
valve, through vanne *f* à passage intégral
valve, with purge vanne *f* à purge
valve lever/handle manette
  ~ **butterfly** ~ papillon
  ~ **flat** ~ plate

Regulation of water pressure
Régulation de la pression de l'eau

filter crépine *f*; filtre *f*
filter, sand filtre *f* à sable
filter, valve crépine *f* à clapet universelle
filter, Y-pattern stainless steel filtre *f* à tamis Y en inox
gauge, axial, for pressure-reducing valve manomètre *m* axial pour réducteur
gauge, radial, for pressure-reducing valve manomètre *m* radial pour réducteur
meter compteur *m* divisionnaire

meter, cold water compteur *m* divisionnaire d'eau froide
meter, hot water compteur *m* divisionnaire d'eau chaude
pressure balancer équilibreur *m* de pression
pressure gauge manomètre *f*
pressure gauge nipple mamelon *f* porte manomètre
pressure reducer réducteur *m* de pression
valve clapet *m*
valve, anti-return check clapet *m* anti-retour
valve, vacuum breaker clapet *m* casse vide
water hammer reducing spring anti-bélier *m* à ressort

Multilayer system
Multicouche système

crimp connector raccord *m* à sertir
joint, automatic push-fit raccord *m* en laition automatique
  ~ **female** ~ femelle
  ~ **male** ~ mâle
joint, brass raccord *m* en laiton
joint, brass, crimp raccord *m* en laiton à sertir
joint, brass compression raccord *m* en laiton à compression
joint, brass elbow raccord *m* en laiton coudé
joint, straight raccord *m* en laiton droit

Plumbing & Heating

joint, tee té *m* en laiton
   ~ equal ~ égal
   ~ reducing ~ réduit
   ~ with fixing plate ~ applique
manifold collecteur *m*
olive, split olive *f* fendue
pipe clip collier *m* simple
pliers, crimping, for multilayer pipe pince *f* à sertir multicouche
sleeve; straight connector, brass manchon *m* en laiton
sleeve; straight connector, brass automatic push-fit manchon *m* en laiton automatique
sleeve; straight connector, brass compression manchon *m* en laiton à compression
stop end, brass bouchon *m* en laiton
stop end, brass automatic push-fit bouchon *m* en laiton automatique
stop end, brass compression bouchon *m* en laiton à compression
tube, multilayer tube *m* d'alimentation multicouche
tube, multilayer, coil of tube *m* d'alimentation multicouche en couronne
tube, multilayer, sheathed tube *m* d'alimentation multicouche gainé
tube, multilayer, straight length tube *m* d'alimentation multicouche en barre
tube, multilayer, unsheathed tube *m* d'alimentation multicouche nu

PER system
PER système

brass ring for slip connector bague *f* en laiton à glissement
connector jonction *f*
connector, straight, reducing jonction *f* de reduction PER
insert, brass, PER pipe insert *m* pour tuyau PER
joint raccord *m*
joint, brass raccord *m* en laiton
joint, brass striated raccord *m* en laiton strié
joint, brass tee raccord *m* en laiton té
   ~ compression ~ à compression
   ~ reducing, slip ~ à sertir réduit
   ~ equal ~ égal
joint, compression raccord *m* en laiton à compression
joint, crimp connector for PER pipe raccord *m* en laiton à sertir PER
joint, elbow raccord *m* en laiton coudé
joint, slip raccord *m* en laiton à glissement
   ~ female ~ femelle
   ~ male, straight ~ mâle droit
manifold nourrice *f*; collecteur *m*

Plumbing & Heating

olive, split olive *f* fendue, for compression joint
pipe bend support; guide *m* tube PER; raccord *m* coudé guide
pipe clip collier *m* simple de fixation PER
pipe reinforcing sleeves douille *f* de renfort en laiton
pliers, PER tube cutting pince *f* coupe tube PER
sleeve/straight connector manchon *m* brass en laiton
~ **compression** ~ à compression
~ **reducing** ~ réduit à glissement
~ **slip connector** ~ à glissement
stop end, brass bouchon *m* en laiton
~ **compression** ~ à compression
tube/pipe cross-linked reticulated polyethylene tube *m*; tuyau *m* ~ en PER (polyéthylène réticulé)
~ **blue (cold water)** ~ bleu
~ **red (hot water)** ~ rouge
~ **sheathed** ~ gainé
~ **unsheathed** ~ nu

Waste water drainage
Évacuation des eaux

PVC pipe & connectors
Tubes & raccords en PVC

access/inspection plug tampon *m* de visite
access/inspection plug, reducing tampon *m* de visite de réduction simple
aerator with PVC membrane aérateur *m* à membrane PVC
anti-return flap valve clapet *m* anti-retour à battant
anti-vacuum device to eliminate noise and odour anti-vide *m* pour tube
basin waste exit (hockey stick shape) sortie *f* de lavabo
collar collier *m*
connector, female/female, with internal stop manchon *f* lèvre FF avec butée
connector, metal and plastic pipe (with spring clips) jonction *f* pour tube métal et plastique
connector, straight manchon *f*
end piece embout *m*
end piece, plastic, male flange embout *m* plastique mâle
end piece, threaded embout *m* fileté
expansion sleeve with flexible seal manchon *f* dilatation
joint raccord *m*
joint, corrugated plastic waste raccord *m* d'évacuation souple
joint, elbow raccord *m* coude
joint, expandable concertina raccord *m* extensible
joint, female/female raccord *m* femelle/femelle (FF)
joint, male/female raccord *m* mâle/femelle (MF)
joint, reducing réduction *m*

Plumbing & Heating

joint, reducing, concentric
  réduction *m* concentrique
joint, reducing, integral
  réduction *m* incorporée
joint, reducing, offset réduction *m* excentrée
joint, trap raccord *m* sur siphon
joint, various angles raccord *m* angle
pipe, PVC tuyau *m* PVC
pipe bracket collier *m* bride; ~ de fixation
repair socket, male/female, for connecting pipe of different diameters manchette *f* réparation MF
saddle connector selle *f* de branchement
siphon/trap, in-line siphon *m* de parcours
sleeve without internal stop coulisse *f* sans butée
stop end bouchon *m*
stop end, rubber bouchon *m* en élastomère
tee té *m*; culotte *f*; culotte *f* de branchement; culotte *f* simple
tee, swept té *m* pied biche
waste connector, Y-shaped raccord *m* Y
waste pipe tube *m* évacuation

Pumps
Pompes

circulating pump, three-speed circulateur *f* trois vitesse
pump pompe *f*
pump, heat pompe *f* à chaleur
pump, circulation pompe *f* de circulation
pump, sump pompe *f* de relevage
pump, electric pompe *f* électrique

Bathroom
Salle de bains

Showers & shower trays
Douches & receveurs

drain; waste outlet bonde *f*
drain; waste outlet, horizontal, with cover bonde *f* à capot horizontale pour douche
drain; waste outlet, shower bonde *f* de douche
  ~ adjustable ~ orientable
  ~ with large horizontal flow ~ flow à grand débit horizontal
  ~ vertical ~ verticale
drain; waste outlet, square bonde *f* carrée
plinth, for shower tray surélévation *f* pour receveur
shower douche *f*
shower bar, vertical, with shower rose barre *f* de douche avec douchette

Plumbing & Heating

shower cabinet cabine *f* de douche
shower cabinet, quarter-circle (corner) cabine *f* de douche quatre de cercle
shower cabinet, rectangular cabine *f* de douche rectangulaire
shower cabinet and integral shower cabine *f* de douche complète
shower column colonne *f* de douche
shower curtain rideau *m* de douche
shower door porte *f* de douche
  ~ **hinged** ~ battante
  ~ **pivoting** ~ pivotante
  ~ **quarter-circle** ~ quatre de cercle
  ~ **sliding** ~ coulissante
  ~ **square** ~ angle carré
shower enclosure paroi *f* de douche
shower handset combiné *f* de douche
  ~ **built-in** ~ à encastrer
  ~ **hydromassage** ~ hydromassante
  ~ **with integral taps** ~ avec robinetterie intégrée douche
shower head pommeau *f* de douche
shower rail barre *f* de douche
shower rose douchette *f*
shower rose, cup bracket support *m* de douchette ventouse
shower rose, overhead pomme *f* haute de douche
shower rose arm, built-in bras *f* de douche à encastrer
shower screen pare-douche *m*
shower set ensemble *f* de douche
shower tap robinet *m* de douche
shower tray receveur *m* de douche
shower tray, floor-mounted receveur *m* de douche bac à poser
shower tray, glazed stoneware receveur *m* de douche en grès émaillé
shower tray, inset receveur *m* de douche à encastrer
shower tray, plastic resin receveur *m* de douche en résine
shower tray, polyurethane receveur *m* de douche en polyuréthane
shower tray, quarter circle (corner) receveur *m* de douche quatre cercle
shower tray, raised receveur *m* de douche surlévé
shower tray, rectangular receveur *m* de douche rectangulaire
shower tray, reinforced acrylic receveur *m* de douche en acrylique renforcé
shower tray, square receveur *m* de douche carré
spray hose metal/plastic/nylon flexible *f* de douche en métal/plastique/nylon

Plumbing & Heating

walk-in shower douche *f* a l'italienne
waste outlet, strip, for douche a l'italienne caniveau (*pl* -x) *m*; canivelle *m*
waste trap siphon *m*
waste trap, horizontal siphon *m* pour sortie horizontale
waste trap, vertical siphon *m* sortie verticale
waste trap, with tiling grille siphon *m* avec grille à carreler

Baths & bidets
Baignoires & bidets

bath baignoire *f*
bath, asymmetric baignoire *f* asymétrique
bath, corner baignoire *f* d'angle
bath, freestanding (with lion's paw feet) baignoire *f* îlot et patte de lion
bath, hip baignoire *f* sabot
bath, oval baignoire *f* ovale
bath, rectangular baignoire *f* rectangulaire
bath feet pieds *m* de baignoire
bath panel tablier *m* de baignoire
bath screen paroi *f* de baignoire; pare-baignoire *f*
 ~ **safety glass** ~ en verre sécurit
 ~ **screen-printed** ~ sérigraphié
 ~ **transparent** ~ transparente
bidet bidet *m*
control wheel, for waste plug volant *m* pour vidage de baignoire
waste outlet, for bath vidage *m* pour baignoire
waste outlet, for bath, cable-operated vidage *m* pour baignoire à câble
waste outlet for bath, freestanding vidage *m* pour baignoire îlot
waste outlet, for bidet, adjustable vidage *m* pour bidet réglable
waste outlet, for hip or corner bath vidage *m* pour baignoire sabot ou d'angle
waste trap siphon *m*
waste trap, angled, for bidet siphon *m* coudé pour bidet
waste trap, for bath siphon *m* pour baignoire
 ~ **slimline** ~ extra-plat

Whirlpools, spas & saunas
Balnéos, spas & saunas

bath, hydrotherapy baignoire *f* à bulle
bath, whirlpool baignoire *f* balnéo
duckboard (sauna) caillebotis *m*
hygrometer and thermometer (sauna) hygromètre *m* et thermomètre *m*
sauna sauna *m*
sauna, infrared sauna *m* à infrarouge
sauna heater poêle *f* pour sauna

Plumbing & Heating

sauna stones pierres *f* pour sauna
spa bath spa *f*
spa bath, floor-mounted spa *f* à poser
spa bath, inflatable spa *f* gonflable
spa bath, interior spa *f* intérieur
spa bath, outside spa *f* extérieur
spa bath, recessed spa *f* à encastrer
steam bath hammam *m*
steam bath cabin cabine *f* hammam
  ~ **with/without floor** ~ avec sol/sans sol
  ~ **ready to tile** ~ prêt à carreler
steam generator générateur *m* vapeur pour hammam

Accessories for showers & baths
Accessoires pour douches & baignoires

bath mat tapis *m* de bain
  ~ **non-slip** ~ antidérapant
duckboard caillebotis *m*
shower rack, hanging étagère *f* de douche à suspendre
shower rack, wall-fixed étagère *f* de douche d'hôte à fixer
squeegee raclette *f* de douche
towel rail porte-serviettes *f*
towel rail, attached porte-serviettes *f* à fixer
towel rail, freestanding porte-serviettes *f* à poser

Toilets & washbasins
WCs & lave-mains

basin; bowl; toilet bowl cuvette *f*
bottle trap siphon *m* de lavabo bouteille
cistern, bowl-mounted réservoir *m* WC attenant
cistern, high level réservoir *m* WC haut
cistern, low level réservoir *m* WC semi-bas
cistern, WC réservoir *m* WC
click-clack basin waste outlet bonde *f* clic-clac
  ~ **without overflow** ~ sans trop plein pour lavabo
macerator broyeur *m* pour WC
overflow tube with waste grille intercalaire *m* de trop-plein avec grille
S-bend outlet, brass siphon *m* de lavabo en S en laiton
toilet WC *mpl*; vécés *mpl*
toilet, chemical WC *m* chimique
toilet, compact, with integral macerator WC *m* compact avec broyeur intégré
toilet, floorstanding WC *m* à poser
toilet, freestanding WC *m* autoportant
toilet, space-saving, horizontal outlet WC *m* 'gain de place', sortie horizontale
toilet, wall-mounted WC *m* suspendu

Plumbing & Heating

toilet seat abattant *m* WC
washbasin lavabo *m*; lave-mains *m*; vasque *f*
washbasin trap siphon *m* de lavabo
washbasin trap, adjustable exit siphon *m* de lavabo réglable sortie
washbasin trap, space-saving, with integral joints siphon *m* de lavabo 'gain de place' avec joints integrés
waste outlet, basin bonde *f*
waste outlet, dome shaped, without overflow bonde *f* à dôme fixe sans trop plein
waste outlet, lever-operated 'mushroom', with overflow bonde *f* champignon à levier avec trop plein pour lavabo
waste outlet, manually-operated pop-up bonde *f* de lavabo à commande manuelle
waste outlet, rotating, without overflow bonde *f* à clapet rotatif sans trop plein
waste outlet and plug bonde *f* pour lavabo à bouchon
waste plug, pop-up clapet *m* rentrant inviolable
WC and cistern complete pack *m* WC
WC control plate plaque *m* de commande WC

WC cistern mechanisms
Mécanismes & evacuation WC

cistern stopvalve robinet *m* WC d'arrêt
float valve and flush mechanism mécanisme *m* à tirette, robinet flotteur à fermeture mécanique
flush mechanism, complete ensemble *m* de mécanisme
flush valve soupape *f* WC
flush valve, pull soupape *f* WC à tirette
flush valve, push soupape *f* WC simple poussoir
outlet pipe pipe *f* WC
outlet pipe, extendable pipe *f* WC souple extensible
outlet sleeve, PVC, replacement manchette *f* de réparation PVC
spray attachment, WC douche *f* pour WC
WC float valve robinet *m* WC flotteur
WC float valve, silent robinet *m* WC flotteur silencieux
WC valve robinet *m* WC
~ **angled** ~ équerre
~ **straight** ~ droit

Bathroom taps
Robinetterie de salle de bain

ceramic disc seal cartouche *f* céramique
mixer, basin mélangeur *m* de lavabo
  ~ **high spout** ~ bec haut
  ~ **low spout** ~ bec bas
  ~ **medium height spout** ~ moyen
  ~ **swivel** ~ bec mobile
mixer, bath mélangeur *m* de baignoire
mixer, bath/shower mélangeur *m* bain/douche
mixer, separate hot and cold taps mélangeur *m*
mixer, shower mélangeur *m* de douche
mixer, single tap mitigeur *m*
mixer, single tap, basin mitigeur *m* de lavabo
  ~ **high spout** ~ bec haut
  ~ **low spout** ~ bec bas
  ~ **medium height spout** ~moyen
mixer, single tap, bath mitigeur *m* de baignoire
mixer, single tap, bath/shower mitigeur *m* bain/douche
mixer, single tap, bidet mitigeur *m* de bidet
mixer, single tap, shower mitigeur *m* de douche
mixer, thermostatic mitigeur *m* thermostatique

  ~ **bath** ~ de baignoire
  ~ **shower** ~ de douche
mixer, two-hole, wall-mounted mitigeur *m* mural deux trous
temperature limiter limiteur *f* de température
washbasin tap robinet *m* de lave-mains
  ~ **high spout** ~ bec haut
  ~ **low spout** ~ bec bas

Kitchen
Cuisine

Kitchen taps
Robinetterie de cuisine

ceramic disc seal cartouche *f* céramique
mixer, kitchen, single tap mitigeur *m* de cuisine; ~ d'évier
  ~ **with spray attachment** ~ avec douchette
mixer, kitchen, two tap mélangeur *m* de cuisine; ~ d'évier
spout bec *m*
  ~ **high swivel** ~ haut mobile
  ~ **inclined** ~ incliné
  ~ **straight** ~ droit
  ~ **swan neck** ~ col de cygne
  ~ **swivelling** ~ rabattable

Plumbing & Heating

Kitchen sinks
Eviers de cuisine

basket strainer, stainless steel
 bonde *f* à panier en inox
 ~ with overflow ~ avec trop plein
connecting tube, double sink outlet tubulure *f* de raccordement, deux cuves
sink évier *m*
 ~ granite ~ en granit
 ~ quartz ~ en quartz
 ~ resin ~ en résine
 ~ sandstone ~ en grès
 ~ stainless steel ~ en inox
sink, corner évier *m* d'angle
sink, surface-mounted évier *m* à poser
sink, two bowl, with drainer évier *m* deux bacs avec un égouttoir
sink, with drainer évier *m* avec égouttoir
sink bowl évier *m* cuve
sink waste vidage *m*
 ~ all-in-one space-saving ~ tout en un 'gain de place'
 ~ cable-operated ~ à câble
 ~ two-bowl, with overflow ~ complet pour évier, deux cuves
strainer, stainless steel, for sink waste, all-in-one panier *m* inox pour bonde tout-en-un
washtub bac *m* à laver
waste assembly with overflow ensemble *m* complet avec trop plein

waste outlet, cable-operated, with overflow bonde *f* à câble avec trop plein
waste outlet, lever-operated bonde *f* à tirette
 ~ with plug ~ à bouchon
 ~ with plug on chain and overflow ~ chaînette avec trop plein
waste outlet, rotating, without overflow bonde *f* à clapet rotatif sans trop plein
waste outlet, sink bonde *f*
waste trap, adjustable siphon *m* réglable pour évier
waste trap, PVC siphon *m* PVC pour évier
waste trap, sink siphon *m*
waste trap, slimline siphon *m* d'évier extra-plat
waste trap, with washing machine connector siphon *m* avec prise machine à laver

Electric heating
Chauffage électrique

convector radiator, electric convecteur *m* électrique
radiant heater radiateur *m* électrique à rayonnement
radiant panel panneau *m* rayonnant
radiator, electric convection radiateur *m* électrique à convection

Plumbing & Heating

radiator, electric inertia radiateur *m* électrique à inertie
  ~ **cast iron radiant/convection** ~ fonte
  ~ **dry** ~ sèche
  ~ **fluid** ~ fluide
  ~ **reconstituted stone heating element** ~ pierre reconstituée
  ~ **soapstone heating element** ~ pierre stéatite
radiator, gentle heat radiateur *m* électrique chaleur douce
underfloor heating, electric plancher *m* chauffant électrique
underfloor heating, for tiling sol *m* chauffant à pose collée

Auxiliary heaters
Chauffage d'appoint

auxiliary heater chauffage *f* d'appoint
auxiliary heater, gas chauffage *f* d'appoint à gaz
auxiliary heater, gas brazier, infrared chauffage *f* d'appoint à brasero infrarouge
auxiliary heater, gas catalytic chauffage *f* d'appoint à catalyse
auxiliary heater, gas infrared chauffage *f* d'appoint à infrarouge
auxiliary heater, terrace chauffage *f* d'appoint de terrasse
auxiliary heater, terrace, electric chauffage *f* d'appoint de terrasse électrique
auxiliary heater, terrace, gas chauffage *f* d'appoint de terrasse à gaz
convector heater, portable electric convecteur *m* mobile
flame-effect fire, electric cheminée *f* électrique
fuel, liquid (for poêle à pétrole) combustible *m* liquide
  ~ **dearomatized** ~ désaromatisé
  ~ **extremely refined** ~ extrêmement raffiné
  ~ **odourless** ~ sans odeur
  ~ **petrol derivative** ~ pétrole
propane heater, for work site générateur *m* d'air chaud
pump pompe *f*
pump, electric, for refilling petrol tank pompe *f* électrique pour pétrole
pump, manual, for refilling petrol tank pompe *f* manuelle pour pétrole
radiant panel heater, electric, mobile panneau *m* rayonnant mobile électrique
radiator/fan heater, portable radiateur *m* soufflant mobile
radiator/heater, electric fan radiateur *m* soufflant électrique
  ~ **bathroom, portable** ~ salle de bain mobile
  ~ **ceramic element** ~ céramique
  ~ **portable** ~ mobile

Plumbing & Heating

radiator/heater, electric fan, bathroom, fixed radiateur *m* soufflant électrique salle de bain fixe
radiator/heater, electric fan, tower unit radiateur *m* soufflant électrique tour
radiator/heater, electric fan, work site radiateur *m* soufflant électrique de chantier
radiator/heater, oil-filled electric radiateur *m* bain d'huile électrique
stove poêle *f*
stove, dual gas/electric poêle *f* infrarouge et électrique
stove, gas poêle *f* à gaz
stove, petrol poêle *f* à pétrole
 ~ electronic injection ~ à injection électronique
stove, real fire effect poêle *f* effet feu de cheminée
stove, wick poêle *f* à mèche
trolley for petrol stove chariot *m* pour poêle à pétrole

Central heating
Chauffage central

bleed valve purgeur *m*
bleed valve, automatic purgeur *m* automatique pour radiateur
bleed valve, finger-operated purgeur *m* à volant mâle
drain valve, adjustable, for radiator robinet *m* de vidange à boisseaux orientable
drain valve, radiator robinet *m* de vidange à boisseaux
lockshield valve coude *f* de réglage
radiator radiateur *m*
radiator, dual hot water/electric radiateur *m* mixte eau chaude/électrique
radiator, hot water radiateur *m* eau chaude
radiator, hot water, aluminium radiateur *m* eau chaude aluminium
radiator, hot water, bimetal radiateur *m* eau chaude bimétal
radiator, hot water, steel radiateur *m* eau chaude acier
radiator, towel radiateur *m* sèche-serviette
radiator bleed key, square-shank clé *m* pour purgeur carré
radiator mounting kit, universal kit *m* de fixation universel pour radiateur
thermostat thermostat *m*

Plumbing & Heating

thermostat, digital programmable thermostat *m* digital programmable
thermostat, electronic thermostat *m* électronique
thermostat, electronic radio/telephone control thermostat *m* électronique programmable radio/tél
thermostat, electronic room stat thermostat *m* électronique d'ambiance
thermostat, high precision thermostat *m* de haute precision
thermostat, mechanical thermostat *m* mécanique
thermostat, programmable thermostat *m* programmable
valve robinet *m*
valve, drain robinet *m* de vidange
valve, radiator robinet *m* de radiateur
valve, radiator, thermostatic robinet *m* de radiateur à tête thermostatique

Boilers & accessories
Chaudières & accessoires

actuator/servomotor servomoteur *m*
air vent, automatic purgeur *m* d'air automatique
boiler bouilleur *m*; chaudière *f*
boiler, cast iron, heating only chaudière *f* fonte chauffage seul
boiler, floorstanding chaudière *f* sol
boiler, floorstanding, condensing chaudière *f* sol à condensation
boiler, floorstanding, oil chaudière *f* sol fioul
boiler, floorstanding, standard gas chaudière *f* sol gaz standard
boiler, floorstanding, with expansion vessel chaudière *f* sol avec ballon
boiler, wall-mounted chaudière *f* murale
boiler, wall-mounted, condensing gas chaudière *f* murale à condensation gaz
boiler, wall-mounted, electric chaudière *f* murale électrique
boiler, wall-mounted, gas chaudière *f* murale gaz
boiler, wall-mounted, with expansion vessel chaudière *f* murale avec ballon
burner brûleur *m*
check valve (preventing thermosiphon effect) clapet *m* anti-thermosiphon
circulation pump circulateur *f*
expansion vessel vase *f* d'expansion; ballon *m*
fireplace insert, wood-burning, with boiler for central heating foyer *m* fermé à bois pour chauffage central
gas, for boiler gaz
oil, for boiler fioul

Plumbing & Heating

pressure gauge manomètre *f* radial
safety valve soupape *f* de sûreté sécurité

Wood heating
Chauffage au bois

adapter, to connect stove to flue pipe, stainless steel adaptateur *m* inox
chimney cheminée *m* (see also: **fireplace**)
chimney flue conduit *m* de cheminée
chimney flue, aluminium conduit *m* de cheminée en aluminium
chimney flue, insulated conduit *m* de cheminée isolé
chimney flue, stainless steel conduit *m* de cheminée en inox
chimney flue, terracotta block conduit *m* de fumée en terre cuite
chimney flue block, terracotta boisseau *m* alvéolé
chimney flue extractor, rotating aspirateur *m*
chimney flue extractor, static aspirateur *m* statique
chimney pot/cap chapeau *m* de cheminée
chimney pot/cap, concrete aspirateur *m* de cheminée en béton
chimney pot/cap, rain chapeau *m* de cheminée pare-pluie

chimney stack, prefabricated sortie *f* de toit
collar, galvanized steel, with screw fixing for wall collier *m* à pointe galvanisé
collar and wall bracket (metal flue) collier *m* mural
collar clamp, for sealing joint between lengths of flue pipe collier *m* de fixation étanchéité
conduit, for stove, fireplace and insert conduit *m* pour poêle, foyer et insert
connector, top of chimney flue raccord *m* haut
~ **stainless steel flue** ~ inox
fireplace (see also: **chimney**)
fireplace; hearth foyer *m*
~ **cast iron** ~ en fonte
fireplace insert foyer-insert *m*; insert *m* de cheminée
fixing bracket, for upper chimney flue cadre *m* de fixation raccord haut
flue liner, flexible tubage *m* de conduit flexible; tubage *m* flexible lisse
flue pipe, aluminium tuyau *m* aluminié
flue pipe, connection sleeve manchon *m* aluminié
flue pipe, matt black, enamelled tuyau *m* émaillé noir mat
flue pipe, reduction, conical, stainless steel réduction *m* conique

Plumbing & Heating

flue pipe, stainless steel tuyau *m* inox
flue pipe, straight, welded, adjustable élément *m* droit réglable soudé
flue pipe bracket support *m* de conduit
flue pipe connection, elbow elément *m* de coude
~ **aluminium pleated, 90°** ~ coude *m* plissé aluminié 90°
~ **enamelled, 45°** ~ émaillé 45°
sealing plate, for chimney flue exiting roof plaque *f* d'étanchéité carrée
smoke pipe conduit *m* fumée
stove poêle *f*
stove, pellet-burning poêle *f* à granulé
stove, wood-burning poêle *f* à bois
stove installation kit, straight sleeve kit *m* de fixation universel pour radiateur manchette droite
tee connector, aluminium, for flue té *m* nu aluminié
tee connector, matt black enamel, for rear of wood stove té *m* tampon émaillé noir mat
tee connector, single-wall té *m* simple paroi

Production of hot water
Production d'eau chaude sanitaire

anti-scald mixer valve, thermostatic mitigeur *m* thermostatique anti-brûlure pour chauffe-eau
ceiling attachment bracket for hot water tank console *f* d'accrochage plafond pour ballon d'eau chaude
element, immersion heater résistance *f* de chauffe-eau thermoplongée
element, water heating résistance *f* de chauffe-eau
element, water heating, reinforced résistance *f* de chauffe-eau blindée
element, water heating, steatite (soapstone) résistance *f* de chauffe-eau stéatite
expansion vessel, hot water vase *f* d'expansion sanitaire
funnel siphon for chauffe-eau entonnoir *m* siphon
heat pump, air/water pompe *f* à chaleur air/eau
hot water tank ballon *m* d'eau chaude
hot water tank, electric ballon *m* d'eau chaude électrique
hot water tank, gas ballon *m* d'eau chaude gaz
pressure gauge manomètre *m*
pressure reducer réducteur *m* de

Plumbing & Heating

pression
stand for water heater trépied *m* chauffe-eau
thermostat, for water heater thermostat *m* pour chauffe-eau
water heater chauffe-eau *m*
water heater, electric chauffe-eau *m* électrique
  ~ **horizontal** ~ horizontal
  ~ **on vertical stand** ~ sur socle
  ~ **over sink** ~ sur évier
  ~ **under-sink** ~ sous-évier
  ~ **vertical** ~ vertical
  ~ **wall-mounted** ~ mural
water heater, electric instantaneous chauffe-eau *m* instantané; ~ rapide
water heater, gas instantaneous chauffe-eau *m* gaz instantané
water heater, instantaneous, combination shower/basin chauffe-eau *m* combi douche/lavabo
water heater installation kit kit *m*; ensemble *m*; ~ sécurité/raccordement chauffe-eau
  ~ **non-solder** ~ sans soudure
  ~ **stainless steel, for aggressive water** ~ inox pour eau agressive
  ~ **Teflon for hard water** Téflon pour eau calcaire
water heater, solar chauffe-eau *m* solaire
water heater with heat pump chauffe-eau *m* thermodynamique

Air conditioning & ventilation

Climatisation & ventilation

air-conditioner climatiseur *m*
air-conditioner, fixed reversible climatiseur *m* fixe réversible
air-conditioner, movable climatiseur *m* local
air freshener rafraîchisseur *m* d'air
condensation duct, for fixed air-conditioner tube *m* condensat pour climatiseur fixe
dehumidifier déshumidificateur *m*
duct, fixed air-conditioner goulotte *f* pour climatiseur fixe
extractor fan aérateur/extracteur *m* d'air
fan, electric ventilateur *m*
fan, electric, bladeless ventilateur *m* sans pales
fan, electric, standard ventilateur *m* sur pied
fan, electric, table ventilateur *m* de table
humidifier humidificateur *m*
humidifier, radiator saturateur *m*

Plumbing & Heating

Water treatment
Traitement de l'eau

anti-corrosion/anti-scale liquid for central heating system inhibiteur *m* chaudière
anti-freeze for central heating system antigel *m* chaudière
anti-hard water device, magnetic anti-calcaire *m* magnétique
  ~ for shower ~ pour la douche
  ~ for washing machine & dishwasher ~ pour machine à laver et lave-vaisselle
anti-hard water silico-phosphate balls billes *f* silico-phosphate anti-calcaire
central heating boiler sludge remover disembouant *f* chaudière
central heating system cleaner nettoyant *m* chaudière liquide
de-limescaling powder, for washing machine/dishwasher poudre *f* détartrante et dégraissante pour lave linge et lave-vaisselle
hard water neutraliser neutraliseur *m* de calcaire
leak stop for central heating system colmatant *m* chaudière liquid
limescale filter, for washing machine filtre *m* anti-tartre pour machine à laver
noise inhibitor liquid for central heating system antibruit *m* liquide pour chaudière
regenerating salt, for water softener sel *m* régénerant pour adoucisseur d'eau
salt tablets, for water softener pastilles *f* de sel pour adoucisseur d'eau
scale inhibitor, electronic anti-tartre *m* électronique
water filter filtrante *f* de l'eau
water filter cartridge cartouche *f* filtrante
water softener adoucisseur d'eau *m*
water softener disinfectant désinfectant *m* pour adoucisseur d'eau

Plumbing & heating tools & accessories
Outils & accessoires pour la plomberie & le chauffage

blowlamp lampe *f* à souder
blowtorch chalumeau (*pl* -x) *m*
blowtorch, cutting (oxyacetylene or oxy-propane) chalumeau *m* soudeur
blowtorch, gas (butane or propane) chalumeau *m* monogaz
cup lighter for blowtorch allume-brûleur *m*

Plumbing & Heating

drain clearing pump pompe *f* à vide
drain clearing tool déboucheur *m*
 ~ **flexible** ~ fléxible
 ~ **flexible, cranked spring** ~ fléxible à manivelle; ~ à crampons
  ~ **piston-operated** ~ à piston
  ~ **pump-operated** ~ à pompe
  ~ **spool type** ~ à tambour
  ~ **suction-operated** ~ ventouse
file lime *f*
flaring tool and clamp appareil *m* à battre les collets
flux flux *f* décapant
gasket/seal joint *m* d'étanchéité
hacksaw scie *f* à métaux
hole-making punch emporte-pièce *m*
hose clip, ratcheted collier *m* à crémallère à vis
leak detector détecteur *m* de fuites
matrix and bracket, for flaring copper tube matrice *f* et étrier (use with: **router for pipe-flaring matrix**)
pipe bending spring ressort *m* à cintrer
pipe bending tool malette *f* cintreuse; pince *f* à cintrer
pipe cutter, blade replacement molette *f* pour coupe-tube cuivre
pipe-cutting gauge gabarit *m* de pose tuyau
pipe wrench serre-tubes *m*

pliers pince *f*
pliers, pipe-cutting (multilayer pipe) pince *f* à coupe tube multicouche
pliers, plumber's; tube tightening clé *m* Suédoise; serre-tubes *m* Suédoise
pliers, wide-jaw, adjustable pince *f* à siphon griptou
plumbline plomb *m*
plunger débouchoir *m*
radiator bleed key clé *m* purgeur à radiateur
radiator valve mounting key clé *m* de montage de radiateur
router for pipe-flaring matrix toupie *f* pour matrice
tube/pipe cutter coupe-tube *f*
 ~ **copper pipe** ~ cuivre
 ~ **PER pipe** ~ PER
valve reseater and mills rodoir *m* et fraises
wrench/spanner clé *m*
wrench/spanner, adjustable clé *m* à molette
wrench/spanner, basin clé *m* lavabo
wrench/spanner, chain clé *m* à chaine
wrench/spanner, monkey clé *m* anglaise
wrench/spanner, rubber strap clé *m* à courroie en caoutchouc
wrench/spanner, Stillson clé *m* Stillson

Plumbing & Heating

Gas & accessories
Gaz & accessoires

bottle, gas, empty bouteille *f* gaz vide
bottle, gas, rechargeable bouteille *f* gaz rechargeable
butane butane *f*
gas cartridge, disposable cartouche *f* jetable
gas regulating tap robinet *m* relais gaz
gas regulator détendeur *m* gaz
pipe, gas tuyau *m* à gaz
pipe, gas, flexible, natural gas tuyau *m* flexible pour gaz naturel
propane propane *f*

Plumbing & Heating

Appendix

REFERENCE
RÉFÉRENCE

Reference

Numbers
Les Numéros

0 **nought** zéro
1 **one** un (une)
2 **two** deux
3 **three** trois
4 **four** quatre
5 **five** cinq
6 **six** six
7 **seven** sept
8 **eight** huit
9 **nine** neuf
10 **ten** dix
11 **eleven** onze
12 **twelve** douze
13 **thirteen** treize
14 **fourteen** quatorze
15 **fifteen** quinze
16 **sixteen** seize
17 **seventeen** dix-sept
18 **eighteen** dix-huit
19 **nineteen** dix-neuf
20 **twenty** vingt
21 **twenty-one** vingt et un (une)
22 **twenty-two** vingt-deux
23 **twenty-three** vingt-trois
24 **twenty-four** vingt-quatre
25 **twenty-five** vingt-cinq
26 **twenty-six** vingt-six
27 **twenty-seven** vingt-sept
28 **twenty-eight** vingt-huit
29 **twenty-nine** vingt-neuf
30 **thirty** trente
31 **thirty-one** trente et un (une)
32 **thirty-two** trente-deux
33 **thirty-three** trente-trois
34 **thirty-four** trente-quatre
35 **thirty-five** trente-cinq
36 **thirty-six** trente-six
37 **thirty-seven** trente-sept
38 **thirty-eight** trente-huit
39 **thirty-nine** trente-neuf
40 **forty** quarante
41 **forty-one** quarante et un (une)
42 **forty-two** quarante-deux
43 **forty-three** quarante-trois
44 **forty-four** quarante-quatre
45 **forty-five** quarante-cinq
46 **forty-six** quarante-six
47 **forty-seven** quarante-sept
48 **forty-eight** quarante-huit
49 **forty-nine** quarante-neuf
50 **fifty** cinquante
51 **fifty-one** cinquante et un (une)
52 **fifty-two** cinquante-deux
53 **fifty-three** cinquante-trois
54 **fifty-four** cinquante-quatre
55 **fifty-five** cinquante-cinq
56 **fifty-six** cinquante-six
57 **fifty-seven** cinquante-sept
58 **fifty-eight** cinquante-huit
59 **fifty-nine** cinquante-neuf
60 **sixty** soixante
61 **sixty-one** soixante et un (une)
62 **sixty-two** soixante-deux
63 **sixty-three** soixante-trois
64 **sixty-four** soixante-quatre
65 **sixty-five** soixante-cinq
66 **sixty-six** soixante-six
67 **sixty-seven** soixante-sept
68 **sixty-eight** soixante-huit
69 **sixty-nine** soixante-neuf
70 **seventy** soixante-dix
71 **seventy-one** soixante et onze

72 **seventy-two** soixante-douze
73 **seventy-three** soixante-treize
74 **seventy-four** soixante-quatorze
75 **seventy-five** soixante-quinze
76 **seventy-six** soixante-seize
77 **seventy-seven** soixante-dix-sept
78 **seventy-eight** soixante-dix-huit
79 **seventy-nine** soixante-dix-neuf
80 **eighty** quatre-vingts
81 **eighty-one** quatre-vingt-un (une)
82 **eighty-two** quatre-vingt-deux
83 **eighty-three** quatre-vingt-trois
84 **eighty-four** quatre-vingt-quatre
85 **eighty-five** quatre-vingt-cinq
86 **eighty-six** quatre-vingt-six
87 **eighty-seven** quatre-vingt-sept
88 **eighty-eight** quatre-vingt-huit
89 **eighty-nine** quatre-vingt-neuf
90 **ninety** quatre-vingt-dix
91 **ninety-one** quatre-vingt-onze
92 **ninety-two** quatre-vingt-douze
93 **ninety-three** quatre-vingt-treize
94 **ninety-four** quatre-vingt-quatorze
95 **ninety-five** quatre-vingt-quinze
96 **ninety-six** quatre-vingt-seize
97 **ninety-seven** quatre-vingt-dix-sept
98 **ninety-eight** quatre-vingt-dix-huit
99 **ninety-nine** quatre-vingt-dix-neuf
100 **a hundred** cent
101 **a hundred and one** cent un
200 **two hundred** deux cents
201 **two hundred and one** deux cent un (une)
300 **three hundred** trois cents
1,000 **a thousand** mille
1,000,000 **a million** un million

1st first 1er premier -ière
2nd second 2e 2ème deuxième
3rd third 3e 3ème troisième
4th fourth 4e 4ème quatrième
5th fifth 5e 5ème cinquième
6th sixth 6e 6ème sixième
7th seventh 7e 7ème septième
8th eighth 8e 8ème huitième
9th ninth 9e 9ème neuvième
10th tenth 10e 10ème dixième
11th eleventh 1 1e 11ème onzième
12th twelfth 12e 12ème douzième

Fractions
Les Fractions
a half un demi
a third un tiers
two-thirds deux tiers
a quarter un quart
a fifth un cinquième
an eighth un huitième
a sixteenth seizième

Percentages
Pourcentages
10% ten per cent 10%; dix pour cent
100% one hundred per cent 100%; cent pour cent

Decimals
Les decimaux
0.5; nought point five 0,5 zéro virgule cinq

Reference

Property
Propriété

apartment appartement *m*
apartment, furnished maison meublée *f*
apartment block maison de rapport *f*
attic comble *m*
auction vente aux enchères *f*
awning; porch auvent *m*
barn grange *f*
barn, sheep bergerie *f*
basement sous-sol *m*
bathroom salle de bain *f*
bedroom chambre *f*
boundary limite du terrain *f*
boundary marker borne *f*
building bâtiment *m*
building land terrain à bâtir *m*
bungalow bungalow *m*; pavillon
buyer; purchaser acheteur; ~euse *mf*
carport abri; ~ voiture *m*
cellar cave *f*
city cité *f*
conveyance of land transfer acte d'achat *m*
cottage cottage *m*
cottage, thatched chaumière *f*
deed of sale acte de vente *m*; ~ authentique de vente *m*
dining room salle à manger *f*
ditch fossé *m*
dovecote; pigeon tower pigeonnier *m*
drainage système d'assainissement *f*

entrance hall vestibule *m*
family room salle de séjour *f*
farm, small; country/weekend cottage fermette *f*
farmhouse ferme *f*; maison du fermier; ~ paysanne)
farmhouse, Provençal mas *m*
fence barrière *f*; cloture *f*
fence post piquet de clôture *f*
field champ *m*
first floor premier étage *m*
for rent à louer *adj*
for sale à vendre *adj*
garage garage *m*
garden jardin *m*
garden, vegetable jardin potager *m*
garden level rez-de-jardin *m*
gatekeeper's lodge maisonnette du garde *f*
granary; attic grenier *m*
ground floor rez-de-chaussée *m*
hamlet hameau *m (pl -x)*
hayloft fenil *m*
house; bungalow; pavilion; gazebo pavillon *m*; bungalow *m*
house, country maison de campagne *f*
house, country manor gentilhommière *f*
house, country (Provence); fortified village bastide *f*
house, dwelling maison d'habitation *f*
house, gentleman's maison de maître *f*
house; home; abode; residence maison *f*

house, small maisonnette *f*
house, suburban maison de banlieue *f*
house, town maison de ville *f*
house, weekend/holiday maison d'amis *f*; ~ de plaisance
houses, semi-detached maisons doubles *fpl*
hunting lodge maison de chasse *f*
junk room débarras *m*
kitchen cuisine *f*
land, plot of; allotment lotissement *m*
land registry cadastre *m*
landowner propriétaire *mf*
larder garde-manger *m*
laundry/utility room buanderie *f*
lean-to appentis *m*
listed building monument historique *m*
living room salon *f*
longhouse; Breton stone-built farmhouse longère *f*
mansion maison bourgeoise *f*
office bureau *m*
outbuilding dépendance *f*
path chemin *m*
pigsty; byre étable *f*; porcherie *f*
planning certificate certificat d'urbanisme *m*
planning permission permis de construire *m*
pond étang *m*
property deed acte notairé *m*
purchase agreement; contract of sale compromis de vente *m*
pylon pylône *m*

rental; lease location *f*
residence, primary résidence primaire *f*
rest home; convalescent home maison de repose *f*; ~ de convalescence *f*
retirement home maison de retrait *f*
roof toit *m*
roof, flat toit-terrasse *m*
sanitation assainissement *m*
sea level niveau de la mer *m*
spring source *f*
stable écurie *f*
staircase escalier *m*
staircase, spiral escalier en colimaçon *m*
telegraph pole poteau télégraphique *m*
town ville *f*; commune *f*
vendor vendeur; ~euse *mf*
veranda véranda *f*
village village *m*; bourg *m*
weekend/holiday home résidence secondaire *f*
workshop atelier *m*

Reference

Trades
Metiers

architect architecte *mf*
blacksmith forgeron *m*
bricklayer maçon *m*
builder constructeur *m*
cabinetmaker ébéniste *mf*
carpenter charpentier *m*
chimneysweep ramoneur *m*
decorator décorateur; ~trice *mf*
draughtsman/woman dessinateur; ~trice *mf*
electrician électricien *m*
estate agent agent immobilier *m*
farmer agriculteur; ~trice *mf*
foreman/woman contremaître; ~esse *fm*; maître d'oeuvre *m*
gardener jardinier; ~ière *mf*
glazier vitrier *m*
engineer ingénieur *m*
handyman/woman bricoleur; ~euse *mf*
heating specialist chauffagiste *m*
interior decorator tapissier décorateur *m*; peintre-décorateur *m*
interior designer ensemblier *m*
iron craftsman/woman ferronnier; ~ière *mf*
ironmonger quincaillier *m*
joiner menuisier *m*
labourer travailleur; ~euse *mf*
landscape gardener paysagiste *mf*
locksmith serrurier; ~ière *mf*
market gardener maraîcher; ~ère *mf*

mechanic/service station worker garagiste *mf*
metalworker métallo *mf*
notary notaire *m*
nurseryman pépiniériste *mf*
painter peintre *m*
plasterer plâtrier *m*
plumber plombier *m*
quantity surveyor métreur; ~euse *mf*
quarryman carrier *m*
removal company déménageur *m*
sewage tanker driver/cesspool cleaner vidangeur *m*
shopkeeper; tradesman/woman marchand; ~e *mf*
surveyor géomètre *mf*
tiler carreleur *m*
upholsterer tapissier; ~ière *mf*
welder soudeur; ~ euse *mf*
workman/worker ouvrier; ~ière *mf*
zinc roofer plombier-zinguer *m*

Colour
Couleur

amber ambré, ~e *adj*
aquamarine bleu-vert *adj*
azure azur *m;* azuré ~e *adj*
beige beige *adj*
black noir, ~e *adj*
blue bleu, ~e *adj*
blue, navy bleu marin *adj*
blue, royal bleu roi *adj*
blue, sky bleu ciel *adj*
blue-green bleu vert *adj*
bluish bleuâtre *adj*
brown brun, ~e *adj;* marron *adj*
cerise cerise *adj*
colour, complementary couleur complémentaire *adj*
colour, of a single unicolore *adj*
colour, main dominante *f* (paint)
colour, primary couleurs fondamentales *fpl*
colour, secondary couleur secondaire *adj*
colour, shade of coloris *m;* nuance *f*
colour chart nuancier *m*
crimson pourpre *adj*
dark foncé, ~e *adj*
fuchsia fuchsia *adj*
gilt doré, ~e *adj;* or *m*
golden doré, ~e *adj*
green vert, ~e *adj*
green, apple vert pomme *adj*
green, bottle vert bouteille *adj*
green, emerald vert émeraude *adj*
green, jade vert jade *adj*
green, olive vert olive *adj*
greenish verdâtre *adj*
grey gris, ~e *adj*
grey, steel gris acier *adj*
greyish grisâtre *adj*
hue coloris *m;* teinte *f*
lavender lavande *adj*
light claire, ~e *adj*
lilac lilac *adj*
maroon bordeaux *adj*
mauve mauve *adj*
mottled jaspé, ~e *adj*
orange orange *adj*
pale pâle *adj*
pastel pastel *m*
pink rosé, ~é *adj*
pinkish rosâtre *adj*
purple violet *m;* ~ette *adj;* pourpre *adj*
red rouge *adj*
red, cherry cerise *adj*
reddish rougeâtre *adj*
russet rousseur *f*
salmon saumon *adj*
sand sable *adj*
silver/silvery argenté, ~e *adj*
slate ardoisé, ~e *adj*
speckled moucheté, ~e *adj*
straw jaune paille *adj*
tint teinte *f*
turquoise turquoise *adj*
two-tone bicolore *adj*
ultramarine outremer *m*
violet violet, ~ette *adj;* purple *m*
white blanc, blanche *adj*
yellow jaune *adj*
yellow, lemon jaune citron *adj*
yellowish jaunâtre *adj*

FRENCH
ENGLISH

MAÇONNERIE
BUILDING

Maçonnerie

Additifs/traitements pour mortier & béton
Additives/treatments for mortar & concrete

accélérateur *m* **rapid** set accelerator
additif *m*; **adjuvant** *m* additive
adjuvant *m* **accélérateur antigel** mortar and concrete cold temperature accelerator additive
adjuvant *m* **des mortiers** mortar and concrete additive
adjuvant *m* **fibres synthétiques** mortar and concrete reinforcing additive
adjuvant *m* **hydrofuge** water repellent additive
adjuvant *m* **plastifiant** mortar and concrete plasticiser additive
adjuvant *m* **pour bétonnage par temps froid** concrete anti-freeze additive
agent *m* agent
agent *m* **décoffrage décoffre** shuttering release agent
agent *m* **décoffrant démoulage** concrete mould release agent
agent *m* **de démoulage** concrete mould release agent
agent *m* **entraîneur d'air** concrete air entraining agent
bitume *m* bitumen
colorant *m* colourant
colorant *m* **béton et mortier** concrete and mortar colourant
colorant *m* **en poudre** powder colourant
colorant *m* **oxyde de fer** iron oxide colourant
durcisseur *m* **de surface fixateur** concrete surface hardener
fixateur *m* setting agent
hydrofuge *m* **liquide** liquid waterproofer
imprégnation *f* **incolore, pavés et dalles béton** colourless waterproofing treatment, for bases
liquide *m* **incolore à base de resins** colourless resin treatment to protect/reinforce concrete slab
pigment *m* pigment
pigment *m* **naturelle** natural pigment
  ~ **ocre jaune** ~ yellow ochre
  ~ **terre d'ombre** ~ umber
  ~ **terre de sienne** ~ sienna
plastifiant *m* plasticiser
réparation *f* **béton** concrete repairer/restorer
résine *f* resin
résine *f* **à base de latex** latex-based resin
résine *f* **d'adjonction** resin binder
retardateur *m* **de prise pour béton** concrete set retarder
revêtement *m* **bitumineux** bituminous liquid
revêtement *m* **d'imperméabilisation pour travaux de cuvelages** waterproofing treatment, for

Maçonnerie

cellars
traitement *m* **caves et sous-sols** waterproofing treatment, for cellars
traitement *m* **façades, murs extérieurs** exterior masonry treatment
traitement *m* **incolore antimousse** colourless anti-moss masonry treatment
traitement *m* **incolore d'imperméabilisant** colourless water repellent, for masonry
traitement *m* **liquide incolore à base de resins** colourless resin protection/reinforcement of concrete slab
traitement *m* **sols** treatment for bases

Traitements du bois
Wood treatments

traitement *m* **anti-termites** anti-termite treatment
traitement *m* **bois intérieurs** interior wood treatment
traitement *m* **contre termites, vrillettes et capricornes** treatment against termites and woodboring beetles
traitement *m* **multi-usages: insecticide, fongicide et anti-termites** treatment against insect, fungal attack and termites

traitement *m* **poutre et charpente** treatment for timber beams and frames

Briques & blocs
Bricks & blocks

bloc *m* block; breezeblock (see also: **parpaing**)
bloc *m* **allégé** alleviated breezeblock
bloc *m* **auto-isolante en terre cuite** cellular terracotta insulating block
bloc *m* **béton cellulaire** concrete cellular insulating block
bloc *m* **creux** hollow block
bloc *m* **creux d'angle** pilaster block (not available in UK)
bloc *m* **creux en béton** hollow concrete block
bloc *m* **de granulats** solid aggregate block
bloc *m* **en béton** solid concrete block
bloc *m* **linteau** lintel block
bloc *m* **perforé** perforated block
bloc *m* **plein** full size block (see also: **parpaing**)
bloc *m* **U** U-shaped channel (not available in UK)
brique *f* brick
brique *f* **à couteau** arch brick
brique *f* **creuse de terre cuite** hollow terracotta brick
brique *f* **de cloison** perforated clay

Maçonnerie

block for partitions (no UK equivalent)
brique *f* **de façade** facing brick
brique *f* **de pavage** paving brick
brique *f* **de type courant** standard brick
brique *f* **de ventilation** ventilation brick
brique *f* **de verre** glass brick
brique *f* **flammée** burnt brick
brique *f* **isolant** insulating brick
brique *f* **perforée** perforated brick
brique *f* **plâtrière** terracotta brick, hollow, for partition walls
brique *f* **pleine** full size brick
brique *f* **terre cuite** terracotta brick
carreau *m* **de plâtre** plaster tile/block (for metal-framed partition walls)
carreau *m* **de plâtre alvéolé** honeycomb plaster block
carreau *m* **de plâtre creux** hollow plaster block
carreau *m* **de plâtre hydrofugé** waterproofed plaster block
carreau *m* **de plâtre plein** solid plaster block
carrelage *m* **en briques** brick paving
demi-brique *f* half-brick
massif *m* **de fondation** foundation block
mulot *m* half-width brick
muret *m* **béton décoratif** decorative concrete walling block
muret *m* **pierre reconstituée** reconstituted stone walling block
parpaing *m* breezeblock (see also: **bloc**)
parpaing *m* **creux à bancher** hollow breezeblock (for filling with mortar)
parpaing *m* **creux béton** hollow concrete breezeblock
parpaing *m* **d'angle** pilaster breezeblock, with hole for reinforcing rod
parpaing *m* **de chaînage** breezeblock, reinforcing, with channel to take reinforcing rods
parpaing *m* **plein** breezeblock, full size
pilier *m* walling pillar
planelle *f* breezeblock, thin profile, hollow (not available in UK)
planelle *f* **perforée** thin profile hollow breezeblock (not available in UK)
plaquette *f* **de parement** facing brick or block

Maçonnerie & granulats
Masonry & aggregates

agrégat/s *m* aggregate/s
agrégat *m* **d'argile expansée** expanded clay aggregate
agrégats *m* **décoratifs en vrac** decorative aggregates, in bulk
bâtard *m* **mortier** cement/lime mix; lime mortar

Maçonnerie

béton *m* concrete
béton *m* **allégé libre** lightweight mortar
béton *m* **à prise rapide** rapid-setting mortar
blocaille *f* ballast (see also: **granulat**)
cailloutage *m* pebbledash
chaux *f* lime
chaux *f* **aérienne** lime, hydrated/slaked
chaux *f* **blanche naturelle** natural white lime
chaux *f* **colorée teintée** coloured lime
chaux *f* **de Saint Astier** St Astier lime
chaux *f* **grise** grey lime
chaux *f* **hydraulique** hydraulic lime
chaux *f* **naturelle formulae** naturally formulated lime
ciment *m* cement
ciment *m* **à maçonner** masonry cement
ciment *m* **bâti prompt** quick setting cement
ciment *m* **blanc** white cement
ciment *m* **fondu** heat-resistant cement
ciment *m* **gris** grey cement
ciment *m* **haute performance** high-performance cement
ciment *m* **joint** tile-joint cement
ciment *m* **milieux agressifs** sulphate-resisting cement
ciment *m* **multi-usages** all-purpose cement
ciment *m* **prêt à l'emploi** dry-mixed cement
ciment *m* **prompt** quick-setting cement
ciment *m* **spécial** special-purpose cement
ciment *m* **super blanc** extra-white cement
crépi/crépissage *m* rendering/roughcast
enduit *m* rendering
enduit *m* **tyrolien** spray-on render (using pneumatic or hand-operated projector)
granulat *m* ballast (see also: **blocaille**)
gravier *m*; **gravillon** *m* gravel
gravier *m* **en vrac** gravel, in bulk
gravier *m* **mignonnette non roulée** fine non-rolled gravel
gravier *m* **roulé** rolled gravel
marbre *m* marble
moellon *m* building stone
mortier *m* mortar; grout
mortier *m* **à prise rapide** quick-setting mortar
mortier *m* **blanc** white mortar
mortier *m* **coloré** coloured mortar
 ~ **beige foncé** ~ dark beige
 ~ **gris profond** ~ dark grey
 ~ **rose ambre** ~ pink amber
 ~ **rouge brique** ~ brick red
mortier *m* **d'imperméabilisation** waterproofing mortar
mortier *m* **de jointoiement** pointing mortar
mortier *m* **de ragréage et de**

Maçonnerie

lissage finishing and smoothing mortar
mortier *m* **de réparation** repair mortar
~ **gris** ~ grey
mortier *m* **fin** fine mortar
~ **blanc** ~ white
mortier *m* **gris** grey mortar
mortier *m* **pierre calcaire** limestone mortar
mortier *m* **prêt à l'emploi** dry-mixed mortar
mortier *m* **prêt mix jointoiement gris** grey ready-mixed pointing mortar
mortier *m* **rapide** quick-setting mortar
mortier *m* **réfractaire** heat-resistant/refractory mortar
polystyrène *m* **adjuvanté** polystyrene aggregate
sable *m* sand
sable *m* **à maçonner** masonry sand
sable *m* **argenté** silver sand
sable *m* **de mélange béton** concreting sand
sable *m* **de rivière** river sand
sable *m* **doux** soft sand
sable *m* **en vrac** sand in bulk
sable *m* **liant/mordant** sharp sand

Pavage
Paving

bloc *m* paving block
bloc *m* **vieilli en béton** aged effect in concrete
bordurette *f* paving edging
brique *f* **de pavage** paving brick
carrelage *f* tiling
carrelage *f* **extérieur** exterior tiling
carrelage *f* **terrasse** terrace/patio tiling
dallage *f* paving
dallage *f* **marbre** marble paving
dallage *f* **multi-formats** paving sets, varying sizes/shapes (e.g. crazy paving)
dalle *f* paving slab
dalle *f* **à engazonner** turf slab
dalle *f* **amortissante** rubber slab
dalle *f* **aspect brique** paving slab, brick pattern
dalle *f* **clipsable** clip-together slab system
dalle *f* **de cheminement en béton** slab path unit
dalle *f* **en ardoise** slate paving stone
dalle *f* **en béton** concrete slab
dalle *f* **en béton, aspect de surface: gravillonné** gravel faced slab
dalle *f* **en pierre** stone slab
~ **naturelle** natural
~ **reconstitutuée** reconstituted
dalle *f* **gazon en polyéthylène** grass-reinforcing slab in polyethylene

Maçonnerie

dalle *f* **gravillons** gravel-faced slab
dallette *f* **pierre** small stone paving slab
frise *f* **galet** pebble frieze
galet *m* **de pierre naturelle** stone pebble
grès *m* **cérame émaillé** stoneware tile
lame *f* **de terrasse en béton** concrete decking
pas *m* **japonais** stepping stone, Japanese style
pavé *m* flagstone; cobblestone
pavé *m* **autobloquant en béton** interlocking concrete paver
pavé *m* **grainaillée** grit finish paver
pavé *m* **vielli en béton** concrete paver with aged effect
rive *f* edging block
trame *f* 'field' slab with moulded design of smaller slabs; separate pieces; woven effect

Plâtrage & de remplissage
Plastering & filling

baguette *f* **d'angle** angle bead
bourrelet *m* **d'étanchéité** angle bead
éclisse *f* **cornière** angle bead
enduit *m* coating; filler; rendering
enduit *m* **à joint** joint filler
~ **prêt à l'emploi** ~ ready to use
~ **prise lente** ~ slow-drying
enduit *m* **à prise rapide** quick-setting filler
enduit *m* **d'étanchéité** waterproof filler
enduit *m* **de finition** finishing filler
enduit *m* **de lissage** fine-surface filler
enduit *m* **de rebouchage** repair filler
enduit *m* **poudre à prise rapide** quick-setting filler, in powder form
enduit *m* **poudre de collage et finition** fine joint filler
enduit *m* **prêt à l'emploi** pre-mixed filler
enduit *m* **surfin** high quality filler
gypse *m* gypsum
gypse *m* **renforcé fibre** fibre reinforced gypsum
mortier *m* mortar; grout
mousse *f* **expansive polyuréthane** expanding polyurethane foam filler
pâte/mastic *m* putty
plâtre *m* plaster
plâtre *m* **à modeler** moulding plaster
plâtre *m* **à projecter** projection plaster
plâtre *m* **allégé** alleviated plaster
plâtre *m* **de Paris** plaster of Paris
plâtre *m* **en poudre** plaster powder
plâtre *m* **fin blanc** fine white plaster
plâtre *m* **gros** backing plaster
plâtre *m* **incendie** fire-resistant plaster

Maçonnerie

plâtre *m* **manuel** hand-mixing plaster
plâtre *m* **multi-usage** multi-finish; universal plaster
plâtre *m* **ponce** pumice plaster
plâtre *m* **prestia** casting plaster
protège *m* **angle galvanisé** galvanized aluminium plaster bead

Plaque de plâtre
Plasterboarding

bande *f* tape
bande *f* **à joint** jointing tape
bande *f* **renfort d'angle** corner jointing tape
panneau (*pl* -**x**) *m* **de doublage plaque de plâtre** plasterboard with central insulating layer
paroi *f* **alvéolaire** cellular core plasterboard (see also: **plaque de plâtre cartonnée**)
plaque de gypse *f* gypsum board
plaque de plâtre *f* plasterboard
plaque de plâtre *f* **acoustique** acoustic plasterboard
plaque de plâtre *f* **cartonnée** cellular core plasterboard
plaque de plâtre *f* **de sol** flooring plasterboard
plaque de plâtre *f* **feu** firecheck plasterboard
plaque de plâtre *f* **haute densité** high density plasterboard
plaque de plâtre *f* **haute résistance** high resistance plasterboard (for timber framed buildings)
plaque de plâtre *f* **hydrofugée** waterproofed plasterboard
plaque de plâtre *f* **ignifugée** fireproofed plasterboard

Cloisons & plafonds
Partition walls & ceilings

Ossatures
Frames

armature *f* **de cloison** galvanized steel frame
attache *f* **universelle** universal fastener (wall and ceiling rails)
bande *f* **résiliente en liège** resilient cork strip to avoid cracks
cavalier *m* galvanized steel bracket for attaching frame to supporting wall
clavette *f* **bois** wooden jointing peg for panels in cellular partition
connecteur *m* **assemblage fourrure** furring strip connector
cornière *f* **d'angle métallique** galvanized steel angle frame
elargisseur *f* **de cloison pour bloc porte** profiled wooden lining for door opening
fourrure *f* **métallique** galvanized metal furring strip

Maçonnerie

lisse *f* **basse en bois** wooden sill
montant *m* metal channel to hold plasterboard
nez *m* **de cloison** partition nosing
nez *m* **de cloison sapin angles arrondis** round-edged nosing in pine
profil *m* **en U pour plafond** U-shaped ceiling rail
raccord *m* **eclisse** connector plate for frames
rail *m* horizontal rail
rail *m* **haut en bois** wooden top rail
rail *m* **U** U-shaped channel
semelle *f* **bois (aggloméré)** chipboard sole plate
suspente *f* galvanized steel suspension bracket (for suspended ceiling)
suspente *f* **articulée** articulated suspension bracket
trappe *f* **de visite** trap door/hatch

Outils pour l'assemblage des cloisons
Tools for assembly of partitions

cisaille *f* **à tôle universelle** metal snips
etai *m* **télescopique** telescopic prop
grignoteuse *f* nibblers for cutting frame pieces
pince *f* pliers
pince *f* **à agrafer** stapling pliers (system Placostil)
pince *f* **à sertir** crimping pliers
vis *f* **plaque de plâtre** plasterboard screws

Matériaux en feuille
Sheet materials

plaque *f* **ondulée** corrugated roof panel
polystyrène *m* **expansé** expanded polystyrene
polystyrène *m* **extrudé** extruded polystyrene
polystyrène *m* **extrudé bord droit** square-edged extruded polystyrene board
polystyrène *m* **extrudé bord rainuré** groove-edged extruded polystyrene board

Les poutres & les supports
Beams & supports

arêtier *m* hip rafter
chevron *m* rafter
latte *f* lath (see also: **volige**)
linteau (*pl* -**x**) *m* lintel
longeron *f* **de faîtage** ridge bar
panne *f* purlin
panne *f* **faîtière** ridge purlin
panne *f* **sablière** eaves purlin
poutre *f* beam

Maçonnerie

poutre *f* **en fer** girder; RSJ (rolled steel joist)
poutre *f* **précontrainte** prestressed concrete girder (see also: **poutrelle**)
poutrelle *f* beam; girder
poutrelle *f* **béton** prestressed concrete beam
poutrelle *f* **béton entrevous céramique** prestressed concrete beam to take ceramic flooring/ceiling blocks between
prelinteau *m* **précontraint** prestressed concrete lintel
sabot *f* **de poutre** joist hanger
solive *f* joist
volige *f* lath (see also: **latte**)

Isolation, la ventilation & l'imperméabilisation
Insulation, ventilation & damp-proofing

bande *f* **de solin** flashing strip; flaunching (see also: **étanchéité**)
couche *f* **isolant** damp-proof course
cour *f* **anglaise** ventilation grille
dalle *f* **isolante/phonique** thermal/sound insulating tile
double vitrage *f* double glazing
étanchéité *f*, **bande de** flashing strip
étanchéité *f*, **bande de indéchirable autocollante** self-adhesive tear-resistant flashing strip
flocons *m* **de laine de roche en vrac** rockwool flakes in bulk
grille *f* **d'aeration** air grille
isolant *m* insulating material
isolant *m* **mince alu réfléchissant** aluminium foil reflective insulation
isolation *m* **à bulle d'air sec** insulation film (aluminium), with air bubble layer
isolation *m* **acoustique** sound insulation
isolation *m* **armé réflecteurs résistants à la déchirure** tear-resistant reflective membrane
isolation *m* **extérieur réflecteur alu** aluminium film, exterior use
isolation *m* **phonique** sound insulation (see also: **isolation acoustique**)
isolation *m* **phonique pour sol humide** sound insulation, for damp floors
isolation *m* **phonique sols** soundproof membrane for floors
isolation *m* **réflecteur intermédiaire** intermediate reflective layer
isolation *m* **thermique** thermal/heat insulation
laine *f* **de chanvre** hemp
laine *f* **de roche** rockwool
laine *f* **de verre** glass wool
mastic *m* **isolation portes-**

Maçonnerie

fenêtres insulating mastic (doors and windows)
panneau *m* **laine de roche** rockwool panel
panneau *m* **laine de roche non revêtue** unsurfaced rockwool panel
pare-vapeur *m*; ~ **kraft** damp-proof membrane
plaque *m* **isolante et réfléchissante** radiator reflector foil
protection *f* **soubassement** damp-proof membrane
rouleau *m* **de laine de verre** glass wool roll
rouleau *m* **multi-réflecteur** reflective roof insulation roll
sous-couche *f* underlay
sous-couche *f* **liège isol carrelage** cork insulating underlay, for tiles
sous-couche *f* **liège isol moquette** cork insulating underlay, for fitted carpet
sous-couche *f* **liège sol isolation phonique** cork soundproofing underlay, for floors
suspente *f* **pour laine de verre** insulation suspension clip
ventilateur *m* ventilator fan
ventilateur *m* **électrique** electric ventilator fan
ventilateur *m* **extracteur** extractor fan
vermiculite *f* vermiculite
vermiculite *f* **enrobée de bitume** bitumen-coated vermiculite
vermiculite *f* **granulé isolant** granulated vermiculite

Adhésifs
Adhesives

ciment *m* **colle** tile adhesive
colle *f* adhesive
colle *f* **à carreau de plâtre** plaster block adhesive
colle *f* **hydro** waterproof adhesive
colle *f* **matériaux d'isolation** adhesive for insulating materials
colle *f* **néoprène** neoprene adhesive

Évacuation des eaux pluviales
Rainwater drainage

caniveau (*pl* -**x**) *m* drainage channel
caniveau *m* **en béton** concrete drainage channel
caniveau *m* **polyester renforcé de fibre de verre** glass fibre reinforced drainage channel
gargouille *f* waterspout
gouttière *f* gutter
regard *m* **de branchement pour eaux pluviales** rainwater gully
tuyau *m* **de descente** downpipe

Maçonnerie

Assainissement
Sanitation

bac *m* **dégraisseur** grease trap
couvercle *m* cover (e.g. for inspection chamber)
drain *m* drain
drain *m* **agricole** land drainpipe
drain *m* **routier** land drainpipe
fosse *f* **d'aisances** cesspool
fosse *f* **septique** septic tank
fosse *f* **septique toutes eaux** septic tank 'all water'
grille *f* **caillebotis en acier galvanisé** galvanized steel mesh grating
kit *m* **de débouchage** drain clearing kit
plaque *f* **d'égout** manhole cover
regard *m* inspection chamber; manhole
~ **béton** ~ concrete
regard *m* **d'assainissement; ~ de drainage** manhole
système *m* **de drainage** drainage system
système *m* **de vidange** waste outlet
système *m* **du tout à l'égout** sewage system
trappe *m* **de visite** manhole (see also: **regard**)
tube *m* **d'assainissement; ~ de drainage** drainpipe

Toiture
Roofing

ardoise *f* roofing slate
ardoise *f* **fibres-ciment** fibre cement roofing slate
armature *f* **à toit** roof truss (see also: **ferme de charpente**)
bardeau (*pl* **-x**) *m* roof shingle
bardeau *m* **verrier-bitumen** bituminous felt
crochet *m* **ardoise** slate fixing hook
écran *m* **de sous-toiture** roof underfelt
ferme *f* **de charpente** roof truss (see also: **armature à toit**)
liteau *m* **couverture** roof tiling batten
tuile *f* roof tile
tuile *f* **à chatière grillagée** ventilator tile (see also: ~ **à douille**)
tuile *f* **à côtes** interlocking ribbed tile
tuile *f* **à douille** ventilator tile (see also: **tuile à chatière grillagée**)
tuile *f* **à emboîtement** interlocking tile
tuile *f* **à emboîtement, grande moule faiblement galbée** interlocking tile, large mould, shallow curve
tuile *f* **à emboîtement, petit moule faiblement galbée** interlocking tile, small mould, shallow curve

Maçonnerie

tuile *f* **à onde douce** interlocking shallow curved tile
tuile *f* **à pureau plat** interlocking flat tile
tuile *f* **canal** pantile; roman tile
tuile *f* **creuse** gutter tile
tuile *f* **de rive** verge tile
tuile *f* **en verre transparente** transparent tile
tuile *f* **faîtière** ridge tile
tuile *f* **grande moule fortement galbée** interlocking roman tile (large mould, deep curve)
tuile *f* **plate** plain tile
tuile *f* **romaine** half-round tile

Outils & equipment
Tools & equipment

Outils à main
Hand tools

agrafe *f* clamp
agrafeuse *f* staple gun
alêne *f* awl
bêche *f* spade
bride *f* clamp
chevillette *f* clamping peg
coupe-boulons *f* bolt cutters
couteau (*pl* -**x**) *f* **à enduire** caulker
fourche *f* **bêche** fork, digging
hache *f* axe
lime *f* file
niveau *m* **à bulle** spirit level
niveau *m* **laser** laser level
pelle *f* shovel
pelle *f* **carrée** square shovel
pelle *f* **ronde** round shovel
pioche *f* pick
pioche *f* **de cantonnier** mattock
pioche *f* **de terrassier** pick-axe (see also: **pioche hache**)
pioche *f* **hache** pick-axe (see also: **pioche de terrassier**)
rabot *m* plane
serre-joint *m* joint clamp
serre-joint *m* **de cimentier** formwork clamp
serre-joint *m* **de maçon** mason's clamp
tournevis *m* screwdriver

Outils de couvreur
Roofer's tools

arrache *m* **liteaux (et lames de parquet)** roof batten remover (and parquet floor lever)
arrache-clou *m* nail puller; slater's ripper
batte *f* **à plomb** lead beater
enclume *f* **de couvrer** roofer's anvil
guillotine *f* **à liteaux** batten guillotine
guillotine *f* **ardoise** slate cutter
marteau (*pl* -**x**) *m* hammer
marteau *m* **à garnier** garnishing hammer
marteau *m* **de couvreur** roofer's hammer
pince *f* pliers
pince *f* **à ardoise** slate-cutting pliers

Maçonnerie

pince *f* à border zinc-bending pliers
poinçonneuse *f* ardoise et tôle punch, for slate/sheet metal roofing

Scies & lames
Saws & blades

lame *f* de scie saw blade
scie *f* saw
scie *f* à métaux hacksaw
scie-cloche *f* hole saw

Truelles & taloches
Trowels & floats

fer *m* à joint brick jointer
fer *m* à joint demi-ronde half-round brick jointer
fer *m* à joint plat flat brick jointer
gâche *f* plaster mixing trowel
platoir *m* trowel; plasterer's float; hawk (see also: **taloche**)
platoir *m* à enduire cement; finishing; flooring; plasterer's trowel
platoir *m* à enduire denté *m* notched trowel
platoir *m* à enduire inoxidable *m* stainless steel float
taloche *f* plasterer's float; hawk (see also: **platoir**)
taloche *f* bois wooden float
taloche *f* plastique plastic float
taloche *f* polystyrène foam float

truelle *f* à brique bricklaying trowel
truelle *f* à maçonner builder's trowel
truelle *f* berthelet no UK equivalent
truelle *f* briqueteuse brick trowel
truelle *f* carrée; ~ italienne carrée bucket trowel
truelle *f* d'angle corner trowel
truelle *f* de couvreur roofer's trowel
truelle *f* de plâtrier à degrossir smoothing trowel
truelle *f* italienne Italian pattern trowel
~ronde round tipped
truelle *f* langue du chat pointing trowel (UK: pointed tip; French: rounded tip). Nearest UK equivalent: gauging trowel
truelle *f* ronde round tipped trowel
truelle *f* triangulaire no UK equivalent

Projecteurs de ciment & d'enduits épais
Projectors of cement & thick coatings

machine *f* à crépir roughcast/render projector
machine *f* à crépir pneumatique avec pistolet pneumatic projector, with pistol
machine *f* à crépir tyrolienne Tyrolien finish projector

Maçonnerie

De mesure & de marquage
Measuring & marking

cordeau *m* **de maçon** builder's string
fausse équerre *f* adjustable/sliding/combination bevel (see also: **sauterelle**)
fil *f* **à plomb maçon** plumbline
mesure *f* measure
mesure *f* **pliante** folding rule
mesure *f* **roulante** *f* retractable tape measure
règle *f* **de maçon** rule (darby)
sauterelle *f* adjustable/sliding/combination bevel (see also: **fausse équerre**)
télémètre *f* **laser** laser measure

Marteaux & hachettes
Hammers & hatchets

décintroir *m* **à pic** small hand-held pick. Not widely available in UK
hachette *f* hatchet
hachette de plâtrier *f* lath/drywall hammer
marteau (*pl* **-x**) *m* hammer
marteau *m* **à boucharder** sculptor's hammer (for dressing concrete, marble, granite)
marteau *m* **à briques** brick hammer
marteau *m* **à garnir** garnishing hammer
marteau *m* **arrache-clou** claw hammer
marteau *m* **de coffreur** packer's/claw hammer
marteau *m* **de couvreur** roofer's hammer
marteau *m* **d'emballeur** packer's hammer
marteau *m* **de maçon** club/lump (see also: **massette**)
martelette *f* small hammer (e.g. slater's)
masse *f* **couple** sledgehammer
massette *f* club/lump hammer (see also: **marteau de maçon**)
merlin *m* poleaxe

Ciseaux de maçon
Masonry chisels

broche *f* masonry chisel (see also: **pointerolle**)
brochette *f* **de carreleur** tiler's chisel
burin *m* cold chisel; engraving chisel
burin *m* **plat** flat bladed cold chisel
burin *m* **pointu** pointed cold chisel
chasse *f* **à pierre** chasing chisel
ciseau (*pl* **-x**) *m* chisel
ciseau *m* **à brique** bolster chisel
ciseau *m* **à pierre** stone; bolster chisel
ciseau *m* **à rainurer** plaster-cutting chisel
ciseau *m* **de maçon** cold chisel

Maçonnerie

pare-coupe *f* protective handgrip/shield for chisel (see also: **poignée**)
poignée *f* protective handgrip/shield for chisel (see also: **pare-coup**)
pointerolle *f* de maçon masonry chisel; bull point chisel (see also: **broche**)
riflard *m* de maçon 'old umbrella' or mushroom hand guard

Pieds de biches
Crowbars

barre *f* à mine straight pry bar
griffe *f* à cintrer pry bar
ouvre-caisse *f* plat crate opener
pied-de-biche *m* crowbar
pince *f* pliers
pince *f* à décoffrer formwork prise
pince *f* à talon claw bar

Équipement motorisé
Equipment, powered

aspirateur *m* eau et poussières vacuum cleaner, water and dust
bétonneuse *f*; bétonnière *f* cement mixer
compresseur *m* d'air air compressor
groupe électrogène *m* generator
malaxeur *m* mixer (paste, plaster, mortar)
monte-matériaux *f* material lift

nettoyeur *m* haute pression high pressure cleaner
plaque *m* vibrante plate compactor
sableuse *f* sandblaster

Outils électriques & accessoires
Power tools & accessories

Perceuses & visseuses
Drills & screwdrivers

perceuse *f* à percussion filaire percussion drill, corded
perceuse *f* à percussion sans fil percussion drill, cordless
perceuse *f* visseuse drill/screwdriver
marteau *m* démolisseur; ~ piqueur demolition drill
marteau *m* perforateur hammer drill
perforateur *m* électropneumatique pneumatic hammer drill
visseuse *f* electric screwdriver

Forets/mèches
Drill bits

coffret *m* de forets/mèches set of drill bits
foret *m* drill bit (see also: **mèche**)
foret *m* à beton masonry drill bit
foret *m* à métaux metal drill bit

mèche *f* drill bit (see also: **foret**)
mèche *f* **à bois** wood bit
mèche *f* **à bois extensible** expansive wood bit
mèche *f* **à bois plate** flat wood bit
mèche *f* **à ogive; ~ carbure; ~ de tungstene** glass/ceramic/porcelain bit
mèche *f* **à spiral unique** auger bit
mèche *f* **hélicoïdal** twist bit

Limes & meuleuses
Files & grinders

lime *f* **électrique** electric filer
meuleuse *f* **electrique** electric grinder
meuleuse *f* **electrique d'angle** electric angle grinder

Scies
Saws

scie *f* **à ruban** band saw
scie *f* **circulaire** circular saw
scie *f* **sabre** sabre saw
scie *f* **sauteuse** jigsaw
tronçonneuse *f* chainsaw

Rabots & defonceuses
Planes & routers

défonceuse *f* router
rabot *m* plane
rainureuse *f* wall chaser attachment

Ponceuses
Sanders

ponceuse *f* sander
ponceuse *f* **à bande** belt sander
ponceuse *f* **delta** delta sander
ponceuse *f* **excentrique** disc sander
ponceuse *f* **vibrantes** orbital sander

Échafaudage, échelles & escabeaux
Scaffolding, ladders & steps

échafaudage *m* scaffolding
échelle *m* ladder
escabeau (*pl* **-x**) *m* stepladder
étai *m* support prop
étai *m* **reglable** adjustable prop
marchepied *m* step/hop-up
planche *f* **d'échafaudage** scaffold board
trétau *m* trestle

Maçonnerie

Equipement & accessoires
Equipment & accessories

auge *f* mixing trough
bâche *m* tarpaulin
balai *m* broom
boîte *f* **à outils** toolbox
ceinture *f* **porte-outils** toolbelt
coin *m* log-splitting wedge
malaxeur *m* **portif** mixing attachment
palin *m* **électrique** motorised hoist
porte-outils *m* toolbox
seau (*pl* -**x**) *m* bucket
seau *m* **de maçon** builder's bucket
tamis *m* sieve

polypropylène renforcée rubble chute, reinforced polypropylene
lève *f* **plaque de plâtre** plasterboard lifter
palin *m* **à chain** chain hoist
pose-dalle *f* slab lifter
poubelle *f* **plastique** rubbish bin, plastic
trémie *f* **de chargement** hopper (for **goulotte**)
treuil *m* **à levier** lever winch

Matériel chantier manuel
Manual construction equipment

benne *f* skip
big bag *m* FIBC (Flexible Intermediate Bulk Container) for bulk delivery of flowable products (sand, gravel etc)
brouette *f* wheelbarrow
coffrage *m* formwork
conteneur *m* **deux roues à basculement** two-wheeled tilting skip
établi *m* workbench
goulotte *f* **à gravats en**

Maçonnerie

Appendice

MENUISERIE
CARPENTRY & JOINERY

Outils de menuiserie
Carpentry tools

Marteaux de charpentier
Carpenter's hammers

marteau *m* hammer
marteau *m* **à menuisier;
hachette** *f* **de charpentier**
carpenter's hammer
marteau *m* **arrache-clou** claw hammer (see also: **marteau de coffreur**)
marteau *m* **de coffreur** claw hammer (see also: **marteau arrache-clou**)
marteau *m* **d'emballeur** packer's hammer
maillet *m* mallet
maillet *m* **d'ébénsite** cabinet maker's (round head mallet
maillet *m* **de menuisier** woodwork mallet (square head)

Ciseaux à bois & gouges
Wood chisels & gouges

bédane *m* **de menuisier** mortise chisel; bedane (woodturning chisel)
ciseau (*pl* -**x**) *m* chisel
ciseau *m* **à bois** wood chisel
ciseau *m* **à grain d'orge** parting chisel (woodturning)
ciseau *m* **à racler arrondis** scraper (woodturning)
ciseau *m* **de charpentier** firmer chisel
ciseau *m* **de menuisier** bevel-edged chisel
ciseau *m* **de sculpteur** bevel-edged chisel
ciseau *m* **droit** straight-edged chisel (woodturning)
gouge *f* gouge (woodturning)
gouge *f* **à creuser** bowl gouge
gouge *f* **à dégrossir** roughing-out gouge
gouge *f* **à profiler** spindle gouge
hache *f* axe
herminette *f* adze

Mesure & traçage
Measuring & marking

compas *m* **d'épaisseur** caliper gauge (woodturning)
fausse *f* **équerre** adjustable/sliding/combination bevel
mètre *m* **pliant** folding rule
mètre *m*; **règle** *m* rule
réglet *f* **inox flexible** flexible steel rule
tarière *f* gimlet
tarière *f* **à gouge** bradawl
trusquin/troussequin *m* marking/mortise gauge
vrille *f* auger (for pilot holes)

Menuiserie

Serre-jointes
Clamps

grand serre-joint *m* sash clamp
pince *f* **à ressort** spring clamp
pince *f* **de serrage** handy clamp
pince *f* **étau à cliquet** ratchet clamp
presse *m* **de mécanicien** G-clamp
presse *m* **mâchoire** F-type gripper clamp (see also: **serre-joint à pompe**)
serre-joint *m* clamp
serre-joint *m* **à pompe** F-type gripper clamp (see also: **presse mâchoire**)
serre-joint *m* **automatique** bar/speed clamp

Scies
Saws

égoïne *f* handsaw (see also: **scie à main**)
égoïne *f* **à denture americaine grosse coupe** handsaw, American pattern, for constructional timber
égoïne *f* **coupe fin** handsaw for mouldings, panelling
égoïne *f* **pour coupe longitudinal** rip saw
égoïne *f* **pour coupe transversal** cross-cut saw
égoïne *f* **universelle** all-purpose saw

scie *f* saw
scie *f* **à araser** gent's/back saw
scie *f* **à chantourner** coping/fret saw (see also: ~ **à défilement**, electric)
scie *f* **à défilement** scroll saw, electric (see also: ~ **à chantourner**)
scie *f* **à dos** tenon saw
scie *f* **à guichet** padsaw; keyhole saw
scie *f* **à main** handsaw (see also: **égoïne**)
scie *f* **à monture de menuisier** frame saw
scie *f* **à onglets** mitre saw
scie *f* **à panneaux** panel saw
scie *f* **à placage** veneer saw
scie *f* **à ruban** band saw
scie *f* **de charpentier** carpenter's saw
scie *f* **sauteuse** jigsaw
tronçonneuse *f* chainsaw

Rabots, râpes & grattoirs
Planes, rasps & scrapers

ciseau *m* **à racler arrondis** (woodturning) scraper (see also: **racloir de finition**)
guillaume *m* plane, rebate/shoulder/bullnose
lime *f* file
rabot *m* plane
rabot *m* **à main;** ~ **manuel** plane, hand/jack

Menuiserie

rabot *m* de charron draw knife
rabot *m* d'ébéniste plane, cabinetmaker's
rabot *m* de poche plane, pocket
rabot *m* en bois plane, wooden
rabot *m* en fonte plane, block; plane, cast iron
rabot *m* en tôle plane, sheet steel
rabot *m* établi plane, bench
rabot *m* métallique plane, smoothing
rabot *m* moulure plane, moulding
racloir *m* acier spokeshave (see also: **vastringue/wastringue**)
racloir *m* de finition (woodturning) scraper (see also: **ciseau** *m* **à racler arrondis**)
râpe *f* rasp
rifloir *m* (or riflard *m*) riffler
Surform *m* planer file (Surform)
varlope *f* plane, jointer/try
vastringue/wastringue *f* spokeshave (see also: **racloir acier**)

Perceuses
Drills

chignole *f* hand drill
perceuse *f* drill
vilebrequin *f* brace

Matériel de menuiserie & accessoires
Carpentry equipment & accessories

boîte *f* à onglets mitre box
cale *f* sandpaper block/wedge
chasse-clou *m*; chasse-pointe *m* nail punch
cheville *f* dowel/pin (see also: **repère de tourillon**)
clip *m* à frisette metal clip for T&G panelling (see also: **crochet à lambris**)
crayon *f* charpente carpenter's pencil
crochet *m* à lambris metal clip for T&G panelling (see also: **clip à frisette**)
établi *m* de bois/de menuisier carpenter's bench
établi-étau *m* portable workbench-vice
établi-étau *m* pliante et reglable folding and adjustable workbench-vice
étau *m* vice
papier *m* de verre glasspaper/sandpaper
planche *f* à dresser shooting board
repère *m* de tourillon dowel pin

Menuiserie

Tours & accessoires
Lathes & accessories

banc *m* lathe bed
bloc-moteur *m* lathe motor block
broche *f* lathe spindle
copieur *m* **universel** copy turning attachment for lathe
éventail *m* lathe tool rest
plateau *m* **de tournage** lathe faceplate
poupée *f* **fixe** lathe headstock
poupée *f* **mobile** lathe tailstock
tour *m* **à bois** lathe

Bois
Wood

bois *m* wood
bois *m* **brut** untreated wood
bois *m* **de charpente** timber
bois *m* **de couverture** roofing timber
bois *m* **dur** hardwood
bois *m* **raboté** planed wood
bois *m* **tendre** softwood
latte *f* lath
planche *f* board; plank; flooring batten
planche *f* **bouvetée** matchboard
planche *f* **de recouvrement** weatherboarding
tasseau (*pl* -**x**) *m* length of wood

Panneaux de bois
Sheet materials

contre-plaqué *m*; **contre-collé** *m* plywood
contre-plaqué *m* **bois exotique** hardwood plywood
dalle *f* **de plancher** floor panel (chipboard or OSB)
fibres *fpl* **dures**; **isorel** *m* hardboard
MDF *m* MDF (medium density fibreboard)
panneau (*pl* -**x**) *m* **d'aggloméré**; **~ de particules** chipboard panel
panneau *m* **d'aggloméré hydrofuge** waterproof chipboard
panneau *m* **d'aggloméré mélaminé** *m* melamine-faced chipboard
panneau (*pl* -**x**) **lattés** *m* blockboard
panneau *m* **OSB** *m* oriented strand board panel

Bois de charpente
Construction timber

bastaing *m* plank
bois *m* **d'ossature** framing timber
chevron *m* rafter
lambourde *f* floor batten; wall plate
liteau *m* roofing batten
madrier *m* large beam

Menuiserie

poutre *f* beam
poutrelle *f* small beam
solive *f* joist
volige *f* lath; strip of cladding

Parquet, plancher & lambris
Woodstrip flooring, floorboards & panelling

contrecollé laminated woodstrip flooring (see also: **stratifié**)
dalle *f* **de plancher** floor panel (chipboard or OSB)
dalle *f* **de plancher isolantes** insulated floor panel
lambris *m* **(avec languettes et rainures)** tongued, grooved and v-jointed (TGV) panelling
lambris *m* **(avec languettes et rainures) aspect brut** unplaned TGV panelling
lambris *m* **(avec languettes et rainures) raboté** planed TGV panelling
parquet *m* parquet flooring
parquet *m* **massif** solid parquet flooring
parquet *m* **plancher** woodstrip flooring
planche *m* board; plank
plancher *m* **déclassé** tongued-and-grooved (T&G) flooring, 'seconds' quality
stratifié laminated woodstrip flooring (see also: **contrecollé**)

Moulure & baguettes
Mouldings & beadings

baguette *f* beading/casing
baguette *f* **d'angle** right-angle moulding
bord *m* **arrondi** nosing
chambranle *m* window frame moulding
champlat *m* cover strip with two rounded edges (see also: **chant plat**)
chant plat *m* (see also: **champlat**)
cheville *f* dowel (see also: **tourillon**)
corniche *f* cornice moulding
encadrement *m* **doucine** ogee moulding
frise *f* **décorative** decorative frieze
jet *m* **d'eau** water bar (window casement or door)
moulure *f* moulding
moulure *f* **demi-rond** half-round moulding
moulure *f* **quart de rond** quarter-round moulding
nez *m* nosing
nez *m* **de cloison** partition nosing
nez *m* **de marche** staircase nosing
pareclose *f* glazing bead
plinthe *f* skirting board
tourillon *m* dowel (see also: **cheville**)
tourillon *m* **cannelé** fluted dowel
tourillon *m* **lisse** smooth dowel

Menuiserie

Variétiés de bois
Wood varieties

acacia *m* acacia
acajou *m* mahogany
aune *m*; **aulne** *m* alder
bambou *m* bamboo
bois *m* **blanc**; **~ de sapin** deal
bois *m* **exotique** exotic wood
bois *m* **vert** unseasoned/green wood
bouleau *m* birch
charme *m* hornbeam
châtaigner *m* sweet chestnut
chêne *m* oak
cyprès *m* cypress
ébène *f* ebony
épicéa *m* spruce
érable *m* maple
frêne *f* ash
hêtre *m* beech
if *m* yew
iroko *m* iroko
marronnier; ~ d'Inde *m* horse chestnut
mélèze *m* larch
méranti *m* meranti
merisier *m* cherry wood
noyer *m* walnut
orme *m* elm
palissandre *m* rosewood
pin *m* pine
pin *m* **sylvestre** scots pine
pitchpin *m* pitch pine
ramin ramin *m*
sapin *m* fir
sapin *m* **de douglas** Douglas fir
saule *m* willow
séquoia *m* redwood
sycomore *m* sycamore
teck *m* teak
thuya *m* thuja; western red cedar
tilleul *m* lime/linden

Escaliers & balustrades
Stairs & stair parts

balustrade *f* balustrade
balustre *f* baluster
barrière *f* **de sécurité enfant** child safety barrier
contremarche *m* riser
échelle *f* ladder
échelle *f* **de grenier** loft ladder
échelle *f* **de meunier** 'miller's' ladder (open tread, with single handrail)
échelle *f* **escamotable** retractable ladder
escalier *m* staircase
escalier *m* **avec contremarche** staircase with risers
escalier *m* **de mezzanine** mezzanine staircase
escalier *m* **droite** straight staircase
escalier *m* **en colimaçon** spiral (see also: **hélicoïdal**)
escalier *m* **en colimaçon carré** square spiral staircase
escalier *m* **en colimaçon rond** round spiral staircase
escalier *m* **gain de place** space-saving staircase

Menuiserie

escalier *m* **hélicoïdal** spiral staircase (see also: **en colimaçon**)
escalier *m* **modulaire** modular staircase
escalier *m* **quart tournant** quarter turn staircase
   ~ **bas** quarter turn at base
   ~ **haut** quarter turn at top
   ~ **milieu** quarter turn at centre
main *m* **courant** handrail
marche *f* tread
palier *m* landing
pas *m* step
pas *m* **décalés** with steps offset
pas *m* **japonais** *m* Japanese style, with steps offset
pilastre *m* newel post (see also: **poteau**)
poteau *m* newel post (see also: **pilastre**)
rambarde *f* railing
rampe *f* rail
trappe *f* **isolée pour échelle escamotable** insulated trapdoor for retractable loft ladder

Menuiserie

Appendice

DÉCORATION
DECORATING

Décoration

Outils de décoration
Decorating tools

Pinceux
Paintbrushes

pinceau *(pl -x) m* paintbrush (see also: **brosse**)
pinceau *m* **à glacis** glaze brush
pinceau *m* **à pochoir** stencil brush
pinceau *m* **à rechampir** pointed brush, for delicate work
pinceau *m* **à vitrifier/vitrificateur** sealing brush
pinceau *m* **acrylique** brush, for acrylic paint
pinceau *m* **aquarelle rond** watercolour brush
pinceau *m* **bois/verni** brush, for varnishing wood
pinceau *m* **d'artiste** artist's paintbrush
pinceau *m* **glycéro** brush, for oil-based paint
pinceau *m* **mate/satinée** brush, for matt/satin finishes
pinceau *m* **nylon plat** flat brush, nylon bristles
pinceau *m* **plat** flat brush
pinceau *m* **radiateur** radiator brush
  ~ **coudé sur chant plat** side-angled, flat
  ~ **plat** forward-angled, flat
pinceau *m* **toute peinture** brush, all paint types
pinceau *m* **universel** brush, universal use
  ~ **plat** flat
  ~ **pouce** round (thumb)

Brosses
Brushes

brosse *f* brush; paintbrush (see also: **pinceau**)
brosse *f* **à badigeon** whitewash/emulsion brush
brosse *f* **à lessiver** cleaning/washing brush
brosse *f* **à plafond** ceiling brush
brosse *f* **à pocher** stippling brush
brosse *f* **à raccords** retouching brush
brosse *f* **à rechampir** pointed brush, for delicate work/mouldings
brosse *f* **à tableau plate/ronde** small flat brush, for retouching/detailed/artistic work
brosse *f* **de pouce** sash brush (round stock; round end to bristles)
brosse *f* **douce** brush, soft, for paint effects
  ~ **synthétique** with synthetic bristles
brosse *f* **en poils de blaireau** badger hair brush
brosse *f* **hermétique** brush with tightly packed bristles
brosse *f* **lasure, traitement bois** brush, for applying stain/wood treatment

Décoration

brosse *f* **plat** flat brush
brosse *f* **plate à lacquer** flat lacquer brush
brosse *f* **plate extra-épaisse** flat, extra-thick brush
brosse *f* **pour effet badigeon** colourwashing brush
brosse *f* **pour effet moucheté** brush, for flecked/dappled paint effect
brosse *f* **radiateur** *m* radiator brush
~ **coudée sur le chant** (side-angled)
~ **coudée sur le plat** (forward-angled)
brosse *f* **rectangulaire** rectangular brush
brosse *f* **rond** round stock brush
brosse *f* **ronde** whitewash/emulsion/paste brush (round stock, large, squared end to bristles)
brosse *f* **spécial acrylique** brush, for acrylic paint
brosse *f* **spécial glycerol** brush, for oil-based paint
brosse *f* **vernis** brush, for varnish
pouce *f* **à rechampir** round stock brush for delicate work/mouldings (see also: **pinceau à rechampir**; **brosse de   pouce**)
queue *f* **anglaise** 'English tail' brush (for large areas and products containing solvents). Nearest UK equivalent: wall brush
queue *f* **de morue** 'codfish tail' brush (for varnish, lacquer and smoothing without loss of hairs)
spalter *m* spalter, for smoothing lacquer and varnish

Rouleaux, tampons de peinture & pistolets à peinture

Rollers, paint pads & sprayguns

bac *m* **à peinture pour rouleaux**
~ **spécial à reservoir** roller tray (see also: **égouttoir**)
égouttoir *m* roller tray (see also: **bac à peinture**)
gant *m* **à peindre en peau de mouton** lambswool painting mitt
manchon *m* roller sleeve
mini rouleau *m* mini roller
monture *f* **rouleau** roller frame
perche *f* **télescopique** telescopic handle for roller frame
pistolet *m* **à peinture** paint spraygun
ralonge *f* **télescopique** extension handle for roller
recharge *f* **rouleau** replacement roller sleeve
rouleau (*pl* -**x**) *m* roller
rouleau *m* **à effet** texturing roller
rouleau *m* **à mèches** polyamide fibre pile roller
rouleau *m* **à peindre** paint roller
rouleau *m* **à radiateur** radiator roller

Décoration

rouleau *m* **à vitrifier** varnish roller
rouleau *m* **alvéolée** honeycomb foam roller
rouleau *m* **angle nervurée** angled ribbed roller
rouleau *m* **anti-gouttes** non-drip roller
rouleau *m* **crépi** texturing roller
  ~ **grain fin** fine grain
  ~ **gross grain** coarse grain
rouleau *m* **cuisine/salle de bain** roller for satin/gloss finish in kitchen/bathroom
rouleau *m* **d'angle à peindre** angled paint roller
rouleau *m* **de mousse synthétique expansée** synthetic foam roller
rouleau *m* **d'une polyamide tissée** polyamide roller
rouleau *m* **effet essuyé** roller for sponged/wiped effect
rouleau *m* **en caoutchouc** rubber roller
rouleau *m* **en mohair** mohair roller
rouleau *m* **façade** exterior roller
rouleau *m* **fibre** fibre roller
  ~ **court** short pile
  ~ **longue** long pile
rouleau *m* **fin** fine finish foam roller
rouleau *m* **finition** finishing roller
  ~ **brilliante** gloss paint
  ~ **mate** matt paint
  ~ **satinée** satin paint
rouleau *m* **floquée** flocked foam roller
rouleau *m* **jetable** disposable roller
rouleau *m* **laqueur** lacquer roller
rouleau *m* **lasure** stain (and other fluids) roller
rouleau *m* **monocouche** one-coat roller
rouleau *m* **mousse** synthetic foam roller
rouleau *m* **mouton laine naturel** natural lambswool roller
rouleau *m* **mur et plafond** wall and ceiling roller
rouleau *m* **pochoir** stencil roller
rouleau *m* **poils courts** short pile roller
rouleau *m* **pour les bois** roller for wood
rouleau *m* **rayé** lined roller
rouleau *m* **toile** roller for ragged effect
rouleau *m* **vernis** varnish roller
roulette *f* small roller
tampon *m* **à peindre** paint pad

Outillage du tapissier
Paperhanging tools & equipment

bac *m* **de trempage** wallpaper soaking tray
balai *m* **de colleur** paperhanging brush (see also: **brosse à tapisser**)
brosse *f* **à encoller** wallpaper pasting brush (see also: **pinceau de tapissier; brosse à mouiller**)
brosse *f* **à mouiller** wallpaper pasting brush (see also: **brosse**

Décoration

à encoller; pinceau de tapissier)
brosse *f* **à tapisser/tapissier** paperhanging brush
ciseaux *f* **de colleur** paperhanger's scissors
couteau (*pl* **-x**) *m* knife
couteau *m* **à colle** adhesive comb
couteau *m* **à emarger** cutting rule
couteau *m* **automatique** extendible blade knife
couteau *m* **lame fixe** fixed-blade knife
décolleuse *f* **à papier peint; ~ à vapeur** wallpaper steam stripper
encolleuse *f* **à papier peint** wallpaper pasting trough
époussette *f* dusting brush
lame *f* **d'arasement** wallpaper trimming wheel (see also: **roulette d'arasement**)
palette *f* **à maroufler** wallpaper smoothing palette (see also: **spatule à maroufler**)
  ~ rigide rigid
  ~ souple flexible
pinceau *m* **de tapissier** wallpaper pasting brush (see also: **brosse à encoller; brosse à mouiller**)
plomb *m* **de tapissier** plumb bob and line
règle *f* rule
règle *f* **de colleur inox** stainless steel rule
règle *f* **de coup** cutting rule/metal straightedge

rouleau *m* roller
rouleau *m* **à colle** paste roller
rouleau *m* **à pointes** spiked roller, for perforating wallpaper prior to stripping
rouleau *m* **débulleur** spiked roller, for removing bubbles)
roulette *f* seam roller
roulette *f* **angle conique** conical seam roller
roulette *f* **angle nervurée** ribbed seam roller
roulette *f* **d'arasement** wallpaper trimming wheel (see also: **lame d'arasement**)
roulette *f* **de tappisier** paperhanger's roller
seau *m* **à colle** paste bucket
seringue *f* **à colle** glue syringe
spatule *f* **à maroufler** wallpaper smoothing spatula
table *f* **à tapissier** pasting table

Outillage du carreleur
Tiling tools

batte *f* float for pressing down tiles
brosse *f* **à joints** joint brush
carrelette *f* tile cutting jig
carrelette *f* **électrique** electric tile cutting jig
disque *f* **diamant carrelage** diamond tile-cutting disc
grille *f* **à poncer** ceramic tile file
jauge *f* **de contour** contour gauge
kit *m* **trepan carbure de**

Décoration

tungstène set of tungsten hole saws
lame *f* **abrasive double face** double-sided tile file
lame *f* **de scie ronde** replacement blade for tile saw
lisseur *m* **de joints** joint smoother
maillet *m* **caoutchouc** rubber mallet (for bedding tiles)
mèche *f* **à percer** extensible drill bit
molette *f* **de rechange** replacement cutting wheel
peigne *m* **à colle** adhesive comb
pierre *f* **à greser double face** double-faced grinding stone
pince *f* **à bec perroquet** ceramic tile nibblers
pince *f* **coupe carreaux;** ~ **carrelage** ceramic tile cutters
pince *f* **de céramiste** ceramic tile cutters for delicate work
pince *f* **mosaïque machoire déportée** tile cutter, jaw offset, for delicate work
pince *f* **mosaïste double molette** double-bladed cutter for mosaics/small tiles
pointe *f* **à tracer** ceramic tile scorer
pointe *f* **à tracer avec système de casse** scorer with tile-breaker
raclette *f* **de carreleur** squeegee
râpe *f* **à céramique** ceramic tile file
scie *f* **de carreleur** tile saw
scie *f* **vilebrequin** cranked tile saw
spatule *f* **à colle** notched glue spatula
taloche *f* **polystyrène expanse** expanded polystyrene float (for smoothing large areas of mortar)
tenaille *f* **de carreleur** tile cutting pliers
ventouse *f* **de préhension** suction pad tile lifter

Matériaux de carrelage
Tiling materials

cales *f* **d'épaisseur** spacing wedges
ciment *m* **joint** grout (see also: **enduit**)
croisillon *m* ceramic tile spacer
enduit *m* grout (see also: **ciment joint**)
joint *m* **en pâte** tile joint sealant
patine *f* **carreaux** tile sheen

Carreaux
Tiles

carreau (*pl* -**x**) *m* **céramique** ceramic tile
carreau *m* **de sol en PVC** PVC floor tiles
carreau *m* **de terre cuite** terracotta tile
carreau (*pl* -**x**) *m* **en grès cérame** stoneware tile
carreau *m* **en marbre antique** antique marble tile
carreau *m* **liège** cork tile
carreau *m* **mural** wall tile
carreau *m* **muraux en faïence**

Décoration

ceramic wall tile
carreau *m* **pierre reconstituée** reconstituted stone tile
carreau *m* **vinyle** vinyl tile
dalle *f* floor tile
dalle *f* **de plafond** ceiling tile
dalle *f* **moquette** carpet tile
plaquette *f* wall tile
plaquette *f* **de parement** plaster wall cladding (interior)

Préparation des murs & plafonds

Preparation for walls & ceilings

accélérateur *m* **de séchage** paint-drying accelerator
antirouille *m* **primaire protecteur** metal primer
cire *f* **carrelage** tile wax/polish
décapant *m* **gel** gel paint stripper
décapant *m* **gel bois** stripper for wood surfaces
décapant *m* **gel carrelage spécial tâches de graisse** grease stain stripper for tiles
décapant *m* **gel carrelage spécial tâches organiques** biological stain stripper
décapant *m* **gel fer** stripper gel for iron surfaces
décapant *m* **gel métal sans grattage** non-scratching gel stripper, for metal surfaces
décapant *m* **gel multi-supports** gel stripper for multiple surfaces
décapant *m* **gel sec confort** dry stripper
décapant *m* **gel universel** gel stripper for all surfaces
décapant *m* **gel voile et laitance ciment carrelage non émaillé** cement stain stripper (unglazed tiles)
décirant *f* polish/shine remover
décolleuse *f* **de papiers peints** chemical wallpaper stripper
décolleuse *f* **de peint** chemical paint stripper
dégraissant *m* degreaser
délaqueur *m* sheen remover
détachant *m* stain remover
diluant *m* paint thinner
diluant *m* **cellulosique** cellulose paint thinner
diluant *m* **synthétique** synthetic paint thinner
dissolvant *m* solvent
enduit *m* filler/coating
enduit *m* **de lissage pâte, prêt à l'emploi** ready-to-use fine paste filler
enduit *m* **de rebouchage** ready-to-use filler
fixateur *m* **de fonds** stabilizer/hardener (friable surfaces)
imperméabilisant *m* **carreaux** tile waterproofer
mastic *m* **de vitrier** putty
mastique *m* **fixation cartouche** joint mastic (in a tube)

Décoration

nettoyant *m* **carreaux** tile cleaner
nettoyant *m* **outils peinture** brush/painting equipment cleaner
résine *f* **armée** polyester resin filler
térébenthine *f* turpentine
white-spirit *m* white spirit
white-spirit *m* **inodore** odourless white spirit

Apprêts & sous-couches
Primers & undercoats

apprêt *m*; **avant-peinture** *m* primer
apprêt *m* **pour plâtre** stabilizing primer
durcisseur *m* hardener
sous-couche *f* undercoat
sous-couche *f* **acrylique** acrylic undercoat
sous-couche *f* **anti-rouille** anti-rust undercoat
sous-couche *f* **avant carrelage** pre-tiling undercoat
sous-couche *f* **bois et fer** undercoat, wood and metal
sous-couche *f* **bois exotiques** undercoat, exotic hardwoods
sous-couche *f* **carrelage/stratifié/PVC/alu/galva** undercoat, smooth surfaces
sous-couche *f* **cuisines et bains, plaque de plâtre** condensation-resistant, anti-mould undercoat (kitchens, bathrooms, plasterboard)
sous-couche *f* **glycéro** oil-based undercoat
sous-couche *f* **grands travaux** undercoat, absorbent or unstable surfaces
sous-couche *f* **intérieur et extérieur** undercoat, interior and exterior woodwork
sous-couche *f* **parpaing/béton** undercoat, blockwork and concrete
sous-couche *f* **pour bois extérieurs** exterior wood primer
sous-couche *f* **plaques de plâtre cartonnées** undercoat for plasterboard
sous-couche *f* **plâtre et ciment** undercoat, plaster and cement
sous-couche *f* **PVC alu galva** undercoat, PVC and galvanized aluminium
sous-couche *f* **supports poreux** undercoat, porous surfaces
sous-couche *f* **universelle** all-surface undercoat

Décoration

Peinture
Paint

badigeon *m* whitewash
badigeon *m* **de chaux** limewash
badigeon *m* **effet douceur blanc à colorer** colourwash (colourant added)
bombe *f* **de peinture** aerosol spray paint
crépi *m* stucco finish
crépi *m* **de façade** exterior stucco
crépi *m* **décollable** peelable stucco
crépi *m* **intérieur décollable** peelable interior stucco
enduit *m* **grain fin** interior wall coat, fine granular finish
peinture *f* paint
peinture *f* **acrylique** acrylic paint
peinture *f* **aérosol radiateur** aerosol radiator paint
peinture *f* **anti-condensation** anti-condensation paint
peinture *f* **antigoutte** non-drip paint
peinture *f* **anti-graffitis finition** anti-graffiti paint
peinture *f* **appui de fenêtre** window sill paint
peinture *f* **bicouche** two-coat paint
peinture *f* **boiseries intérieures** interior wood paint
peinture *f* **brillante** gloss paint
peinture *f* **émulsion** emulsion paint
peinture *f* **en aérosol** spray paint
peinture *f* **en flacon** bottle of paint (for stencils)
peinture *f* **en tube** tube of paint (for stencils)
peinture *f* **façade** masonry paint
peinture *f* **façade martelée en aérosol** hammered metal finish, aerosol
peinture *f* **façade mate** matt paint
peinture *f* **façade métallisée** metallic paint
peinture *f* **façade microporeuse** microporous paint
peinture *f* **façade monocouche** one-coat paint
peinture *f* **façade murs fissurés ou crépis** masonry paint, for cracked/stuccoed walls
peinture *f* **fluo** fluorescent paint
peinture *f* **glycéro** oil-based paint
peinture *f* **haute température** high temperature paint, ferrous metal and copper
peinture *f* **inodore** odourless paint
peinture *f* **laquée** lacquer
peinture *f* **murs et boiseries** paint, walls/woodwork
peinture *f* **murs et plafonds** paint, walls/ceilings
peinture *f* **plafond** ceiling paint
peinture *f* **radiateurs** radiator paint
peinture *f* **satinée** satin paint
peinture *f* **sol intérieur/extérieur** interior/exterior paint, bases
peinture *f* **soubassement et murets** paint, basement/small walls

Décoration

peinture *f* **spécial fer** metalwork paint
peinture *f* **traitement anti-humidité** anti-humidity paint

Peintures décoratives
Paint for decorative effects

céruse *f* **murale** 'white lead' effect paint
cirer *f* **murale** wax coating
dorure *f* gilding
enduit *m* **à cirer** wax wall coating
gel *m* **à craqueler** crackle finish gel
glacis *m* glaze
glacis *m* **à craqueler** crackle glaze
glacis *m* **à huile** oil glaze
glacis *m* **à la cire** wax glaze
glacis *m* **acrylique** acrylic glaze
patine *f* **de finition** finishing glaze, semi-transparent
peinture *f* **à vieillir** paint, aged patina
peinture *f* **effet de chaux** paint, limewash effect
peinture *f* **effet glacis** paint, glaze effect
peinture *f* **effet nacrée** paint, pearl finish
peinture *f* **tableau** *f* blackboard paint

Lasure, vernis, huile & cire
Stain, varnish, oil & wax

bouche-pores *f* wood grain filler
cire *f* wax
cire *f* **effet blanchi** wax, bleached effect
cire *f* **teintée pour meuble** wax, tinted, for furniture
crème *m* **ferronerie-font** grate polish
huile *f* oil
huile *f* **de teck** teak oil
huile *f* **pour plan de travail** oil, for worktops
lasure *f* stain
lasure *f* **badigeon** semi-opaque stain, bleached/aged wood effect
lasure *f* **bois intérieur** interior wood stain
  ~ **opaque** opaque finish
  ~ **satiné** satin finish
  ~ **transparente** transparent finish
teinte *f* tint; stain
teinte *f* **à bois** wood stain
teinte *f* **pour meuble** furniture stain
vernis *m* varnish
vernis *m* **brillant** gloss varnish
vernis *m* **ciment** cement varnish
vernis *m* **clair** clear varnish
vernis *m* **coloré** coloured varnish
vernis *m* **extérieur** exterior varnish
vernis *m* **intérieur** interior varnish
vernis *m* **intérieur cuisines et**

Décoration

bains moisture-resistant varnish, for kitchens/bathrooms
vernis *m* **marin** yacht/marine varnish
vernis *m* **mat** matt varnish
vernis *m* **pierre** stone varnish
vernis *m* **pour meuble et objets** varnish for furniture/objects
vernis *m* **satiné** satin finish varnish

Papier peints & revêtements muraux

Wallpapers & wallcoverings

frise *f* frieze
frise *f* **adhésive** frieze, adhesive backed
frise *f* **murale** frieze, wall
liège *m* **mural** cork wallcovering
papier peint *m* wallpaper
papier peint *m* **à peindre** wallpaper, for painting
papier peint *m* **effet pommelé** wallpaper, dappled effect, for painting
papier peint *m* **effet tissé** wallpaper, woven effect
papier peint *m* **en grès cérame** wallpaper, ceramic effect
papier peint *m* **expansé sur papier** wallpaper, expanded vinyl, paper-backed
papier peint *m* **gaufré** wallpaper, embossed
papier peint *m* **intissé** wallpaper, non-woven
papier peint *m* **lavable** wallpaper, washable
papier peint *m* **motif naturel (incrustation de copeaux de bois)** wallpaper, woodchip
papier peint *m* **motif textile** wallpaper, textile effect
papier peint *m* **mur d'image** wallpaper, mural
papier peint *m* **préencollé** wallpaper, pre-pasted
papier peint *m* **vinyle** wallpaper, vinyl
  ~ **expansé** ~ expanded
  ~ **non-woven** ~ sur intissé
  ~ **vinyl lourd sur intissé** ~ heavy, non-woven back
revêtement *m* **de lissage; ~ de rénovation** wallcovering, for smoothing rough surfaces
revêtement *m* **mural** wallcovering
revêtement *m* **mural à peindre** wallcovering, for painting
revêtement *m* **mural fibre de verre** wallcovering, glass fibre (see also: **voile de verre**)
  ~ **anti-fissure** ~ anti-crack
revêtement *m* **mural fibre de verre maille** wallcovering, glass fibre mesh
revêtement *m* **mural fibre de verre mini-maille** wallcovering, glass fibre, fine
revêtement *m* **mural fibre de verre non-inflammable**

Décoration

wallcovering, glass fibre, non-inflammable
revêtement m **mural fibre de verre prépeinte** wallcovering, glass fibre, pre-painted
structure f **à peindre sur intissé maille** wallcovering, non-woven textured (for painting)
toile f **de verre** glass cloth
voile m **de renfort** reinforcing glass fibre wallcovering
voile m **de verre** wallcovering, glass fibre (see also: **revêtement mural fibre de verre**)

Outils & matériaux de décoration
Decorating tools & materials

Masquage
Masking tape

adhésif m **de protection** masking tape (see also: **masquage**)
adhésif m **de protection antidérapant** masking tape, non-slip
adhésif m **de protection électrique** insulating tape; electrical masking tape
adhésif m **de protection peinture** masking tape, painting
adhésif m **de protection peinture gros oeuvre murs/façades** masking tape, painting, heavy duty for large areas (e.g. walls)
adhésif m **de protection peinture lignes droites** masking tape, painting straight lines (see also: **masquage lignes droites**)
adhésif m **de protection peinture spécial courbes** masking tape, painting curves
adhésif m **écologique kraft** masking tape, kraft paper, solvent free
adhésif m **emballage kraft** parcel tape, adhesive
masquage m masking tape (see also: **adhésif de protection**)
masquage m **bois** masking tape, for wood
masquage m **lignes droites** masking tape, painting straight lines (see also: **adhésif de protection peinture lignes droites**)
toile f **adhesive de protection** masking tape, fabric

Bâches & accessoires de protection
Dust sheets & protective accessories

adhesive f **de protection** dust sheet
adhesive f **de protection avec fermeture** dust sheet, with zip closer (masking/sealing doorways)

Décoration

adhesive *f* **de protection couloirs & passages** dust sheet, hallways
adhesive *f* **de protection sols & fenêtres** dust sheet, floors/windows
bâche *f* tarpaulin
bobine *f* **de protection** dust sheet, roll
combinaison *f* **de bricolage protective** overalls, one-piece (including hood!)
sacs *m* **à gravats** rubble bags, tough plastic
support *m* **extensible pour bâche** prop, extendable, to secure dust sheet to walls

Outils & accessoires de décoration
Decorating tools & accessories

boîte *f* **à coupe** mitre box (cutting mouldings)
brosse *m* **à decaper** rotary wire brush (for power drill)
brosse *m* **à la main métallique** wire brush
cale *m* **à poncer** sanding block
cisailles *fpl* wirecutters
ciseaux *fpl* scissors
coupe-verre *f* glass cutter
couteau *m* knife
couteau *m* **à enduire** smoothing knife (for filler)
couteau *m* **de peintre** paint stripping knife
éponge *f* sponge
éponge *f* **naturelle** natural sponge
éponge *f* **synthétique** synthetic sponge
gants *m* **de caoutchouc** rubber gloves
genouillères *f* knee pads
grattoir *m* scraper
grattoir *m* **à fissures triangulaire** triangular shave hook
grattoir *m* **à lame** scratching blade
laine *f* **d'acier** wire wool
malaxer *m* **de peinture** paint mixer
mélangeur *m* **à peinture** paint stirrer
nuancier *m* **chromatique** paint colour chart
pistolet *m* **décapeur à air chaud** hot air gun
raclette *m* squeegee
raclette *m* **à emmancher; ~ à joint** rubber bladed squeegee
racloir *m* scraper; paint scraper
règle *f* **à émarger** metal rule
sabre *m* **de tapissier** palette knife
spatule *f* spatula
spatule *f* **à maroufler** paint shield
spatule *f* **crantée** notched spatula
taloche *f* hawk; flat trowel

Décoration

Outils pour les effets spéciaux de peinture
Tools for special paint effects

boisette *m* wood graining roller
outil *m* **à veiner effet bois** wood graining veiner
peigne *m* **en caoutchoc** rubber comb (combed effect)
peigne *m* **en carton** corrugated card comb (combed effect)

Colle à papier peint
Wallpaper paste

colle *f* (see also: **pâte**) glue; paste
colle *f* **corniche et rosace** glue, cornices and roses
colle *f* **frise** glue for border/frieze
colle *f* **murale liège; ~ pour liège** cork glue
colle *f* **papier peint** wallpaper paste
colle *f* **papier peint intissé** paste for non-woven wallcoverings
colle *f* **papier peint raccords** wallpaper glue, joins
colle *f* **papier peint vinyle** paste, vinyl wallpaper
colle *f* **pour dalles polystyrène** glue, polystyrene tile
colle *f* **renforcée** glue, reinforced
 ~ **frise** ~ for border/frieze
 ~ **raccord** ~ for touch-up
colle *f* **revêtement textiles muraux** glue, textile wallcovering
colle *f* **toile de verre** glass cloth glue
colle *f* **tous papiers peints** all-purpose wallpaper glue
pâte *f* paste (see also: **colle**)
pistolet *m* **à colle** glue gun
seringue *f* **à colle** glue syringe

Moquette & sol vinyle
Carpet & vinyl floorcoverings

dalle *f* floor tile
dalle *f* **de moquette** carpet tile
dalle *f* **PVC** PVC floor tile
dalle *f* **vinyle auto-adhésive** adhesive-backed vinyl tile
lame *f* **PVC** PVC strip floorcovering
lame *f* **PVC auto-adhésive** adhesive-backed PVC strip floorcovering
moquette *f* carpet
moquette *f* **aiguilletée** needle pile carpet
moquette *f* **à la coupe** cut pile carpet
moquette *f* **à relief** raised pile carpet
moquette *f* **berbère** Berber carpet
moquette *f* **bouclée** looped pile carpet
moquette *f* **fibres do coco** cocoa fibre carpet
moquette *f* **imprimée** printed carpet

Décoration

moquette *f* **laine** raised wool carpet
moquette *f* **tressée** woven carpet
moquette *f* **velours** velvet pile carpet
rabane *f* **jonc** rafia matting
rabane *f* **jonc de mer** seagrass floorcovering
rabane *f* **jonc de montagne** rush floorcovering
revêtement *f* **de sol** floorcovering
revêtement *f* **de sol en vinyle rouleaux** vinyl floorcovering, on roll
revêtement *f* **de sol PVC** PVC floorcovering
revêtement *f* **de sol sisal** *m* sisal floorcovering

Appendice

ÉLECTRICITÉ
ELECTRICITY

Électricité

Gaines & accessoires électriques
Electrical sheathing & accessories

fixation *m* **pour gaines** (see also: **stop gaine**) sheath bracket, screw-in
gaine *f*; **~ électrique; ~ de protection** polypropylene corrugated flexible cable sheathing
gaine *f* **avec tire-fil** sheathing, with cable pull-through
gaine *f* **plastique rigide** sheathing, rigid plastic
gaine *f* **précablée** sheathing, pre-installed with circuit cable
gaine *f* **préfilée** sheathing, pre-installed with cable cores
gaine *f* **préfilée téléphone ADSL vert** sheathing, pre-installed with ADSL telephone cable, green
gaine *f* **préfilée TV coaxial vert** sheathing, pre-installed with TV coaxial cable, green
gaine *f* **vide** sheathing, empty
lubrifiant *m* **pour tirage de fils** lubricant for feeding cores and cables through sheathing
manchon *m* **ouvrable** sheathing connector, clip-on
stop gaine *m* sheath bracket, screw-in (see also: **fixation pour gaines**)
~ double ~ double
~ simple ~ single
tire-fil *f* **en nylon** nylon cable pull-through

Moulures & goulottes
Mouldings & trunking

baguette *f* **de distribution** (see also: **tube**) cable conduit
baguette *f* **de distribution sol** (see also: **passage de plancher**) cable conduit, floor-mounted
boîte *f* **de dérivation plinthe** skirting junction box
cache-câble *f* **en PVC, auto-adhésif** cable conduit, self-adhesive
clou *m* **spécial moulure** moulding fixing bracket
goulotte *f* trunking, PVC
goulotte *f* **pour installation en saillie** trunking, surface-fixed (with clip-on cover)
moulure *f* **angle** moulding, angled (corner fixing)
moulure *f* **plafond** moulding, ceiling
moulure *f* **PVC** moulding, PVC
passage *f* **de plancher** (see also: **baguette de distribution sol**) cable conduit, floor-mounted
plinthe *f* **décor** skirting board, decorative
tube *m* cable conduit (see also: **baguette de distribution**)

Électricité

tube *m* **tulipé** cable conduit, flared end, for connection to adjoining length

Accessoires: moulures & goulottes
Accessories: mouldings & trunking

Goulottes
Trunking

cornet *m* **de plafond** ceiling duct, conical
embout *m* push-in end piece
support *m* **de prise électrique** electric socket mount

Moulures
Mouldings

adaptateur *m* **pour moulure** adapter (switch/socket installation)
boîte *f* **de dérivation pour moulure** junction box for moulding
boîte *f* **pour point lumineux** junction box for ceiling light
embout *m* **pour moulure** moulding, end piece
jonction *f* **couvercle** moulding, junction cover
moulure *f* **angle** moulding, angle
moulure *f* **angle, extérieur** moulding, exterior angle connector
moulure *f* **angle, intérieur** moulding, interior angle connector
moulure *f* **avec séparation** moulding, partitioned
moulure *f* **en té** moulding, tee connector
moulure *f* **plat** moulding, flat right-angle joint
té *m* **de dérivation pour moulure** tee junction box

Plinthes
Skirting boards

agrafe *f* **décorative** decorative joint clip
chambranle *f* **décorative** decorative junction between skirting and moulding

Tubes
Conduit

clip *m* clip-in bracket
coudes *m* **équerre** right-angle elbow connector
courbe *m* curved connector
fixation *m* **pour tube** screw-in bracket
manchon *f* sleeve for connecting lengths

Électricité

manchon *f* **ouvrable** snap-on hinged sleeve
té *m* tee-connector

Câble & fil d'installation
Cable & wire

câble *m* **d'alimentation rigide** rigid cable core
câble *m* **de terre, cuivre nu** earth wire, bare copper
câble *m* **électrique** electric cable
câble *m* **électrique à la coupe** electric cable, by the length
câble *m* **électrique au mètre** electric cable, by the metre
câble *m* **électrique de distribution** mains cable
câble *m* **électrique de mise a la terre, cuivre nu** bare copper earth wire
câble *m* **électrique en couronne** cable, reel of
câble *m* **électrique multifilaire** multi-core cable
câble *m* **électrique rigide** rigid cable
câble *m* **électrique silicone** silicone-sheathed cable (use in hot atmospheres)
câblette *m* **de terre** earth cable
conducteur *m* cable core
fil *m* wire; filament
fil *m* **nu** bare cable core

Câble souple & cordon d'alimentation
Flex & power cords

câble *m* **coaxial tv hertzien et satellite** cable, coaxial terrestrial and satellite TV cable
câble *m* **haut parleur, translucide, méplat** twin-core sheathed hi-fi cable, flat
câble *m* **multimédia** multimedia cable
câble *m* **multimédia hi-fi** multimedia hi-fi cable
câble *m* **multimédia téléphone** multimedia telephone cable
câble *m* **multimédia téléphone, internet et informatique** telephone, internet and computer cable
câble *m* **multimédia téléreport armé** EDF-installed telephone cable for meter connection
câble *m* **souple** flex
câble *m* **souple au mètre** PVC-sheathed flex, by the metre
câble *m* **souple en bobine** flex, in a reel
câble *m* **unifilaire souple** PVC-sheathed flex core (not available in UK)

Électricité

Fixation des gaines & câbles
Conduit & cable fixings

attache-fil *m* cable clip (nail fixing)
clip *m* **double** twin clip (for parallel cables)
collier *m* **de fixation; ~ de serrage** cable tie (use with: **embasse**)
embasse *f* clip, head piece (use with: **collier**)
embasse *f* **à cheville; ~ a visser** clip, head piece, screw fixing
embasse *f* **à frapper** clip, head piece, nail fixing
serre-câble *m* **à cheville** cable clip (screw fixing)

Boîtes de dérivation
Junction boxes

boîte *f* **de dérivation** (see also: **coffret de dérivation**) junction box
boîte *f* **de dérivation à encastrer** junction box, recessed
boîte *f* **de dérivation à sceller** junction box, sealed (in masonry)
boîte *f* **de dérivation cloison sèche à encastrer** junction box, drywall recessed
boîte *f* **de dérivation en saillie** junction box, surface-mounted
boîte *f* **de dérivation étanche** junction box, waterproof
boîte *f* **de dérivation maçonnerie à encastrer** junction box, for masonry
boîte *f* **de distribution** branch box; connection box (see also: **boîte de jonction en saillie**)
boîte *f* **de jonction en saillie** branch box; connection box (see also: **boîte de distribution**)
coffret *m* **de dérivation** (see also: **boîte de dérivation**) junction box
couvercle *m* **de finition** junction box, cover
  ~ à clipser ~ clip-on
  ~ à visser ~ screw-on
entrée *f* **étanche en saillie** grommet

Boîtes d'encastrement
Mounting boxes

boîte *f* mounting box
boîte *f* **appliquée** mounting box, surface-fixed
boîte *f* **appliquée cloison sèche** mounting box, surface-fixed, partition wall
boîte *f* **avec patte de chambranle** mounting box, door/window frame
boîte *f* **d'encastrement** mounting box, flush
boîte *f* **d'encastrement à sceller** mounting box, flush, recessed, sealed
boîte *f* **d'encastrement deux**

Électricité

postes mounting box, flush, double
boîte *f* **d'encastrement multi-matériaux** mounting box, flush, all materials (see also: **boîte d'encastrement tout type de matériaux**)
boîte *f* **d'encastrement tout type de matériaux** mounting box, flush, all materials (see also: **boîte d'encastrement multi matériaux**)
boîte *f* **d'encastrement plaque de plâtre** mounting box, flush, for plasterboard wall
boîte *f* **d'encastrement point de centre pour plafond** mounting box, flush, for ceiling
boîte *f* **d'encastrement pour mur creux** mounting box, flush, for hollow walls
boîte *f* **d'encastrement pour mur plein** mounting box, flush, for solid wall
boîte *f* **d'encastrement quatre postes** mounting box, flush, quadruple
boîte *f* **d'encastrement trois postes** mounting box, flush, triple
boîte *f* **plafond** mounting box, ceiling
plaque *f* **d'obturation** blanking plate

Interrupteurs & prises
Switches & sockets

cache *f* **pour interrupteur** switch faceplate
cache *f* **pour prise** faceplate, for socket outlet
interrupteur *m* switch
interrupteur *m* **à distance** switch, remote control
interrupteur *m* **à encastrer** switch, recessed
interrupteur *m* **à pied** switch, foot-operated
interrupteur *m* **bipolaire** switch, two-pole
interrupteur *m* **combiné pac saillie** switch, surface-mounted
interrupteur *m* **de contrôle** switch, control
interrupteur *m* **différentiel** switch, consumer unit main
interrupteur *m* **étanche** switch, two-way, waterproof exterior
interrupteur *m* **va-et-vient** switch, two-way
obturateur *m* faceplate, junction box
plaque *f* **simple** cover plate
poussoir *m* push button/switch
poussoir *m* **à bascule** toggle switch
poussoir *m* **à encastrer** push button/switch, recessed
poussoir *m* **à voyant, témoin ou lumineux** push button/switch, luminous

Électricité

poussoir *m* **étanche** push button switch, waterproof
prise *f* **électrique** socket outlet
prise *f* **électrique à distance** socket outlet, remote control
prise *f* **électrique à encastrer** socket outlet, recessed
prise *f* **électrique avec terre** socket outlet, earthed
~ **automatique à encastrer** ~ recessed
prise *f* **électrique deux pôles & terre (P+T)** socket outlet, two-pole, with earth pin
prise *f* **électrique double** socket outlet, double
~ **avec terre** ~ earthed
~ **deux pôles** ~ two-pole
prise *f* **électrique en appliqué** socket outlet, surface-mounted
prise *f* **électrique murale** socket outlet, wall fixed
prise *f* **électrique plinthe** socket outlet, recessed, skirting board
prise *f* **électrique programmable** socket outlet, programmable
~ **digital** ~ time switch, digital
~ **mécanique** ~ time switch, mechanical
prise *f* **électrique sans terre** socket outlet, two-pole, without earth
prise *f* **électrique trois P+T** socket outlet, three-pole, plus earth
prise *f* **informatique** socket outlet, telephone/computer
prise *f* **téléphone** socket outlet, telephone
prise *f* **TV/FM/SAT** socket outlet, television/stereo/satellite
sortie *f* **de câbles** cable outlet
variateur *m* dimmer switch

Fiches électriques & douilles
Plugs & lampholders

douille *f* lampholder
douille *f* **à baïonnette** lampholder, bayonet fitting
douille *f* **à vis** lampholder, screw fitting
douille *f* **acier laitonné** lampholder, brass finish
douille *f* **double bague** lampholder, two retaining rings
douille *f* **étanche** lampholder, waterproof
douille *f* **simple bague** lampholder, one retaining ring
fiche *f* **électrique** plug
fiche *f* **électrique caoutchouc** plug, rubber
fiche *f* **électrique caravanne** plug, caravan
fiche *f* **électrique femelle** plug, female
~ **2 pôles** ~ 2-slot
~ **2 pôles + terre** ~ 2-slot plus earth pin
fiche *f* **électrique mâle** plug, male
~ **2 pôles** ~ 2-pin

Électricité

~ **2 pôles +terre** ~ 2-pin plus earth
~ **3 pôles + terre** ~ 3-pin plus earth

Tableaux électriques
Consumer units

borne *f*; **bornier** *f* terminal
borne *f* **d'alimentation** terminal, phase/neutral
borne *f* **d'arrivée** terminal, principal consumer unit
borne *f* **de raccordement** terminal, consumer unit
cloison *f* **de séparation** consumer unit, partition
coffret *m* **de chantier** box, 'builder's', temporary site consumer unit
coffret *m* **de communication** box, to distribute TV/multimedia systems, computer network & telephone (see also: **coffret multimédia**)
coffret *m* **multimédia** box, to distribute TV/multimedia systems, computer network & telephone (see also: **coffret de communication**)
obturateur *m* **coffret** blanking plate
peigne *f* terminal block strip
~ **horizontal reversible**
~ horizontal reversible
~ **vertical** ~ vertical

support barrette *f* **pour cache borne** support bar for terminal cover
tableau *m* **de commande principal** switch board, main
tableau *m* **de protection** consumer unit (see also: ~ **électrique**; ~ **de répartition**)
tableau *m* **de répartition** consumer unit (see also: ~ **de protection**; ~ **de répartition**)
tableau *m* **électrique** consumer unit (see also: ~ **de protection**; ~ **de répartition**)
tableau *m* **électrique chauffe-eau câblé** consumer unit, for water heater, cabled
tableau *m* **électrique d'atelier** consumer unit, for workshop
tableau *m* **électrique étanche** consumer unit, waterproof
tableau *m* **électrique nu** consumer unit, empty casing
tableau *m* **électrique prééquipé et précâblé** consumer unit, pre-installed and pre-cabled

Disjoncteurs
Circuit breakers

coupe-circuit *m* circuit breaker, fused
disjoncteur *m* circuit breaker
disjoncteur *m* **différentiel** residual current device (RCD)
disjoncteur *m* **divisionnaire**

Électricité

différentiel miniature circuit breaker
interrupteur *m* **différentiel** circuit breaker, switched
parafoudre *m* ~ **modulaire**; ~ **de secteur** lightning surge protector
recharge parafoudre *m* lightning surge protector, replacement cartridge (after many triggers)

Ampoules & tubes
Light bulbs & tubes

ampoule *f* (see also: **lampe**) light bulb
ampoule *f* **clair** light bulb, clear
ampoule *f* **demi argentée** light bulb, half silvered standard
ampoule *f* **dépoli** light bulb, frosted
ampoule *f* **économie d'énergie (éco)** light bulb, energy efficient
ampoule *f* **flamme** light bulb, flame effect
ampoule *f* **flamme coup de vent** light bulb, 'candle in the wind'
ampoule *f* **globe** light bulb, globe
ampoule *f* **halogène** light bulb, halogen
 ~ **spot** ~ spotlight
ampoule *f* **halogène TBTS (très basse tension)** light bulb, low voltage
ampoule *f* **incandescent** light bulb, incandescent
ampoule *f* **LED** light bulb, LED (light-emitting diode)
ampoule *f* **lotus** light bulb, lotus-shaped
ampoule *f* **réflecteur** light bulb, reflector
ampoule *f* **Soft Tone** light bulb, Soft Tone
ampoule *f* **sphérique** light bulb, spherical
ampoule *f* **spirale** light bulb, spiral
ampoule *f* **spot** light bulb, spotlight
ampoule *f* **standard** light bulb, standard
culot *m* light bulb, cap
culot *m* **B bayonnette** bayonet cap
culot *m* **E** E-type (Edison screw) cap
culot *m* **G** G-type bi-pin cap
lampe *f* light bulb (see also: **ampoule**)
tube *m* **fluorescent** tube, fluorescent
 ~ **blanc** ~ white
tube *m* **halogène** tube, halogen
 ~ **éco** ~ energy-efficient
tube *m* **incandescent** tube, incandescent
 ~ **dépoli** ~ frosted
 ~ **opale** ~ opal

Électricité

Fusibles
Fuses

adaptateur *m* **porte-fusible à broches** fuse adapter (porcelain fuseholders)
coupe-circuit *m* **á broche** cartridge fuse (see also: **fusible à cartouche**)
fil *m* **fusible plomb** fuse wire
fusible *m* fuse
fusible *m* **à cartouche** cartridge fuse (see also: **coupe-circuit á broche**)
fusible *m* **céramique** fuse, ceramic
   ~ **avec voyant** ~ with indicator
   ~ **sans voyant** ~ without indicator
fusible *m* **verre** fuse, glass
porte-fusible *m* fuse holder

Accessoires électriques
Electrical accessories

barrette *f* **de connexion** (see also: **peigne d'alimentation**) terminal block strip
bloc *m* **ménager** trailing socket
bloc *m* **multiprise** multiple socket extension lead
   ~ **parafoudre** ~ with lightning protection
borne *f* terminal
borne *f* **automatique** terminal, automatic push-in core connector
borne *f* **de câble** terminal, cable socket
borne *f* **de jonction** terminal, junction box
câble *m* **connecteur** cable connector
câble *m* **enrouler** cable reel
chargeur de piles *m* battery charger
cosse *f* crimp connector
cosse *f* **clip femelle** crimp connector, female
cosse *f* **clip plat mâle** crimp connector, flat
cosse *f* **fiche mâle** crimp connector, male, flat
cosse *f* **fourche** crimp connector forked
dés *m* **de raccordement (domino)** connector block
détecteur *m* **de coupure de courant** detector, electrical current cut
détecteur *m* **de fumée** detector, smoke
détecteur *m* **de gel** detector, frost
détecteur *m* **d'inondation** detector, flood
détecteur *m* **de monoxide de carbone** detector, carbon monoxide
détecteur *m* **de panne de congélateur** freezer alarm
écrou *f* terminal nut
embout *m* **de câble** terminal, cable
enrouleur *m* extension reel
fiche *f* **multiprise** plug adapter

Électricité

générateur *m* generator, electrical (see also: **groupe électrogène**)
groupe électrogène *m* generator, electrical (see also: **générateur**)
parafoudre *m* **de secteur** surge/lightning protector
parafoudre *m* **pour ligne téléphonique** surge/lightning protector, telecommunications equipment
peigne *f* **d'alimentation** terminal block strip (see also: **barrette de connexion**)
pile *f* battery
pile *f* **alcaline** battery, alkaline
pile *f* **bouton** battery, button
pile *f* **lithium** battery, lithium
pile *f* **rechargeable** battery, rechargeable
piquet *m* **de terre** earth spike
prise *f* **parasurtenseur** surge/lightning protector, socket-mounted
prolongateur *m* **électrique** long extension lead
raccord *m* **auto-dénudant** wire connector, self-stripping
rallonge *m* **électrique** extension lead
ruban *m* **adhésif**; **~ isolant** insulating tape

Outils d'électricien
Electrician's tools

ampèremètre *m* ammeter
coupe-câble *m* cable cutter
couteau *m* **à degainer** sheathing cutter
couteau *m* **d'électricien** knife, electrician's
dénundeur *m* **de câble** cable stripper
 ~ coaxial ~ coaxial cable
détecteur *m* **de câbles** detector, cable
détecteur *m* **de metaux** detector, metal
détecteur *m* **de phase** detector, phase
marteau *m* **d'électricien** hammer, electrician's
multimètre *f* **digital** circuit tester
ohmmètre *m* ohmmeter
pince *f* pliers; pincers
pince *f* **à cosses** pliers, crimp connector (see also: **pince** *f* **à sertir**)
pince *f* **à dénuder** wirestrippers
pince *f* **à dénuder et coupe-fil** wirecutters
pince *f* **à dénuder et coupe-fil à becs** wirecutters, side-cutting
pince *f* **à dénuder et coupe-fil automatique** wirecutters, automatic
pince *f* **à dénuder et coupe-fil reglable** wirecutters, adjustable
pince *f* **à sertir** pliers, crimp

Électricité

connector (see also: **pince** *f* **à cosses**)
pince *f* **coupante** pliers, cutting
pince *f* **crocodile** crocodile clip
pince *f* **de serrage pour collier** pliers, cable tie
testeur *m* **de cartouche fusible** cartridge fuse tester
testeur *m* **de courant** tester, current
testeur *m* **de tension** tester, voltage
tournevis *m* **électricien** screwdriver, electrician's
  ~ **Phillips** ~ Phillips pattern
  ~ **plat électricien** ~ flat blade
  ~ **Posidriv** ~ Pozidriv pattern
  ~ **pour vis à fente** ~ slotted screws
voltmètre *m* voltmeter
wattmètre *m* wattmeter

Électricité

Appendice

QUINCAILLERIE & VISSERIE
IRONMONGERY & HARDWARE

Adhésifs
Adhesives

adhésif *m* adhesive (see also: **colle**)
adhésif *m* **mastic de fixation néoprène** neoprene adhesive mastic
adhésif *m* **mastic sans solvant** adhesive mastic, solvent-free
bâton *m* **de colle** glue stick
bâton *m* **de colle à chaud** hot melt glue stick
cartouche *f* **de colle** glue cartridge
colle *f* glue (see also: **adhésif**)
colle *f* **à bois** wood glue
colle *f* **à bois en biberon** wood glue, in a baby's bottle!
colle *f* **à bois en boîte** wood glue, in a pot
colle *f* **à bois extérieur** wood glue, exterior
colle *f* **à bois milieu humide** vinyl wood glue, outdoor, moderate humidity
colle *f* **à bois polyurethane** wood glue, polyurethane
colle *f* **à bois prise rapide** wood glue, quick-setting
colle *f* **à bois rapide vinylique** wood glue, quick-setting vinyl
colle *f* **à carrelage spéciale terrasse** tile adhesive for terraces
colle *f* **à froid bitumineuse** cold bituminous adhesive
colle *f* **acrylique** acrylic glue
colle *f* **acrylique pour sous-couche** acrylic glue, for underlay
colle *f* **bardeau** adhesive, wooden shingles
colle *f* **basse température (matériaux délicats)** low temperature hot melt glue, delicate materials
colle *f* **caoutchouc** adhesive, rubber
colle *f* **carreaux de plâtre** adhesive for plaster slabs (not available in UK)
colle *f* **carrelage** adhesive, tile
colle *f* **carrelage rénovation sans poussière** dust-free tiling adhesive
colle *f* **carrelage sol et mur intérieur** wall and floor tile adhesive, interior
colle *f* **carrelage sol intérieur/extérieur** floor tile adhesive, interior and exterior
colle *f* **contact intérieur** contact adhesive, interior
colle *f* **corniche et rosace** adhesive, cornice and ceiling rose
colle *f* **cuir** leather glue
colle *f* **cyanoacrylate** cyanoacrylate glue, plastics
colle *f* **cyanoacrylate porcelaine et faïence** cyanoacrylate glue, porcelain and earthenware
colle *f* **dalles de plafond** adhesive, ceiling tile
colle *f* **dalles polystyréne** glue, polystyrene tile

Quincaillerie & Visserie

colle *f* **de blocage** glue, gap-filling
colle *f* **élastomères synthétiques** glue, synthetic rubber
colle *f* **époxy** epoxy glue
colle *f* **époxy pour bois** epoxy glue, wood
colle *f* **époxy pour métal** epoxy glue, metal
colle *f* **époxy pour verre** epoxy glue, glass
colle *f* **époxy rapide** epoxy glue, rapid-setting
colle *f* **époxy universelle** epoxy glue, universal
colle *f* **et joint spéciale douche à l'italienne et piscine** glue and joint for showers and swimming pools
colle *f* **fibre de verre** adhesive, fibreglass wallcovering
colle *f* **fixation étanchéité** glue cartridge, for sealing and caulking
colle *f* **Fixer sans Percer; ~ Ni Clou Ni Vis** proprietary 'no nail, no screw' glue
  ~ démontable removable
colle *f* **frises décoratives** adhesive, decorative friezes
colle *f* **instantanée universelle** instant all-purpose superglue
colle *f* **intérieur/extérieur sous abris** glue, all materials, inside outside, sheltered aspect
colle *f* **isolants minces polystyrène expansé** glue, expanded polystyrene insulation

colle *f* **joint foyers et inserts** fire cement
colle *f* **latex naturel pour tissu** glue, natural latex, for fabrics
colle *f* **liège** cork glue
colle *f* **l'insonorisation** acrylic resin, for insulating materials
colle *f* **maquette** modelmaker's glue
colle *f* **métaux** metal glue
colle *f* **miroir** mirror glue
colle *f* **moquette** carpet glue
colle *f* **moquette et fibre naturelle** glue, carpet and natural fibre floorcoverings
colle *f* **moquette et plastique/PVC** glue, carpet and plastic/PVC floorcoverings (tile or roll)
colle *f* **murale universelle** adhesive, interior walls
colle *f* **néoprène** neoprene adhesive
colle *f* **néoprène gel multi-usages** neoprene gel adhesive, multi-purpose
colle *f* **néoprène liquide** neoprene liquid adhesive
colle *f* **néoprène pour manchon d'isolation** neoprene adhesive, for pipe lagging
colle *f* **nez de marche** stair nosing adhesive
colle *f* **objets lourds intérieur/extérieur** adhesive, heavy objects inside/outside
colle *f* **papier peint** wallpaper paste/glue

colle *f* papier peint adhérence élevée high bond wallpaper glue
colle *f* papiers peints épais glue, thick wallpaper
colle *f* papiers peints intissé glue, non-woven wallpaper
colle *f* parquet glue, elastic, for parquet flooring
colle *f* parquet contrecolles mince/et mosaiques glue, for thin laminate flooring/mosaics
colle *f* pâte glue paste
colle *f* pâte mur intérieur glue paste, for interior wall tiling
colle *f* pâte spéciale liège murs/plafonds glue, for cork walls/ceilings
colle *f* phonicolle polystyrene soundproofing adhesive (not available in UK)
colle *f* plaquettes et parement wallboard adhesive
colle *f* plastique plastic adhesive
colle *f* plastique rigide adhesive, for rigid plastic
colle *f* polymère universelle polymer adhesive
colle *f* polystyrène polystyrene adhesive, ceilings and panelling
colle *f* PVC PVC adhesive
colle *f* PVC raccords et gouttières rigide adhesive, PVC joint and guttering
colle *f* raccords tous papiers peints adhesive, wallpaper joints
colle *f* réfractaire refractory adhesive
colle *f* renforcée frise reinforced adhesive, for friezes
colle *f* repositionnable adhesive, repositionable
colle *f* résine époxydique epoxy resin adhesive
colle *f* revêtement muraux spéciaux adhesive, special wallcoverings
colle *f* revêtement muraux sur intissés adhesive, non-woven wallcovering
colle *f* rouleaux isolants adhesive, insulation roll
colle *f* sans solvant solvent-free adhesive
colle *f* silicone silicone adhesive
colle *f* sol polyvalente adhesive, multi-purpose flooring
colle *f* sol pour fibres naturelles adhesive, natural fibre floorcoverings
colle *f* sols plastiques, PVC, vinyles adhesive, plastic, PVC and vinyl floorcoverings
colle *f* spéciale blocage pour bois wood fibre penetrating adhesive
colle *f* spéciale plastique souple glue, soft plastic items
colle *f* spéciale pochoir adhesive, repositionable, for stencils
colle *f* spéciale tissus latex glue, for special fabrics
colle *f* spéciale tuyaux PVC glue, for PVC pipes
colle *f* spéciale verre glue, for glass

Quincaillerie & Visserie

colle *f* **spéciale vibrations et hautes températures** glue, items subject to vibration and high temperatures (e.g. washing machine/oven)
colle *f* **stratifié et flottant** adhesive, laminate and floating floors
colle *f* **textile** glue, textiles
colle *f* **textile muraux** glue, textile wallcovering
colle *f* **textile thermofusible** hot melt glue
colle *f* **textile UV matériaux transparent** ultra-violet glue, for glass, crystal, transparent plastics
colle *f* **tissu** adhesive, fabric
colle *f* **toile de verre** adhesive, fibreglass fabric
colle *f* **tous papiers peints** adhesive, all wallpaper types
colle *f* **transparente après séchage** glue, transparent drying
colle *f* **universelle instantanée** superglue
fixer *m* **mousse double face** adhesive foam pad
liant *m* **colle** flexible adhesive, for plaster tiles, cement, terracotta tiles
mastic *m* mastic
mastic *m* **colle** mastic adhesive
mastic *m* **colle auto/marine** mastic adhesive, auto/marine
mastic *m* **colle verre-vitrage cartouche** mastic adhesive cartridge, glass and window
mastic *m* **polyester standard** polyester putty/glue/sealer for slight indentations
mortier *m* **adhésif pour plaque de plâtre et doublage** adhesive mortar for plasterboard
mortier *m* **colle** adhesive mortar
mortier *m* **colle béton cellulaire** adhesive mortar, cellular concrete
mortier *m* **colle gris** adhesive mortar, grey, for floor tiles
mortier *m* **colle vinylique** vinyl adhesive mortar
mortier *m* **colle vinylique pour bois extérieur** vinyl adhesive mortar, exterior wood
mortier *m* **colle vinylique pour bois intérieur** vinyl adhesive mortar, interior wood
mortier *m* **colle vinylique pour papier et carton** vinyl adhesive mortar, paper and cardboard
pastilles *f* **adhésives** self-adhesive pads
pâte *f* **à coller** resin and hardener for fixing, patching, reshaping, repairing

Quincaillerie & Visserie

Ruban adhésifs
Adhesive tapes

ruban *m* adhésif adhesive tape
ruban *m* adhésif alu/aluminium adhesive tape, aluminium, for chimney hoods and flues
ruban *m* adhésif anti-dérapant adhesive tape, anti-slip
ruban *m* adhésif anti-fuites adhesive tape, leak repair
ruban *m* adhésif auto-grippant adhesive tape, self-adhesive
ruban *m* adhésif de masquage masking tape
ruban *m* adhésif de masquage bois/murs/peints masking tape, woodwork, walls
ruban *m* adhésif de masquage courbe protection masking tape, for corners and curves
ruban *m* adhésif de masquage crêpe masking tape, crepe
ruban *m* adhésif de masquage droit protection masking tape, for straight edges
ruban *m* adhésif de masquage lisse masking tape, smooth, for flat surfaces
ruban *m* adhésif de masquage protection toutes peintures masking tape, for all paintwork
ruban *m* adhésif de masquage vitres/carrelages masking tape, for glass and tiles
ruban *m* adhésif double face adhesive tape, double sided
~ **extérieur** ~ exterior grade
~ **extra fort** ~ extra strong
~ **miroirs** ~ mirror-fixing
~ **multi-usages** ~ multi-purpose
~ **plinthe** ~ skirting boards
ruban *m* adhésif fin intérieur/extérieur adhesive tape, fine (indoor/outdoor use)
ruban *m* adhésif isolant adhesive tape, insulating
ruban *m* adhésif laine de roche adhesive tape, for mineral fibre insulation
ruban *m* adhésif laine de verre adhesive tape, for mineral fibre and glass fibre insulation
ruban *m* adhésif multi-usages adhesive tape, all-purpose
ruban *m* adhésif perforé pour plaque adhesive tape, perforated, for sealing polycarbonate roof panels
ruban *m* adhésif pour plaque adhesive tape, non-perforated, for sealing polycarbonate roof panels
ruban *m* adhésif pour sous-couche adhesive tape, for underlay
ruban *m* adhésif PVC souple adhesive tape, supple PVC
ruban *m* adhésif PVC spécial extérieur adhesive tape, PVC exterior grade
ruban *m* adhésif raccord plaques de plâtre adhesive tape, plasterboard jointing

Quincaillerie & Visserie

ruban *m* **adhésif réparer/renforcer** adhesive tape, repairing and reinforcing
ruban *m* **adhésif rigid PVC** adhesive tape, PVC rigide
ruban *m* **adhésif spécial emballage lourds** packing tape, heavy duty glass fibre
ruban *m* **adhésif toilé** adhesive tape, canvas-backed repair/reinforcing
ruban *m* **adhésif translucide** adhesive tape, translucent

Outils pour adhésifs
Adhesive tools & equipment

couteau *m* **de colle** applicator, notched
peigne *f* **à colle** glue comb
pistolet *m* **à colle** glue gun
   ~ à basse température ~ low temperature
   ~ avec sélecteur de température ~ variable temperature
   ~ buse pour pistolet à colle ~ nozzle
   ~ haute température ~ high temperature
   ~ sans fil ~ cordless
rouleau *m* **à colle** glue roller
seau *m* **à colle** paste bucket
seringue *m* **à colle** glue syringe
spatule *f* **à colle** glue spatula

Abrasifs
Abrasives

bande *f* **abrasif** abrasive paper band, for belt sander
bloc *m* **à poncer** sanding block (see also: **cale**; **~ à poncer**)
cale *f*; **~ à poncer** sanding block (see also: **bloc à poncer**)
cale *f* **à poncer de plâtre** sanding block, for plasterwork
cale *f* **et grille** abrasive sanding block, with abrasive grille
disque *m* **abrasive autogrippant** sanding disc, Velcro-backed, for power sander
éponge *f* **abrasive** abrasive sponge
   ~ perméable ~ waterproof
feuille *f* **abrasive** abrasive paper, sheet of
   ~ abrasive vernis/peintures
   ~ varnish/paintwork
   ~ bois ~ woodwork
   ~ de finition ~ finishing
   ~ décapage peinture
   ~ paintwork
   ~ préparation surfaces brutes
   ~ rough surfaces
garniture *f* **papier abrasive** garnet paper
   ~ à plâtre ~ for plasterwork
paille *m* **de fer** steel wool
   ~ synthétique ~ synthetic
papier *m* **abrasif** abrasive paper
papier *m* **abrasif anti-encrassant** abrasive paper, anti-clogging

Quincaillerie & Visserie

papier *m* **abrasif carbure de silicium** abrasive paper, silicon carbide
papier *m* **abrasif corindon** corundum paper
papier *m* **abrasif fin grain** abrasive paper, fine grain
papier *m* **abrasif gros grain** abrasive paper, coarse grain
papier *m* **abrasif moyen grain** abrasive paper, medium grain
papier *m* **abrasif perforé** abrasive paper, perforated (for dust extraction)
papier *m* **abrasif silex** abrasive paper, flint
patin *m* **abrasive** abrasive pad
patin *m* **abrasive scotchbrite** abrasive pad, Scotchbrite
toile *f* **abrasive** abrasive cloth
toile *f* **émeri** emery cloth

Fixations
Fixings

Clous
Nails

bande *f* **pré-clouée plastique** band, for regular alignment of upholstery tacks
clou *m* (see also: **pointe**) nail
clou *m* **à bateaux** nail, flooring
clou *m* **à béton** nail, masonry
clou *m* **à tête bombeé** nail, domed head
clou *m* **à tête d'homme** nail, oval wire
　~ en acier inoxydable ~ stainless steel
　~ en acier laitonné ~ brass-plated steel
　~ en acier poli ~ polished steel
　~ en acier trempé ~ tempered steel
　~ en acier zingué ~ zinc-plated steel
clou *m* **à tête diamant** clout nail, diamond head
clou *m* **à tête perdue** brad; nail, lost head
clou *m* **à tête plate** nail, round wire
　~ en acier poli ~ polished steel
clou *m* **à tête plate en cuivre** nail, copper, flat head
clou *m* **à tête plate, extra large** clout nail, extra large head
clou *m* **à tête plate large en acier zingué** nail, large head zinc-plated wire
clou *m* **à tête ronde** nail, round head
clou *m* **cache vis tête martelée** screw head cover, hammer-on
clou *m* **de bouche; ~ de soufflet** tack (see also: **petit clou; semence**)
clou *m* **de Paris** nail, wire
clou *m* **de plinthes/lambris en acier poli, tête homme** nail, round head, polished steel for skirting/panelling
clou *m* **de vitrier** glazing sprig

Quincaillerie & Visserie

clou *m* **découpé/étampé** nail, cut
clou *m* **doré** nail, brass head
clou *m* **étêté** nail, headless
clou *m* **maçon acier brut** nail, masonry, steel
clou *m* **pour shingles, acier zingué** nail, zinc-plated steel, for roof shingles
clou *m* **ondulé** corrugated fastener
clou *m* **tapissier** upholstery pin
~ **bronze vieilli** ~ aged bronze
~ **laitonné** ~ brass
~ **nickelé** ~ nickel
~ **rosace bronze** ~ bronze, with rosette head
clou *m* **torsadé** nail, twisted shank
conduit *m* staple (see also: **crampillon**)
conduit *m* **acier zingué** staple, zinc-plated steel
crampillon *m* staple (see also: **conduit**)
crampillon *m* **en acier galvanisé** staple, galvanized steel
petit clou *m* tack (see also: **clou de bouche**; ~ **de soufflet**; **semence**)
pointe *f* nail; tack (see also: **clou**)
pointe *f* **à ardoise** slate peg
pointe *f* **à placage acier zingué** nail, zinc-plated steel, headless
pointe *f* **décorative à tête bombée** upholstery pin, dome headed
pointe *f* **moulures** moulding pin
pointe *f* **striée béton acier zingué** nail, masonry, steel, ribbed, zinc-plated

pointe *f* **tête fraisée acier galvanisé** nail, countersunk head, galvanized
pointe *f* **tête homme acier brut** nail, steel oval
pointe *f* **tête plate** nail, flat head
~ **acier brut** ~ steel
~ **inox** ~ stainless steel
pointe *f* **tête plate large galvanisée** nail, large head galvanized
pointe *f* **tête ronde acier zingué** nail, steel round head, zinc-plated
pointe *f* **tête ronde béton acier trempé** nail, round head, tempered steel
pointe *f* **tête ronde laiton** nail, brass round head
pointe *f* **torsadée acier brut** nail, twisted shank steel
~ **acier zingué** ~ zinc-plated steel
pointe *f* **vitrier acier zingué** nail, glazing, zinc-plated steel
punaise *f* tack, thumb
semence *f* tack (see also: **clou de bouche**; ~ **de soufflet**; **petit clou**)
semence *f* **chaussure acier bichromaté** tack, cobbler's/upholsterer's bichromate steel
semence *f* **de tapissier** tack, upholstery
~ **acier bleui** ~ tempered steel
~ **cuivre** ~ copper

Quincaillerie & Visserie

Screws
Vis

tire-fond *f* coach screw; lag screw
~ **acier** ~ plated steel bichromaté
~ **acier zingué** ~ galvanized steel
vis *f* screw
vis *f* **à bois** woodscrew
vis *f* **à bois et aggloméré; ~ agglo** screw, chipboard
~ **tête cylindrique pozi** ~ cylindrical head (Posidriv)
~ **tête fraisée pozi** ~ countersunk head (Posidriv)
vis *f* **à métaux cylindrique pans creux** machine screw (Allen pattern)
vis *f* **à tête fendue** screw, slot-headed
vis *f* **à tête ronde fendue** screw, dome-headed
vis *f* **à tôle autoperceuse** screw, self-drilling, self-tapping
~ **tête cylindrique** ~ cylindrical head
~ **tête cylindrique pozi** ~ pan head Posidriv
~ **tête fraisée** ~ countersunk head
~ **tête fraisée bombée inox** ~ dome-headed stainless steel countersunk head
~ **tête fraisée bombée pozi inox** ~ dome-headed stainless steel countersunk Posidriv
~ **tête trompette** ~ trumpet-head
vis *f* **à tôle tête hexagonale à collerette** screw, flanged, for sheet metal
vis *f* **empreinte cruciforme (Phillips)** screw, cross-headed Phillips
vis *f* **empreinte cruciforme (Posidriv)** screw, Posidriv
vis *f* **empreinte cruciforme (TORX)** screw, TORX
vis *f* **fraisée bombée** screw, round topped
vis *f* **indesserrable** screw, non-removable
vis *f* **penture empreinte étoile acier noir** screw, steel star-pattern, black (for hinges on shutters, gates etc)
vis *f* **plaque de plâtre** screw, plasterboard
~ **acier phosphaté** ~ steel, phosphate
vis *f* **plate, fraisée et fendue** screw, countersunk head, slotted
vis *f* **pour tasseau** screw, batten-fixing
vis *f* **pozi acier bichromaté tête fraisée** screw, countersunk head Posidriv, plated steel
vis *f* **tête fraisée fendue laiton** screw, brass slotted countersunk head
vis *f* **tête ronde acier zingué** screw, galvanized steel round headed

Quincaillerie & Visserie

Chevilles
Plugs

boulon *m* **à expansion** expansion bolt
cartouche *f* **de scellement chimique** chemical anchor, cartridge of
cheville *f* wallplug; anchor; pin
cheville *f* **à ancrage et verrouillage de forme** cavity fixing, expanding locking steel, for plasterboard
cheville *f* **à bascule appui sur support** spring toggle, suspended light fitting
~ **avec vis, piton ou crochet** ~ with screw, eye or hook
cheville *f* **à écartement** plasterboard fixing, light to medium loads (no pre-drilling)
cheville *f* **à frapper** wallplug, hammer-in plug/screw
cheville *f* **auto-foreuse/auto-perceuses** wallplug, self-drilling
cheville *f* **auto-foreuse/auto perceuses à ancrage** wallplug, self-drilling, for plasterboard (medium load)
cheville *f* **auto foreuse/auto-perceuses à bascule** wallplug, self-drilling toggle, plasterboard
cheville *f* **auto-foreuse/auto-perceuses en acier à visser** wallplug, self-drilling steel
cheville *f* **en acier à ressort** spring toggle, steel
~ **avec crochet** ~ with hook
~ **avec piton** ~ with eye
~ **avec vis** ~ with screw
cheville *f* **en fonte** wallplug, cast iron heavy duty
cheville *f* **en laiton** wallplug, brass corrosion-resistant
cheville *f* **fendue pour plafond suspendu** wallplug, expanding brass, for suspended ceiling
cheville *f* **métallique** anchor fixing, metal
cheville *f* **métallique à expansion** anchor fixing, metal, hollow wall
cheville *f* **métallique et vis** anchor fixing, metal, with screw
cheville *f* **métallique mini** anchor fixing, metal, small hammer-in
cheville *f* **nylon** plug, nylon
~ **à ancrage et écartement** ~ expanding, spreading
~ **à clouer** ~ hammer-in
~ **à expansion** ~ expanding
~ **à visser** ~ screw-in auger bolt (for plasterboard)
~ **avec vis** ~ with screw
~ **fendue** split, expanding
~ **fendue pour encadrement de portes et fenêtres** ~ frame-fixing, doors and windows
~ **sans vis** ~ without screw
~ **spécial béton cellulaire** ~ for breezeblocks
cheville *f* **parois minces** wallplug, expanding, thin walls
cheville *f* **plaque de plâtre** wallplug, plasterboard

Quincaillerie & Visserie

cheville *f* **polypropylène** wallplug, polypropylene
cheville *f* **pour WC** wallplug, screw & cover, fixing WC cistern to wall
cheville *f* **rallongée à tire fond** frame fixing, long, with coach screw
cheville *f* **traversante, expansion au vissage** frame fixing, long, with screw
cheville *f* **universelle** wallplug, basic
douille *f* **filetée pour scellement chimique** chemical anchor, threaded sleeve
embout *m* **mélangeur pour cartouche de scellement chimique** chemical anchor cartridge, mixing tip
goujon *m* **d'ancrage à expansion** anchor stud, expanding
scellement *f* **chimique** chemical anchor
tamis *f* **avec centreur pour scellement chimique** chemical anchor sleeve
tige *f* **filetée pour scellement chimique** chemical anchor, threaded rod

Accessoires pour des chevilles
Accessories for plugs

crochet *m* **à collerette à boulonner** hook for spring toggle fixings, with flange
gond *m* hinge pin, right-angle, for spring toggle fixings
patte *f* **à vis** threaded stud, for pipe collar
pistolet *m* **pour cartouche de scellement chimique** gun for chemical fixing cartridge
piton *m* **à collerette à boulonner** screw eye for spring toggle fixings, with flange
suspension *f* **Speedy-Fix** proprietary screw-eye for suspending chain, wire, hooks and carabiners

Boulonnerie
Nuts & bolts

boulon *m* bolt
boulon m **à clavette** bolt, cotter
boulon *m* **à croc** bolt, hook
boulon *m* **à écrou** screwbolt
boulon *m* **à tête carrée** bolt, square-headed
boulon *m* **acier zingué** bolt, galvanized steel
boulon *m* **cylindrique** bolt, cylindrical-headed
boulon m **d'ancrage** bolt, anchor

Quincaillerie & Visserie

boulon *m* **d'assemblage** bolt, fastener
boulon *m* **de fondation** bolt, foundation
boulon *m* **de retenue** bolt, retaining
boulon *m* **en nylon** bolt, nylon
boulon *m* **fraisée** bolt, countersunk head
boulon *m* **hexagonale** bolt, hexagonal-headed
boulon *m* **inox** bolt, stainless steel
boulon *m* **poëlier acier zingué** bolt, tap
boulon *m* **ronde** bolt, round-headed
  ~ **collet carré** ~ with square collar
cache écrou *f* **à pointe** nut cover, hammer-in
circlip *m* **extérieur** circlip/snap ring
cuvette *m* **laiton nickelé** cup washer, nickel-plated
écrou *m* nut
écrou *m* **à embase** nut, flange
écrou *m* **à oreilles** nut, wing
écrou *m* **à six pans** nut, hexagonal
écrou *m* **autobloquant** locknut (see also: **écrou contre-écrous;** ~ **indesserrable de blocage**)
écrou *m* **borgne** nut, blind
écrou *m* **carré** nut, square
écrou *m* **contre-écrous** locknut (see also: **écrou autobloquant;** ~ **indesserrable de blocage**)
écrou *m* **indesserrable de blocage** locknut (see also: **écrou autobloquant;** ~ **contre-écrous**)
écrou *m* **ordinaire** nut, standard
goupille *f* **fendue acier zingué** cotter pin, galvanized steel
manchon *f* **acier bichromaté** sleeve, plated steel, for connecting threaded rod
rondelle *f* washer
rondelle *f* **à denture/dentelée** washer, serrated
rondelle *f* **à ressort/frein à ressort** washer, spring/split
rondelle *f* **carroissier** washer, large
rondelle *f* **en feutre** washer, felt
rondelle *f* **isolation** washer, insulation
rondelle *f* **plate** washer, flat
  ~ **plate étroite** ~ thin
  ~ **plate étroite nylon** ~ thin nylon
  ~ **plate large** ~ large
rondelle *f* **pour vis plaque de plâtre** washer, for plasterboard screw
rondelle *f* **trés large** washer, very large!
tige *f* **filetée** rod, threaded
vis *f* **de pression** screw, headless threaded, for use with Allen key

Quincaillerie & Visserie

Crochets, pitons & gonds de fixation
Screw hooks, pegs & eyes

anneau-écrou *m* **à visser** ring nut, screw-on
crochet *m* hook
crochet *m* **à tableau** hook, picture
crochet *m* **à visser** hook, screw
  ~ **en acier inoxydable** ~ stainless steel
  ~ **en acier zingué** ~ galvanized steel
  ~ **en epoxy blanc/noir** ~ with white/black epoxy coating
  ~ **en laiton** ~ brass
gond *m* hinge
gond *m* **à visser** hinge pin, screw-in
gond *m* **en acier inoxydable** hinge, stainless steel
gond *m* **en acier zingué** hinge, galvanized steel
gond *m* **en epoxy blanc/noir** hinge, with white/black epoxy coating
gond *m* **en laiton** hinge, brass
piton *m* **à visser** screw eye
  ~ **en acier inoxydable** ~ stainless steel
  ~ **en acier zingué** ~ galvanized steel
  ~ **en epoxy blanc/noir** ~ with white/black epoxy coating
  ~ **en laiton** ~ brass

vis *f* **patte de jonction à visser** connecting strip, screw threaded

Fixation & assemblage
Fixing & assembly

coin *m* **métallique** bracket, corner, triangular metal; flange bracket
équerre *f* bracket, angle
équerre *f* **d'angle** bracket, corner plate
équerre *f* **d'assemblage; ~ de chassis** bracket, flat plate
  ~ **coudée** ~ elbow
équerre *f* **de chaise** bracket, right-angled chair
équerre *f* **de renfort** bracket, right-angled reinforcement
  ~ **acier plastifié** ~ plastic-coated
équerre *f* **demi ronde** bracket, half-round
patte *f* **d'assemblage forte** plate, flat rectangular
  ~ **plastique** ~ plastic
  ~ **tronquée** ~ reinforced
platine *f* **pour poteau** bracket, for post

Rivetage & agrafage
Riveting & stapling

agrafe *f* staple
agrafe *f* **bébé** staple, small
agrafe *f* **cavalier** staple, oval
agrafe *f* **étroite** staple, narrow

Quincaillerie & Visserie

agrafe *f* **galvanisée** staple, galvanized steel
agrafe *f* **grillage verte;**
~ **plastifiée verte** staple, green for wire mesh fence
agrafeuse *f* staple gun
agrafeuse-cloueuse *f* stapler/nailer
~ **électrique** ~ electric
~ **manuelle** ~ manual
~ **pneumatique** ~ pneumatic
~ **sans fil** ~ cordless
dégrafeur *f* staple remover
écrou *m* **aveugle acier** blind nut, steel
extracteur *m* **(clous, punaises, agrafes)** extractor (nails, tacks, staples)
pince *f* **à écrou** pliers, blind nut crimping
pince *f* **à riveter** pliers, riveting
~ **tête pivotante** ~ pivoting-head
pince *f* **à sertir** pliers, crimping
pointe *f* staple, single point
rivet *m* rivet
rivet *m* **à tête ronde** rivet, round-headed
rivet *m* **aveugle** rivet, blind
~ **acier** ~ steel
~ **alu/acier** ~ aluminium/steel
~ **cannelé alu/acier** ~ corrugated aluminium/steel
~ **étanche** ~ waterproof
~ **inox** ~ stainless steel
~ **plastique/alu** ~ plastic/aluminium

rivet *m* **spécial plaque d'immatriculation** rivet, for attaching car number plate
rivet *m* **tubulaire mâle et femelle** rivet, tubular male/female

Sécurité
Security

barre *f* **antipanique pour porte** bar, anti-panic, for door
barre *f* **de sécurité pour persienne** bar, security, for louvre shutter
barre *f* **de sécurité pour volet** bar, security, for shutter
barre *f* **de sécurité renforcée** bar, security, reinforced
béquille *f* **à cylindre pour barre antipanique** cylinder lock, for anti-panic bar, crutch-handled
bloque-poignée *f* **de placard** cupboard door stay (child safe)
bride *f* **de renfort** bar, lock reinforcement
câble *m* **antivol à clé** cable lock, key-operated
cadenas *m* padlock
cadenas *m* **à clé** padlock, key-operated
cadenas *m* **à combinaison** padlock, combination
cadenas *m* **anse haute** padlock, long shackle
cadenas *m* **anse protégée** padlock, closed shackle

Quincaillerie & Visserie

chaîne *f* **antivol à clé** chain lock, key-operated
combine *f* **double verrouillage pour porte de garage** garage door, double lock
crémone *f* window latch
crémone *f* **à barillet (porte-fenêtre)** lock, barrel, for French window
crémone *f* **à encastrer sans pêne carré** window latch, recessed, without square bolt
crémone *f* **à larder** window latch, mortise
crémone *f* **à têtière** French window, top lock
crémone *f* **pompier à poignée rotative** window latch, for fire door, with rotating handle
crémone *f* **serrure** door lock, entry
cylindre *f* **de serrure** cylinder lock
cylindre *f* **de serrure débrayable** cylinder lock, disengaging (allows key operation from outside even if a key is inserted on the inside)
entrebâilleur *m* **à chaîne** door chain
entrebâilleur *m* **de sécurité pour volets** stay, for shutters
entrebâilleur *m* **fenêtre** stay, for window
  ~ **serpentin** ~ serpentine
entrebâilleur *m* **fixe** stay, for door
ferme-porte *f* door closer
ferme-porte *f* **à pignon et crémaillère** door closer, rack and pinion
ferme-porte *f* **à ressort** door closer, spring
gâche *f* keep plate
gâche *f* **électrique** keep plate, electrically-operated door lock
gâche *f* **rouleaux** keep plate, for roller shutter
gâche *f* **universelle à encastrer** keep plate, recessed
gorge *f* lock tumbler
goupille *f* pin (in cylinder lock)
grille *f* **de hublot** window grille
judas *m* door viewer
loquet *m* **de portail à clé** gate latch, key-operated
pêne *f* bolt/lock (see also: **targette; verrou**)
plaque *f* **de renfort à cylindre** cylinder plate, reinforcing
  ~ **profilée** ~ for profiled cylinder
poignée *f* handle; doorknob
poignée *f* **à condamnation par barrilet** window handle, locking
  ~ **à bouton** ~ button-operated
  ~ **à clé** ~ key-operated
porte-cadenas *m* hasp and staple
protège *f* **gonds de fenêtre** window hinge protector
  ~ **battante ou oscillo-battante** ~ side hung or pivoting
rosace *f* **de finition à trou de cylindre** rosette trim for cylinder hole
  ~ **profilé** ~ for profiled cylinder
serrure *f* lock
serrure *f* **à bandeau** locking bar,

Quincaillerie & Visserie

multi-point
serrure *f* **à encastrer** lock, mortise
  ~ à clé ~ key-operated
  ~ à condamnation ~ WC or bathroom
  ~ à cylindre ~ with cylinder
serrure *f* **bas de porte** door lock, base
serrure *f* **électrique** lock, electrically-operated
serrure *f* **en applique** lock, rim
  ~ horizontale ~ horizontal
  ~ verticale ~ vertical
serrure *f* **haut de porte** door lock, top
serrure *f* **monopoint** lock, single point
  ~ à appliquer ~ face-fixed
  ~ à encastrer ~ recessed
serrure *f* **multipoint** lock, multiple point (i.e. with connecting bars to secure top and bottom of door)
  ~ à appliquer ~ face-fixed
  ~ à encastrer ~ recessed
serrure *f* **tubulaire bec-à-cane à condamnation** lock, tubular, button-operated, with locking nib (WC or bathroom)
targette *f* bolt/lock (see also: **pêne; verrou**)
targette *f* **à pêne plat** bolt, flat latch
targette *f* **à pêne ronde** bolt, round
verrou *m* bolt/lock (see also: **pêne; targette**)
verrou *m* **à bouton** bolt, button-operated

~ avec cylindre ~ night latch with cylinder
~ sans entrée de clé extérieur ~ night latch without exterior key entry
~ sûreté à bouton ~ night latch with sliding bar
verrou *m* **à code mécanique** lock, mechanical, code-operated
verrou *m* **à cylindre** lock, cylinder
  ~ verticale ~ vertical
verrou *m* **à pêne dormant** cylinder rim lock, deadbolt
verrou *m* **automatique** latch, automatic
verrou *m* **cambré bouton cylindre** cylinder rim lock, button-operated
verrou *m* **cylindre** cylinder rim lock
verrou *m* **cylindre clés protégées et plaque** cylinder rim lock and plate, key operated
verrou *m* **de cabine** bolt, WC door
verrou *m* **de condamnation pour menuiserie** bolt, locking, for window
verrou *m* **d'écurie** bolt, stable
verrou *m* **de fenêtre** window lock
verrou *m* **de fenêtre battante ou baie coulissante** window lock, swinging/sliding
verrou *m* **double cylindre clés réversibles** cylinder rim lock, double, with reversible keys
verrou *m* **double entrée** lock double entry

Quincaillerie & Visserie

verrou *m* **embouti bouton cylindre** cylinder lock, pressed steel, button-operated
verrou *f* **en applique** bolt, face-fixed
verrou *m* **médial à bouton avec cylindre** rim lock, button-operated, with separate cylinder rim lock
verrou *m* **pour fenêtre oscillant battante** window lock, swinging/pivoting
verrou *m* **vertical** bolt, sliding, vertical

Charnières & paumelles
Hinges

bagues *f* **pour paumelles en laiton** brass spacers for lift-off hinges
charnière *f* hinge
charnière *f* **à congé** hinge, flap
charnière *f* **à lamelles** hinge, flush
   ~ de meubles ~ furniture
   ~ pour porte ~ for door
charnière *f* **à ressort** hinge, spring
   ~ à visser avec ressort pour
   ~ double action ~ double action
porte de meuble ~ screw-on spring furniture hinge, door
charnière *f* **amovible** hinge, removable
charnière *f* **bichromate** hinge, bichromate finish
charnière *f* **contre coudée** hinge, cranked
charnière *f* **de caisse d'étui; ~ de coffre** hinge, box/chest
charnière *f* **de lit** hinge, bed (not a UK category, but similar to a butt or backflap hinge)
charnière *f* **de table** hinge, table, drop leaf
charnière *f* **démontable** hinge, demountable (loose pin backflap)
charnière *f* **double action** hinge, double action
charnière *f* **en acier** hinge, steel
charnière *f* **en acier zinguées** hinge, galvanized steel
charnière *f* **en inox** hinge, stainless steel
charnière *f* **en laiton** hinge, brass
charnière *f* **festonnée** hinge, scallop-edged decorative
charnière *f* **invisible** hinge, concealed clip-on
charnière *f* **paravent** hinge, screen/windbreak
charnière *f* **piano** hinge, piano
charnière *f* **pivot** hinge, pivot
charnière *f* **pour porte** hinge, door
charnière *f* **pour porte en verre** hinge, glass door
charnière *f* **universelle** hinge, universal (butt and flap)
fiche *f* **à visser** (see also: **gond**) screw hinge
   ~ à tourillon à visser ~ with swivel pin

Quincaillerie & Visserie

gond *m* screw hinge (see also: **fiche à visser**)
paumelle *f* hinge, lift-off
paumelle *f* **à bout rond** hinge, round end
paumelle *f* **à vase** hinge, lift-off, with decorative pin
paumelle *f* **de table** hinge, table
paumelle *f* **pour porte** hinge, lift-off, for door
   ~ **légère** ~ lightweight door
   ~ **rentrante** ~ inset
   ~ **va-et-vient** ~ two-way
paumelle *f* **universelle** hinge, universal
penture *f* strap hinge
penture *f* **anglaise** strap hinge, English pattern
penture *f* **droite bout carré** strap hinge for shutter
penture *f* **queue de carpe** strap hinge, fishtail pattern

Accessoires pour volets
Shutter accessories

anneau (*pl* -**x**) *m* **de tirage** pull ring
arrêt *m* **de volet à poignée** retainer, pivoting, with stop handle
arrêt *m* **marseillais à tourniquet** retainer, pivoting, Marseille pattern (leaf motif)
arrêt *m* **tête de bergère à tire-fond** retainer, shepherdess figure, coach screw fixing
arrêt *m* **volet automatique** retainer, automatic
barre *f* **de sécurité** security bar
butée *f* **surmoulée** retainer, base
cardan *m* **de manivelle** gimbal for roller shutter crank
clou *m* **tête diamant** nail, diamond-headed
crémaillère *f* retaining bracket/hook
crochet *m* hook
crochet *m* **de contrevent** hook and brace
entrebâilleur *m* **de sécurité pour volets** hasp and staple
espagnolette *f* **complète** lock set
fermeture *f* **de volet à loquet** latch
gond *m* hinge
gond *m* **à sceller double feuille** hinge bracket for solid wall fixing
   ~ **à platine verticale** ~ plate fixing, vertical
   ~ **à vis bois** ~ screw-in
   ~ **chimique** ~ chemical adhesive
guide *f* **de sangle** roller shutter guide
lame *f* **à volet roulant** roller shutter slat
manivelle *f* **métal pour volet roulant** roller shutter crank
poignée *f* **de fleau** shutter catch
ferrure *f* **de volet** shutter lock
penture *f* **droite bout carré** strap hinge
portail *m* **à bascule** (see also: **tourniquet à visser**) retainer, pivoting

Quincaillerie & Visserie

sangle *f* **pour volet** roller shutter strap
serrure *f* **de crémone** espagnolette lock
té droit/paire d'équerres T-shaped bracket (slots onto hinge)
tourniquet *m* **à visser** retainer, pivoting (see also: **portail à bascule**)
verrou *m* bolt
verrou *m* **à tige réglable cadenas** bolt, adjustable
verrou *m* **baïonnette** bolt, bayonet
verrou *m* **d'écurie** bolt, stable
verrou *m* **de pied** bolt, foot
verrou *m* **de serrage pour volet roulant** bolt, for roller shutter

Accessoires de porte
Door accessories

arrêt *m* **de porte** doorstop (see also: **butée de porte; butoir**)
~ **fixe à encastrer** ~ recessed
barre *f* **de tirage** pull handle
béquille *f* handle, crutch
bouton *m* knob; button
bouton *m* **de porte** doorknob
~ **d'entrée** ~ for entrance door
bouton *m* **de sonnette** doorbell pushbutton
~ **filaire** ~ wired
~ **sans fil** ~ wireless
butée *f* **de porte** doorstop (see also **arrêt de porte; butoir**)
butoir *m* doorstop (see also **arrêt de porte; butée de porte**)
carillon *m* chime; doorbell
carillon *m* **enfichable** chime, plug-in
carillon *m* **filaire** chime, wired
carillon *m* **sans fil** chime, wireless
carré *m* **de poignée** spindle, door handle
cuvette *f* **doigt têtière** finger latch
ensemble *m* **de porte** handle set
ferme-porte *f* door closer
~ **à ressort** ~ spring
~ **automatique** ~ automatic
interphone *m* intercom
~ **audio** ~ audio
~ **vidéo** ~ video
marteau *m* **de porte** knocker
poignée *f* handle; doorknob
poignée *f* **béquille réversible** handle, reversible for right- or left-hand fixing
poignée *f* **de cuvette serrure** handle, bowl lock
poignée *f* **de porte sur plaque à clé** handle and keyhole plate assembly
poignée *f* **de porte sur plaque à cylindre** handle and cylinder plate assembly
poignée *f* **de porte sur plaque sans condamnation** handle, non-locking
poignée *f* **sur rosace** handle and rosette assembly
poussoir *m* push button
rosace *f* rosette escutcheon
rosace *f* **à cylindre** escutchon,

Quincaillerie & Visserie

for cylinder lock (see also: **rosace de protection; ~ de sécurité**)
rosace *f* **à serrure** escutcheon, for lock
rosace *f* **de porte à clé** escutecheon, keyhole
rosace *f* **de porte à condamnation** escutcheon, lockable (for use inside WC or bathroom)
rosace *f* **de porte à décondamnation** escutcheon, unlockable with screwdriver from outside (should occupant of WC or bathroom become trapped)
rosace *f* **de protection** escutechon, for cylinder lock (see also: **rosace de protection; ~ à cylindre**)
rosace *f* **de sécurité** escutechon, for cylinder lock (see also: **rosace à cylindre; ~ de sécurité**)

Accessoires de fenêtre
Window accessories

boîtier *m* **crémone** handle (to connect **tringle**)
crémone *f* window latch
  ~ serrure ~ lockable
espagnolette *f* **crémone** French window catch
poignée *f* **de sécurité** window handle, lockable
tringle *f* **pour crémone** metal rod for operating espagnolette

Moustiquaires
Mosquito nets

fibre *m* **de verre blanc** net, white glass fibre
kit *m* **de liaison moustiquaire** mosquito net kit
moustiquaire *f* mosquito net
moustiquaire *f* **à enroulement** mosquito net, for window, vertical roller
moustiquaire *f* **à enroulement latéral** mosquito net side-rolling, for door
moustiquaire *f* **alu** mosquito net, aluminium
moustiquaire *f* **battante** mosquito net, for hinged doors
moustiquaire *f* **cadre fixe pour fenêtre** mosquito net, fixed, for window
moustiquaire *f* **de toit** mosquito net, for roof window
moustiquaire *f* **fenêtre et baie coulissante** mosquito net, for sliding window and door
moustiquaire *f* **plissée** mosquito net, folding
moustiquaire *f* **porte-rideau** mosquito net, door curtain
moustiquaire *f* **pour fenêtre** mosquito net, for window
moustiquaire *f* **pour lit** mosquito net, for bed
moustiquaire *f* **pour porte-fenêtre** mosquito net, for French window

Quincaillerie & Visserie

moustiquaire *f* pour porte/fenêtre avec fixation velcro mosquito net, for door/window, Velcro fixing
store *m* moustiquaire enroulable roller blind screen
toile *f* de remplacement pour moustiquaire net replacement

Corde, sangle, sandow, chaîne & câble

Rope, webbing, chain & cable

câble *f* cable
câble *f* acier galvanisé cable, galvanized steel
câble *f* gainé cable, sheathed
câble *f* levage acier cable, steel lifting
câble *f* qualité levage cable, lifting; traction; leverage
carotte *f* de drisse rope, knot of
chaîne *f* chain
chaîne *f* de lustrerie chain, chandelier
chaîne *f* de signalisation chain, signalling
 ~ en plastique ~ plastic
chaîne *f* droite soudée chain, straight welded
chaîne *f* maillons courts chain, short link
chaîne *f* maillons longs chain, long link
chaîne *f* torsadée chain, twisted
cordage *f* rope
cordage *f* chanvre rope, hemp
 ~ naturel ~ natural
 ~ torsadée ~ twisted
cordage *f* polypropylène rope, polypropylene
cordage *f* sisal rope, sisal
corde *f* rope; string; cord
corde *f* à linge washing line
cordeau *m* de maçon stringline, mason's
corde *f* tressée rope, braided
drisse *f* en polypropylène halyard, polypropylene
ficelle *m* string
fil *m* wire
fil *m* cuivre wire, copper
fil *m* en bottillon wire, reel of
fil *m* galvanisé wire, galvanized steel
fil *m* laiton wire, brass
fil *m* plastifié wire, plastic-coated
pelote *f* de cordeau string, plumbline, ball of
pelote *f* de ficelle string, ball of
sandow *m* bungee cord
sandow *m* à crochet bungee cord, with hooks
sandow *m* multicolore bungee cord, multicoloured
sangle *f* belt strap
sangle *f* à cliquet belt strap, with ratchet
sangle *f* bagagère belt strap, for luggage rack
sangle *f* d'arrimage belt strap, for stowage

Quincaillerie & Visserie

~ **avec came à griffes** ~ with cam buckle
~ **boucle surmoulée** ~ with moulded buckle
sangle *f* **pince autobloquante** belt strap, with self locking clamp
sangle *f* **pour volet roulant** belt strap, for roller shutter

Accessoires: corde, sangle, sandow, chaîne & câble

Accessories: rope, webbing, chain & cable

anneau *m* metal ring
anneau *m* **brisé** metal split ring
anneau *m* **de corde à rampe** metal ring, for rope handrail
arrêt *f* **de cordon pour store** cleat (for blind)
boucle *f* **à ouverture rapide** buckle, quick release (for webbing)
boulon *m* **oeil** eye-bolt
bride *f* **de fixation** fixing collar
cosse-coeur *f* cable loop support
crochet *m* hook
crochet *m* **de levage à oeil et linguet de sécurité** hook and eye, lifting, with safety latch
crochet *m* **pour sandow** hook, for bungee cord
esse *f*; ~ **égale** S-hook
esse *f* **de boucher** butcher's hook
goupille *f* cotter pin
maillon *m* link

maillon *m* **de jonction** link, connecting
maillon *m* **rapide** carabiner (quick link)
manille *f* **droite** D-shackle
mousqueton *m*; ~ **à linguet** snap clasp; carbine hook
mousqueton *m* **à vis** snap clasp, screwed
mousqueton *m* **pompe à touret** snap clasp, with swivel
mousqueton *m* **pompier** snap clasp, 'firefighter's'
poulie *f* pulley
poulie *f* **à crochet** pulley, with suspension hook
poulie *f* **à visser** pulley, with suspension screw
serre-câble *f* cable clamp
serre-câble *f* **étrier** cable clamp, stirrup
serre-câble *f* **plat** cable clamp, flat
tendeur *m* **à cage** cable tightener
touret *m* **double** swivel rings, twin

Stockage & transport: les outils & les matériaux

Storage & transport: tools & materials

armoire *f* **de rangement métal** tool storage cupboard, metal
barette *f* **porte-outils magnétique** tool rack, magnetic

Quincaillerie & Visserie

boîte *f* **à outils** toolbox (see also: **coffre à outils; caisse à outils; coffre de chantier fixe**)
boîte *f* **à outils sur roulettes** toolbox, wheeled
caisse *f* **à outils** toolbox (see also: **boîte à outils; coffre à outils; coffre de chantier fixe**)
ceinture *f* **porte-outil** tool belt
coffre *m* **à outils** toolbox (see also: **boîte à outils; caisse à outils; coffre de chantier fixe**)
coffre *m* **de chantier fixe** toolbox (see also: **boîte à outils; coffre à outils; caisse à outils**)
cantine *f* **renforcée** toolchest, reinforced
chariot *m*; ~ **de transport** trolley
chariot *m* **pliant** trolley, folding
diable *m* barrow
diable *m* **porte sac** barrow, sack
étagère *f* shelf unit
lève meuble *f* furniture lifter, with roller
malette *f* **mousse de protection** case, with foam insert with tool profile cutout
module *f* **de rangement** storage case, with drawers for screws, nails etc.
organisateur *m* **à plateau** tray, pivoting with divided compartments
panier *m* **porte-outils** tool basket
panneau *m* **mural alvéolé** tool board wall panel
porte-outils *m* **magnétique** tool holder, wall mounted or portable, magnetic
rangement *m* **des outils** tool storage
ratelier *m* **pour outils** tool rack
servante *f* **à outils** toolbox, wheeled suitcase-type
support *m* **mural avec crochets autobloquants** wall bracket, with locking tool clips support
support *m* **roulant pivotant** roller support, pivoting
trousse *f* tool roll
ventouse *f* **double** suction lifter, double

Escabeaux & marchepieds
Ladders & stepladders

échafaudage *m* scaffolding
échafaudage *m* **d'intérieur** scaffolding, interior use
échelle *f* **télescopique** ladder, telescopic
escabeau *m* stepladder
marchepied *m* step; hop-up
pied *m* **d'éléphant** hop-up, elephant foot

Quincaillerie & Visserie

Établis & accessoires
Workbenches & accessories

cale *f* **de serrage** clamping wedge
établi *m* workbench
établi *m* **de mécanicien** workbench, mechanic's
établi *m* **pliant** worbench, folding
établi-étau *m* workbench-vice, portable
mâchoires *f* **d'étau** vice jaws
mâchoires *f* **d'étau en aluminium** vice jaws, aluminium
mâchoires *f* **d'étau en plastique** vice jaws, plastic
servante *f* **à rouleau** roller stand
tréteau-support *m* trestle support

Calfeutrage
Draughtproofing; weatherseal

bas *m* **de porte** excluder strip, door (draught/rain/sound)
~ **eau/air/bruit adhésif** ~ adhesive
bas *m* **de porte à bavette** excluder strip, flap
~ **gros espace** ~ for large gap
bas *m* **de porte à clouer** excluder strip, pin on
bas *m* **de porte à lèvres** excluder strip, lipped
bas *m* **de porte à visser** excluder strip, screw on
bas *m* **de porte argent, brosse dure** excluder strip, silver heavy-duty brush
bas *m* **de porte bronze (brosse dure)** excluder strip, door (draught/rain/sound), bronze heavy duty brush
bas *m* **de porte brosse** excluder strip, brush
~ **souple** ~ soft
bas *m* **de porte de garage** excluder strip, garage
~ **grande bavette** ~ thermoplastic flap
~ **grande brosse** ~ brush
~ **petite bavette** ~ small brush seal
bas *m* **de porte pivotant** excluder strip, pivoting
bourrelet *m* draught strip, foam
dessous *m* **de porte** draught excluder, under-door
isolant *m* **trappe de visite** loft hatch insulation
joint *m* **adhésif** weatherstrip, adhesive
~ **caoutchouc profil E** ~ rubber E-profile
~ **caoutchouc profil P** ~ rubber P-profile
~ **longue durée combles** ~ long lasting foam
joint *m* **adhésif de porte, fenêtre et placard coulissants** weatherstrip, for doors, windows

and sliding closet doors
joint *m* **adhésif fenêtre petites rainures** weatherstrip, grooved (windows)
joint *m* **adhésif mousse universel** weatherstrip, foam
joint *m* **adhésif portes et fenêtres PVC** weatherstrip, PVC (doors and windows)
joint *m* **de calfeutrage** weatherstrip
mousse *f* **adhésive d'isolation** foam insulation, adhesive

Roues & roulettes
Wheels & castors

roue *f* wheel
roue *f* **caoutchouc** wheel, rubber
roue *f* **de brouette** wheel, wheelbarrow
roue *f* **de poussette** wheel, pushchair
roue *f* **gonflable** wheel, inflatable
roue *f* **jockey télescopique** wheel, jockey, telescopic
roue *f* **manutention très souple sur tous sols** wheel, flexible handling on all surfaces
~ **légere** ~ light loads
~ **moyenne** ~ medium loads
roue *f* **plastique** wheel, plastic
roue *f* **tondeuse** wheel, lawnmower
roulette *f* castor
roulette *f* **à œil** castor, slot-on
roulette *f* **à tige filetée carénée** castor, with threaded shank
roulette *f* **à tige lisse** castor, with smooth shank
roulette *f* **d'ameublement double galet** castor, twin-wheeled, furniture
roulette *f* **galet** roller wheel
roulette *f* **platine** castor, with mounting plate
~ **fixe** ~ with fixed plate
~ **pivotante** ~ with pivoting plate
~ **pivotante et frein** ~ pivoting, braked

Ferrures de meubles
Furniture fittings

anneau *m* **rond** ring pull handle
bouton *m* **de meuble** knob/button
bouton *m* **de tiroir** knob/button, drawer
coulisse *f* **de tiroir** drawer slide
crochet *m* **en métal pour cassettes et caisses** hook, metal, for cassettes or boxes
embout *m* **plastique** end piece, plastic
~ **entrant** ~ push-in cap for hollow leg
~ **enveloppant** ~ push-on cap for solid leg
équerre *f* **carrée métal, trou taraudé** bracket, metal, square, with threaded hole

Quincaillerie & Visserie

loquet *m* latch
loquet *m* **à bille en métal** roller catch, metal
loquet *m* **en plastique** latch, door, plastic
pastille *f* **mousse/caoutchouc anti-bruit adhésive** foam/rubber pads, noise cushioning
patin *m* **à clouer plastique** pin-on pad, plastic
patin *m* **alvéolaire** foam pad
patin *m* **anti-dérapant et anti-vibration** anti-slip/anti-vibration pad
patin *m* **feutre adhésif/auto collant** felt self-adhesive pad
patin *m* **glisseur lisse** slider/furniture glide
pied *m* foot/leg
~ **avec embout taraudé** ~ with threaded socket
~ **avec vis filetée** ~ with threaded shank
~ **de meuble plastique** ~ plastic
pied *m* **de lit** foot/leg, for bed
pied *m* **de table** foot/leg, for table
~ **de table réglable** ~ adjustable
~ **rabattable** ~ folding
poignée *f* **à encastrer** handle, recessed
poignée *f* **coquille** handle, shell-shaped pull
poignée *f* **à patte** handle, finger-pull
poignée *f* **de meuble;**
~ **d'ameublement** handle, furniture
poignée *f* **pendant** handle, pendant
porte-étiquette *f* **classeur** filing cabinet, label holder
vérin *m* foot plate, pivoting/adjustable
verrou *m* **en métal pour cassettes et caisse**s catch, two-part, metal, for cassettes or boxes

Appendice

FERRONNERIE
METALWORK

Ferronnerie

Métal
Metal

Types de métal
Types of metal

acier *m* steel
acier *m* **galvanisé** steel, galvanized
acier *m* **laminé** steel, laminated
acier *m* **nickelé** nickel-plated steel
acier *m* **zinguée** steel, zinc-coated
aluminium *m* aluminium
argent *m* silver
bronze *m* bronze
chrome chromium *m*
cuivre *m* copper
cuivre *m* **jaune** brass (see also: **laiton**)
cuivre *m* **recuit** copper, annealed
electrozinguée zinc, electroplated
étain *m* tin
fer *m* iron
fer *m* **de fonte** iron, cast
fer *m* **galvanisé** iron, galvanized
inox *m* stainless steel
laiton *m* brass (see also: **cuivre jaune**)
métal *m* **ferreux** metal, ferrous
métal *m* **non ferreux** metal, non-ferrous
nickel *m* nickel
nickel-argent *m* nickel-silver
or *m* gold
platine *m* platinum
plomb *m* lead
tungstène *m* tungsten
zinc *m* zinc

Sections métalliques
Metal sections

acier *m* **laminé à chaud** steel, hot-rolled section
acier *m* **laminé à froid** steel, cold-rolled section
barre *f* **en métal** bar, metal
barre *f* **plat métal** bar, flat metal
barre *f* **ronde serrurier** bar, round metal
cornière *f* angle iron (see also: **fer d'angle**)
cornière *f* **égale** angle iron, equal sides
cornière *f* **inégale** angle iron, unequal sides
fer *f* **carré** iron, square section
fer *f* **d'angle** angle iron (see also: **cornière**)
fil *m* wire
fil *m* **massif** wire, solid
tôle *f* sheet metal
  ~ **electrozinguée** ~ electroplated
  ~ **galvanisée** ~ galvanized
  ~ **perforée** ~ perforated
tube *m* tube
tube *m* **carré** tube, square hollow section
tube *m* **métal rectangulaire** tube, rectangular hollow section
tube *m* **rond** tube, round
U *m* **à conge** U-shaped metal channel

Outils à main ferronnerie
Metalwork hand tools

batte *f* **de tôlier-carrossier** panel beater
burin *m* **de mécanicien** cold chisel
calibre *m* **d'epaisseur** feeler gauge
clé *f* spanner
clé *f* **à molette** monkey wrench; adjustable
clé *f* **à pipe** spanner, box/socket
~ **débouchée** ~ through
clé *f* **cliquet** speed wrench
clé *f* **étoile** star key
clé *f* **mixte** spanner, combination
coffret *m* **de tarauds et filières** tap and die set
compas *m* compasses
compas *m* **à pointes sèches** spring divider
coupe-boulons *mpl* bolt cutters
douille *f* socket spanner
ergoscie *f* keyhole saw
lime *f* file
lime *f* **aiguille** file, needle
lime *f* **carrée** file, square
lime *f* **de precision** file, mini
lime *f* **mi-ronde** file, half-round
lime *f* **plate à main** file, flat
lime *f* **ronde** file, round
lime *f* **tiers point** file, saw
maillet *m* mallet (see also: **masse; massette**)
maillet *m* **à tête plastique** mallet, plastic-headed
maillet *m* **cuivre** mallet, copper-headed
marteau *m* hammer
marteau *m* **à piquer les soudures** hammer, chipping
marteau *m* **boule 'anglais'/'americain'** hammer English/American pattern ball pein
marteau *m* **de forgeron** hammer, blacksmith's
marteau *m* **de mecanicien** hammer, mechanic's
marteau *m* **rivoir** hammer, riveting
masse *f* mallet (see also: **maillet; massette**)
massette *f* mallet (see also: **maillet; masse**)
monture *f* **scie à métaux** hacksaw frame
pied *m* **à coulisse** calliper
pied *m* **à coulisse compas d'épaisseur** calliper, outside spring
pied *m* **à coulisse digital** calliper, digital vernier
pied *m* **à coulisse vernier** calliper, vernier
pince *f* pliers
pince *f* **à bec demi-rond de longueur** pliers, long-nosed
pince *f* **à becs coudes effiles** pliers, bent-nose
pince *f* **à becs plats** pliers, flat long-nose
pince *f* **à becs ronds** pliers, round-nosed
pince *f* **coupante** pliers, cutting
~ **de coté** ~ side-

Ferronnerie

~ **de devant** ~ front
~ **diagonale** ~ diagonal
~ **mécanicien** ~ mechanic's
pince *f* **multifonctions** pliers, multi-purpose
pince *f* **multiprise de longueur** pliers, water pump
pince *f* **reglable** pipe wrench, adjustable
pince *f* **universelle** pliers, general purpose
pince-étaux *f* pliers, locking
~ **bec courts** ~ short-nosed
~ **bec longs** ~ long-nosed
point *m* **à tracer** scriber
pointeau *m* ~ **de précision** centre punch
porte-lame *f* hacksaw, mini
rapporteur *m* **d'angle échancré** protractor
scie *f* **à métaux** hacksaw
scie *f* **à métaux junior** hacksaw, junior
tenaille *f* pincers
tournevis *m* **lame magnétique** screwdriver, magnetic tip

Accessoires pour outillage à main ferronnerie

Accessories for metalwork hand tools

caisse *f* **mécanicien** toolbox, mechanic's
équerre *f* set square
~ **acier** ~ steel
~ **alu** ~ aluminium
équerre *f* **simple à 90°** set square, 90° square **réglet** *m* rule
étau *m* vice
lame *f* **de scie** saw blade
mètre *m* **ruban** tape measure
réglet *m* **inox flexible** rule, flexibe stainless steel
réglet *m* **semi-rigides inox** rule, stainless steel

Outils électriques ferronnerie

Metalwork power tools

fer *m* **à souder électronique** soldering iron, electric
fraiseuse *f* milling machine
lime *f* **électrique** filer, electric
meule *f* grinding disk/wheel
~ **grain fin** ~ fine grain
meule *f* **à eau** whetstone
meuleuse *f* **d'angle** angle grinder
perceuse *f* drill
perceuse *f* **d'établi** drill, bench
perceuse *f* **manuelle** drill, manual
perceuse *f* **sur colonne** drill press
pistolet *m* **à souder** soldering gun, electric
plateau *m* **pour disques** angle grinder backing pad
scie *f* saw
scie *f* **à ruban** metal saw, metal-cutting band
scie *f* **circulaire métal** saw, metal-

Ferronnerie

cutting circular
scie *f* **sabre** saw, sabre
scie *f* **sauteuse** jigsaw
scie *f* **sauteuse laser** jigsaw, laser
scie *f* **sauteuse pendulaire** jigsaw, pendular
socle *m* **pour touret** pedestal stand grinder
touret *m* **à meuler** bench grinder
touret *m* **à meuler mixte** bench grinder, with wire wheel
tronçonneuse *f* metal saw, cut-off

Accessoires pour outils électriques ferronnerie
Accessories for metalwork power tools

disque *m* **à lamelles** disk, flap
disque *m* **à tronçonner** disk, cutting
disque *m* **sisal** disk, sisal polishing
lame *f* **pour scie à ruban métal** blade, band saw
lame *f* **pour tronçonneuse métal** blade, cut-off saw
outils *m* **à pastilles carbure démontables** lathe cutting tools
support *m* **de perçage** drill stand
support *m* **touret a meuler** bench
support *m* **tronçonnage de meuleuse** angle grinder cutting stand
tête *f* **de filière** die head for thread cutting on lathe

Accessoires ferronnerie
Metalwork accessories

bouchons *mpl* **d'oreille** ear plugs
casque *m* **antibruits** ear defenders
débilitre *m* **à colonne** gas flow meter
économiseur *m* **de gaz** gas economiser
foret *m* drill bit
foret *m* **HSS** drill bit, high speed steel (HSS)
foret *m* **métaux** drill bit, metal
~ **queue hexag** ~ hexagonal shank
~ **queue réduite** ~ reduced shank
huile *f* oil
huile *f* **hydraulique** oil, hydraulic
huile *f* **soluble** oil, soluble
lettres *f* **et chiffres à frapper** letters and numbers punch set
mastic *m* **soudre à froid universel** epoxy resin mastic
pâte *f* **à polir** polishing paste
propane *m* propane
tampon *m* **de nettoyage** cleaning rag

Soudage & de brasage
Soldering, welding & brazing

anti-retour *f* **pare-flamme oxygène** flame arrestor, oxygen, non-return
bague *f* **de soudage** welding ring
baguette *f* brazing rod
baguette *f* **d'aluminium enrobé** brazing rod, aluminium
baguette *f* **de brasage, cuivre/ phosphor argent** brazing rod, copper, phosphorous, silver brazing rod
baguette *f* **de métal d'apport et étain** welding rod
baguette *f* **en cuivre phosphore** brazing rod, phosphorus copper
bouteille *f* **gaz rechargeable** gas bottle, refillable
brasure *f* **aluminium basse temperature** brazing rod, aluminium, low temperature
brosse *f* **métallique** wire brush
brûleur *m* burner
brûleur *m* **à bec plat** burner, flat beak
brûleur *m* **à flamme enveloppante** burner, enveloping
brûleur *m* **à pointe super fine** burner, extra-fine point
brûleur *m* **grande flamme** burner, large flame
buse *f* **de soudage** welding nozzle
cartouche *f* **gaz jetable** gas bottle, disposable
cartouche *f* **oxygène** oxygen canister
chalumeau *m* gas welding/ soldering/cutting torch
　~ **avec levier** ~ lever-operated
　~ **chauffeur** ~ heating
　~ **monogaz** ~ gas
　~ **soudure** ~ welding
décapant *m* flux
détendeur *m* regulator
eau à souder *f* liquid flux
fer *f* **à souder** soldering iron
fer *f* **à souder autonome à gaz** soldering iron, gas
fer *f* **à souder électrique** soldering iron, electric
lampe *f* **à souder** blowtorch
lance *f* **de soudage** soldering lance
lunettes *f* **de soudage/de protection** goggles
manchette *f* **équipée** torch hose, small bore (not available in UK)
masque *m* **de soudure, arc/MIG** headshield, arc/MIG welding
oxygène *m* oxygen
pare-flamme *f* welding blanket
pâte *f* **décapante** flux paste
pierre *f* **ammoniacale** ammonia stone for cleaning soldering iron
pistolet *m* **à souder** soldering gun
pompe *f* **à dessouder** desoldering pump
poste *f* **à souder oxyacétylénique** oxyacetylene welder
robinet *m* **relais** regulating tap

Ferronnerie

soudure *m* étain en bobine tin solder, bobbin of
table *f* de soudage welding table
tuyau *m* acétylène hose, acetylene
tuyau *m* butane/propane hose, butane/propane
tuyau *m* oxygène hose, oxygen

Soudure à l'arc
Arc welding

électrode *f* electrode
électrode *f* enrobée electrode, fluxed
gants *m* spécial pour soudure à l'arc gauntlets, welding
générateur *m* rectifier
marteau *m* pique soudure hammer, welder's
pince *f* porte électrode electrode holder
positionneur *m* aimant spécial soudure magnetic welding positioner
poste *m* de souder à l'arc arc welder
prise *f* de masse earth clamp
redresseur *m* à courant continu DC DC inverter
tablier *m* de protection pour soudure à l'arc apron, protective

Soudure MIG
MIG welding

adaptateur *m* de fil MIG wire adapter
bobine *f* fourré welding wire, bobbin of
  ~ pour poste sans gaz ~ gasless MIG
buse *f* de souder welding nozzle
électrode *f* electrode
fil *m* fourré acier sans gaz gasless MIG wire
pince *f* MIG pliers
poste *m* à soudage MIG welder
poste *m* de soudage à l'arc sans gaz welder, gasless
spray *m* anti-adhérent anti-spatter spray
torche *f* MIG torch
tube *m* contact vissé contact tube

Soudure à gaz
Gas welding

acétylène *m* acetylene
allume-brûleur *m* cup lighter
anti-retour *m* pare-flamme flame arrestor
chalumeau *m* welding torch
chalumeau *m* bi-gaz two-gas welding kit
chalumeau *m* coupeur cutting torch
chariot *m* cylinder trolley

Ferronnerie

écran *m* **thermique** anti-thermic screen
gel *m* **thermique anti-chaleur** heat gel
poste *m* **à souder bi-gaz** dual gas welder (brazing and gas welding) flashback arrestor
raccord *m* **rapide** quick-fit connector
stylo *m* **soudure gaz** pencil flame torch
tête *f* **à aleser** reamer head

Abrasifs ferronnerie
Metalwork abrasives

abrasif *m* abrasive
carbure *m* **de silicium** silicon carbide paper
corindon *m* corundum paper
feuille *f* **abrasive** abrasive sheet
garniture *f* garnet paper
papier *m* **émeri** emery paper

Ferronnerie

Appendice

PLOMBERIE & CHAUFFAGE
PLUMBING & HEATING

Tuyaux & tubes
Pipe & tube

barre *f* **cuivre** pipe, copper, length of
barre *f* **multicouche** pipe, length of multilayer plastic
couronne *f* **cuivre recuit** copper pipe, coil, annealed
  ~ revêtu (or **gainé**) ~ sheathed
  ~ sans carbone ~ carbon free
flexible *f* pipe, flexible
flexible *f* **sanitaire tressé en acier inoxydable** pipe, flexible braided stainless steel (sanitary use)
  ~ femelle/femelle ~ two female connectors
  ~ femelle/jonction cuivre sans soudure ~ one female; one compression fitting
  ~ mâle/femelle ~ one male, one female connector
gaine *f* sheath
gaine *f* **sanitaire ivoire** sheath, ivory, for plastic and copper pipe
gaine *f* **translucide** sheath, translucent
tube *m* tube
tube *m* **d'alimentation** pipe, feed
tube *m* **d'alimentation en polyéthylène** pipe, feed, polyethylene
tube *m* **d'alimentation gainé en PER** pipe, feed, sheathed PER pipe
tube *m* **d'alimentation multicouche** pipe, feed, multilayer plastic
  ~ en barre ~ bar
  ~ en couronne ~ coil
tube *m* **de cuivre** tube, copper
tube *m* **écroui** tube, copper, hard
tube *m* **en cuivre recuit** tube, copper, annealed
tube *m* **en PVC-C** tube, CPVC
tuyau *m* pipe
tuyau *m* **à gaz** pipe, gas
tuyau *m* **cuivre** pipe, copper
tuyau *m* **d'arrosage** garden hose
tuyau *m* **de trop plein** pipe, overflow
tuyau *m* **flexible d'alimentation souple** pipe, hand-bendable
tuyau *m* **flexible pour gaz naturel** pipe, flexible, for natural gas
tuyau *m* **polyéthylène eau potable** pipe, MDPE blue, water
tuyau *m* **pour robinetterie sanitaire** tap connector, flexible
tuyau *m* **PVC** pipe, PVC (polyvinylchloride)

Raccords d'alimentation
Plumbing connectors

Raccords à souder
Solder fittings

bouchon *m* end cap
bouchon *m* **à souder en laiton pour cuivre** end cap, brass
bouchon *m* **femelle à souder** end cap, female
bouchon *m* **mâle à souder** end

Plomberie & Chauffage

cap, male
chapeau *m* **de gendarme à souder en laiton pour cuivre, femelle/femelle** brass 'cocked hat' fitting for bypassing another pipe (female joints)
clarinette *f* **à souder en laiton pour cuivre, mâle/femelle** S-shaped brass fitting for bypassing another pipe
coude *m* **à souder** elbow, soldered
coude *m* **à souder en laiton pour cuivre, 45°/90°** elbow, soldered, brass, for copper pipe 45°/90°
~ **femelle/femelle** ~ female/female
~ **mâle/femelle** ~ male/female
courbe, 90° curve *f* 90°
douille *f* **cuivre avec emboîture à braser écrou prisonnier taraudé** capillary socket/threaded captive nut
manchon *m* connector, straight
~ **sans lèvre** ~ without lip
raccord *m* joint
raccord *m* **coude cuivre à souder** joint, elbow, soldered
raccord *m* **courbe cuivre à souder** joint, angle, soldered
raccord *m* **cuivre à souder** joint, copper capillary
raccord *m* **droit à souder à écrou prisonnier** joint, straight, with captive compression nut
té *m* tee
té *m* **cuivre à souder** tee, soldered copper
té *m* **cuivre à souder égal** tee, equal
té *m* **cuivre à souder réduction** tee, reducing
té *m* **femelle réduit** tee, female reducing
té *m* **pied biche** tee, swept
té *m* **purgeur droit à souder** gate valve

Raccords en plastique
Plastic fittings

coude *f* elbow
coude *f* **de jonction polyéthylène plastique** elbow, plastic
raccord *m* joint
raccord *m* **polyéthylène à visser** joint, polyethylene, screwed
~ **femelle** ~ female
~ **mâle** ~ male
té *m* **de jonction polyéthylène plastique** tee connector, plastic

Raccords sans souder bicône
Compression fittings

bague *f* **bicône** olive (see also: **olive bicône**)
bouchon *m* pipe stop end
contre-écrou *m* **à plateau** locknut
coude *f* elbow
coude *f* **applique** elbow, wall plate
coude *f* **bicône** elbow, with olives

Plomberie & Chauffage

coude *f* **fer cuivre femelle** elbow, iron/copper
coude *f* **mâle** elbow, male sockets
coude *f* **mâle/femelle** elbow, male/femelle
écrou *m* **et olive bicône** nut and olive
mamelon *f* nipple
mamelon *f* **double mâle réduit** nipple, double male reducing
mamelon *f* **égal** nipple, equal
~ **femelle** ~ female
~ **mâle** ~ male
~ **mâle/femelle** ~ male/female
manchon *f* **fer/cuivre** straight connector, iron to copper
~ **femelle** ~ female
~ **mâle** ~ male
nourrice *f* **entrée quatre départs mâles** manifold, four male outlets
olive *f* **bicône** olive (see also: **bague bicône**)
raccord *m* joint
raccord *m* **à joint mixte mâle** joint, copper/PER
raccord *m* **à olive** joint, brass compression, with olive
raccord *m* **en laiton à visser** compression fitting
raccord *m* **tournant bicône** tap connector
raccord *m* **union bicône** joint, straight, with olives
~ **égal** ~ equal
~ **femelle** ~ female
~ **mâle** ~ male

~ **réduit** ~ reducing
réduction *m* **mâle/femelle** reduction connector, male/female
ruban *m* **Téflon d'étanchéité** PTFE joint sealing tape
té *m* tee connector
té *m* **bicône** tee, with olives
té *m* **joint mixte** tee, copper/PER
~ **femelle** ~ female
~ **mâle** ~ male
union *m* **mâle sans outil** connector, male, hand-tightening

Raccords sans souder américains
American system fittings

joint *m* (or **jonction** *f*; **raccord** *m*) **rapide U.S.** American pattern quick joint
manchon *m* **en laiton rapide** American pattern, straight brass connector
raccord *m* **<<gripp>>** American pattern, proprietary fitting
raccord *m* **instantané ou américain** American pattern, or instant joint
~ **coudé en laiton rapide** ~ elbow, brass
~ **réduit rapide U.S.** ~ reducing connector
té *m* **en laiton rapide** American pattern, tee fitting, brass

Plomberie & Chauffage

Raccords sans souder automatique
Automatic push-fit fittings

bouchon *m* **automatique** stop end, push-fit
douille *f* **de renfort automatique** pipe insert, reinforcing
raccord *m* (or **jonction** *f*) **automatique** automatic (push-fit) joint
raccord *m* **coude/mamelon/ manchon/droit/té automatique** automatic elbow/nipple/sleeve/straight/tee joints

Raccordements pour machine à laver & lave-vaisselle
Connections for washing machine & dishwasher

bride *f* **de vidange coudée auto perceuse** waste connector, self-cutting
entonnoir *m* **d'évacuation double pour machine à laver et lave-vaisselle** steam outlet, dual, for washing machine and dishwasher
raccord *m* **de jonction en Y pour tuyau d'alimentation** Y-junction feed pipe connector
robinet *m* tap
robinet *m* **de machine à laver auto perceur pour tube cuivre** tap, self-cutting, for copper pipe
robinet *m* **pour machine à laver** tap, washing machine
siphon *m* **pour machine à laver** trap and upstand, for washing machine
tuyau *m* pipe/hose
tuyau *m* **d'alimentation** pipe/hose, supply
tuyau *m* **de vidange** drain hose

Vannes & robinets d'arrêt
Valves & stop taps

clapet *m* **anti-pollution** anti-pollution valve
manette valve lever/handle
  ~ **papillon** ~ butterfly
  ~ **plate** ~ flat
robinet *m* **à boisseau** stoptap; stopcock (see also: ~ **d'arrêt**)
robinet *m* **autoperceur** tap, self-cutting
robinet *m* **d'arrêt** stoptap; stopcock (see also: **robinet** *m* **à boisseau**)
robinet *m* **d'arrêt à raccord sans purge** stoptap, without drain valve
robinet *m* **d'arrêt avec purge** stoptap, with drain valve
robinet *m* **d'arrêt de puisage** stoptap, with hose connector

Plomberie & Chauffage

robinet *m* de jardin tap, garden
robinet *m* extérieur tap, outside
robinet *m* poussoir tap, push
tête *m* de robinet; ~ à potence tap head
vanne *f* valve
vanne *f* à boisseau sphérique ballvalve (see also: ~ à sphere)
vanne *f* à passage intégral valve, through
vanne *f* à purge valve, with purge
vanne *f* à sphere ballvalve (see also: vanne à boisseau sphérique)
vanne *f* à sphere avec purge ballvalve, with drain
vanne *f* à sphere puisage ballvalve, with hose connector
vanne *f* à sphere raccord bicône ballvalve, with compression connections
vanne *f* d'arrêt stopvalve

Régulation de la pression de l'eau
Regulation of water pressure

anti-bélier *m* à ressort water hammer reducing spring
clapet *m* valve
clapet *m* anti-retour valve, anti-return check
clapet *m* casse vide valve, vacuum breaker
compteur *m* divisionnaire meter
compteur *m* divisionnaire d'eau chaude meter, hot water
compteur *m* divisionnaire d'eau froide meter, cold water
crépine *f* filter (see also: **filtre**)
crépine *f* à clapet universelle filter, valve
équilibreur *m* de pression pressure balancer
filtre *f* filter (see also: **crépine**)
filtre *f* à sable filter, sand
filtre *f* à tamis Y en inox filter, Y-pattern stainless steel
mamelon *f* porte manomètre pressure gauge nipple
manomètre *f* pressure gauge
manomètre *m* axial pour réducteur gauge, axial, for pressure-reducing valve
manomètre *m* radial pour réducteur gauge, radial, for pressure-reducing valve
réducteur *m* de pression pressure reducer

Multicouche système
Multilayer system

bouchon *m* en laiton stop end, brass
bouchon *m* en laiton à compression stop end, brass compression
bouchon *m* en laiton automatique stop end, brass automatic push-fit

Plomberie & Chauffage

collecteur *m* manifold
collier *m* **simple** pipe clip
manchon *m* **en laiton** sleeve; straight connector, brass
manchon *m* **en laiton à compression** sleeve; straight connector, brass compression
manchon *m* **en laiton automatique** sleeve; straight connector, brass automatic push-fit
olive *f* **fendue** olive, split
pince *f* **à sertir multicouche** pliers, crimping, for multilayer pipe
raccord *m* **à sertir** crimp connector
  ~ mâle ~ male
raccord *m* **à sertir en laiton** joint, brass, crimp
raccord *m* **en laiton** joint, brass
raccord *m* **en laiton à compression** joint, brass compression
raccord *m* **en laition automatique** joint, automatic push-fit
  ~ femelle ~ female
  ~ mâle ~ male
raccord *m* **en laiton coudé** joint, brass elbow
raccord *m* **en laiton droit** joint, straight
té *m* **en laiton** joint, tee
  ~ applique ~ with fixing plate
  ~ égal ~ equal
  ~ réduit ~ reducing
tube *m* **d'alimentation multicouche** tube, multilayer
tube *m* **d'alimentation multicouche en barre** tube, multilayer, straight length
tube *m* **d'alimentation multicouche en couronne** tube, multilayer, coil of
tube *m* **d'alimentation multicouche gainé** tube, multilayer, sheathed
tube *m* **d'alimentation multicouche nu** tube, multilayer, unsheathed

PER système
PER system

bague *f* **en laiton à glissement** brass ring for slip connector
bouchon *m* **en laiton** stop end, brass
  ~ à compression ~ compression
collecteur *m* manifold (see also: **nourrice**)
collier *m* **simple de fixation PER** pipe clip
douille *f* **de renfort en laiton** pipe reinforcing sleeves
guide *m* **tube PER** pipe bend support (see also: **raccord coudé guide**)
insert *m* **pour tuyau PER** insert, brass, PER pipe
jonction *f* connector
jonction *f* **de reduction PER** connector, straight, reducing
manchon *m* **brass en laiton** sleeve/ straight connector

Plomberie & Chauffage

~ **à compression** ~ compression
~ **à glissement** ~ slip connector
~ **réduit à glissement**
~ reducing
nourrice *f* (see also: **collecteur**) manifold
olive *f* **fendue** olive, split, for compression joint
pince *f* **coupe tube PER** pliers, PER tube cutting
raccord *m* joint
raccord *m* **coudé guide** pipe bend support (see also: **guide tube PER**)
raccord *m* **en laiton** joint, brass
raccord *m* **en laiton à compression** joint, compression
raccord *m* **en laiton à glissement** joint, slip
~ **femelle** ~ female
~ **mâle droit** ~ male, straight
raccord *m* **en laiton à sertir PER** joint, crimp connector for PER pipe
raccord *m* **en laiton coudé** joint, elbow
raccord *m* **en laiton strié** joint, brass striated
raccord *m* **en laiton té** joint, brass tee
~ **à compression** ~ compression
~ **à sertir réduit** ~ reducing, slip
~ **égal** ~ equal
tube *m* **en PER (polyéthylène réticulé)** tube/pipe cross-linked reticulated polyethylene

(see also: **tuyau en PER**)
~ **bleu** ~ blue (cold water)
~ **gainé** ~ sheathed
~ **nu** ~ unsheathed
~ **rouge** ~ red (hot water)
tuyau *m* **en PER** (see also: **tube en PER**) tube/pipe cross-linked reticulated polyethylene

Évacuation des eaux
Waste water drainage

Tubes & raccords en PVC
PVC pipe & connectors

aérateur *m* **à membrane PVC** aerator with PVC membrane
anti-vide *m* **pour tube** anti-vacuum device to eliminate noise and odour
bouchon *m* stop end
bouchon *m* **en élastomère** stop end, rubber
clapet *m* **anti-retour à battant** anti-return flap valve
collier *m* collar
collier *m* **bride; ~ de fixation** pipe bracket
coulisse *f* **sans butée** sleeve without internal stop
culotte *f* tee (see also: **té; culotte de branchement; culotte simple**)
culotte *f* **de branchement** tee (see also **culotte; culotte simple; té**)

Plomberie & Chauffage

culotte *f* **simple** tee (see also: **té; culotte; culotte de branchement**)
embout *m* end piece
embout *m* **fileté** end piece, threaded
embout *m* **plastique mâle** end piece, plastic, male flange
jonction *f* **pour tube métal et plastique** connector, metal and plastic pipe (with spring clips)
manchette *f* **réparation MF** repair socket, male/female, for connecting pipe of different diameters
manchon *f* connector, straight
manchon *f* **dilatation** expansion sleeve with flexible seal
manchon *f* **lèvre FF avec butée** connector, female/female, with internal stop
raccord *m* joint
raccord *m* **angle** joint, various angles
raccord *m* **coude** joint, elbow
raccord *m* **d'évacuation souple** joint, corrugated plastic waste
raccord *m* **extensible** joint, expandable concertina
raccord *m* **femelle/femelle (FF)** joint, female/female
raccord *m* **mâle/femelle (MF)** joint, male/female
raccord *m* **sur siphon** joint, trap
raccord *m* **Y** waste connector, Y-shaped

réduction *m* joint, reducing
réduction *m* **concentrique** joint, reducing, concentric
réduction *m* **excentrée** joint, reducing, offset
réduction *m* **incorporée** joint, reducing, integral
selle *f* **de branchement** saddle connector
siphon *m* **de parcours** siphon/trap, in-line
sortie *f* **de lavabo** basin waste exit (hockey stick shape)
tampon *m* **de visite** access/inspection plug
tampon *m* **de visite de réduction** simple access/inspection plug, reducing
té *m* tee (see also: **culotte; culotte de branchement; culotte simple**)
té *m* **pied biche** tee, swept
tube *m* **évacuation** waste pipe
tuyau *m* **PVC** pipe, PVC

Pompes
Pumps

circulateur *f* **trois vitesse** circulating pump, three-speed
pompe *f* pump
pompe *f* **à chaleur** pump, heat
pompe *f* **de circulation** pump, circulation
pompe *f* **de relevage** pump, sump
pompe *f* **électrique** pump, electric

Plomberie & Chauffage

Salle de bains
Bathroom

Douches & receveurs
Showers & shower trays

barre *f* **de douche** shower rail
barre *f* **de douche avec douchette** shower bar, vertical, with shower rose
bonde *f* drain; waste outlet
bonde *f* **à capot horizontale pour douche** drain; waste outlet, horizontal, with cover
bonde *f* **carrée** drain; waste outlet, square
bonde *f* **de douche** drain; waste outlet, shower
~ **flow à grand débit horizontal** ~ with large horizontal flow
~ **orientable** ~ adjustable
~ **verticale** ~ vertical
bras *f* **de douche à encastrer** shower rose arm, built-in
cabine *f* **de douche** shower cabinet
cabine *f* **de douche complète** shower cabinet and integral shower
cabine *f* **de douche quatre de cercle** shower cabinet, quarter-circle (corner)
cabine *f* **de douche rectangulaire** shower cabinet, rectangular
caniveau (*pl* -**x**) *m* (or **canivelle** *f*) waste outlet, strip, for **douche à l'italienne**)

colonne *f* **de douche** shower column
combiné *f* **de douche** shower handset
~ **à encastrer** ~ built-in
~ **avec robinetterie intégrée douche** ~ with integral taps
~ **hydromassante**
~ hydromassage
douche *f* shower
douche *f* **a l'italienne** walk-in shower
douchette *f* shower rose
ensemble *f* **de douche** shower set
flexible *f* **de douche en métal/plastique/nylon** spray hose metal/plastic/nylon
pare-douche *m* shower screen
paroi *f* **de douche** shower enclosure
pomme *f* **haute de douche** shower rose, overhead
pommeau *f* **de douche** shower head
porte *f* **de douche** shower door
~ **angle carré** ~ square
~ **battante** ~ hinged
~ **coulissante** ~ sliding
~ **pivotante** ~ pivoting
~ **quatre de cercle** ~ quarter-circle
receveur *m* **de douche** shower tray
receveur *m* **de douche à encastrer** shower tray, inset
receveur *m* **de douche bac à poser** shower tray, floor-

Plomberie & Chauffage

mounted
receveur *m* **de douche carré** shower tray, square
receveur *m* **de douche en acrylique renforcé** shower tray, reinforced acrylic
receveur *m* **de douche en grès émaillé** shower tray, glazed stoneware
receveur *m* **de douche en polyuréthane** polyurethane shower tray, polyurethane
receveur *m* **de douche en résine** shower tray, plastic resin
receveur *m* **de douche quatre cercle** shower tray, quarter circle (corner)
receveur *m* **de douche rectangulaire** shower tray, rectangular
receveur *m* **de douche surlévé** shower tray, raised
rideau *m* **de douche** shower curtain
robinet *m* **de douche** shower tap
siphon *m* waste trap
siphon *m* **avec grille à carreler** waste trap, with tiling grille
siphon *m* **pour sortie horizontale** waste trap, horizontal
siphon *m* **sortie verticale** waste trap, vertical
support *m* **de douchette ventouse** shower rose, cup bracket
surélévation *f* **pour receveur** plinth, for shower tray

Baignoires & bidets
Baths & bidets

baignoire *f* bath
baignoire *f* **asymétrique** bath, asymmetric
baignoire *f* **d'angle** bath, corner
baignoire *f* **îlot et patte de lion** bath, freestanding (with lion's paw feet)
baignoire *f* **ovale** bath, oval
baignoire *f* **rectangulaire** bath, rectangular
baignoire *f* **sabot** bath, hip
bidet *m* bidet
pare-baignoire *f* bath screen (see also: **paroi de baignore**)
paroi *f* **de baignoire** bath screen (see also: **pare-baignoire** *f*)
~ **en verre sécurit** ~ safety glass
~ **sérigraphié** ~ screen-printed
~ **transparente** ~ transparent
pieds *m* **de baignoire** bath feet
siphon *m* waste trap
siphon *m* **coudé pour bidet** waste trap, angled, for bidet
siphon *m* **pour baignoire** waste trap, for bath
~ **extra-plat** ~ slimline
tablier *m* **de baignoire** bath panel
vidage *m* **pour baignoire** waste outlet, for bath
vidage *m* **pour baignoire à câble** waste outlet, for bath, cable-operated
vidage *m* **pour baignoire îlot** waste outlet for bath, freestanding

Plomberie & Chauffage

vidage *m* **pour baignoire sabot ou d'angle** waste outlet, for hip or corner bath
vidage *m* **pour bidet réglable** waste outlet, for bidet, adjustable
volant *m* **pour vidage de baignoire** control wheel, for waste plug

Balnéos, spas & saunas
Whirlpools, spas & saunas

baignoire *f* **à bulle** bath, hydrotherapy
baignoire *f* **balnéo** bath, whirlpool
cabine *f* **hammam** steam bath cabin
~ **avec sol/sans sol** ~ with/without floor
~ **prêt à carreler** ~ ready to tile
caillebotis *m* duckboard (sauna)
générateur *m* **vapeur pour hammam** steam generator
hammam *m* steam bath
hygromètre et thermomètre *m* hygrometer and thermometer (sauna)
pierres *f* **pour sauna** sauna stones
poêle *f* **pour sauna** sauna heater
sauna *m* sauna
sauna *m* **à infrarouge** sauna, infrared
spa *f* spa bath
spa *f* **à encastre** spa bath, recessed
spa *f* **à poser** spa bath, floor-mounted

spa *f* **extérieur** spa bath, outside
spa *f* **gonflable** spa bath, inflatable
spa *f* **intérieur** spa bath, interior

Accessoires pour douches & baignoires
Accessories for showers & baths

caillebotis *m* duckboard
étagère *f* **de douche à suspendre** shower rack, hanging
étagère *f* **de douche d'hôte à fixer** shower rack, wall-fixed
porte-serviettes *f* towel rail
porte-serviettes *f* **à fixer** towel rail, attached
porte-serviettes *f* **à poser** towel rail, freestanding
raclette *f* **de douche** squeegee
tapis *m* **de bain** bath mat
~ **antidérapant** non-slip

WCs & lave-mains
Toilets & washbasins

abattant *m* **WC** toilet seat
bonde *f* waste outlet, basin
bonde *f* **à clapet rotatif sans trop plein** waste outlet, rotating, without overflow
bonde *f* **à dôme fixe sans trop plein** waste outlet, dome shaped, without overflow
bonde *f* **champignon à levier avec trop plein pour lavabo** waste

Plomberie & Chauffage

outlet, lever-operated 'mushroom', with overflow
bonde *f* **clic-clac** click-clack basin waste outlet
   ~ sans trop plein pour lavabo ~ without overflow
bonde *f* **de lavabo à commande manuelle** waste outlet, manually-operated pop-up
bonde *f* **pour lavabo à bouchon** waste outlet and plug
broyeur *m* **pour WC** macerator
clapet *m* **rentrant inviolable** waste plug, pop-up
cuvette *f* basin; bowl; toilet bowl
intercalaire *m* **de trop-plein avec grille** overflow tube with waste grille
lavabo *m* washbasin (see also: **lave-mains; vasque**)
lave-mains *m* washbasin (see also: **lavabo; vasque**)
pack *m* **WC** WC and cistern complete
plaque *m* **de commande WC** WC control plate
réservoir *m* **WC** cistern, WC
réservoir *m* **WC attenant** cistern, bowl-mounted
réservoir *m* **WC haut** cistern, high level
réservoir *m* **WC semi-bas** cistern, low level
siphon *m* **de lavabo** washbasin trap
siphon *m* **de lavabo bouteille** bottle trap
siphon *m* **de lavabo en S en laiton** S-bend outlet, brass
siphon *m* **de lavabo 'gain de place' avec joints integrés** washbasin trap, space-saving, with integral joints
siphon *m* **de lavabo réglable sortie** washbasin trap, adjustable exit
vasque *f* washbasin (see also: **lavabo; lave-mains**)
vécés *mpl* toilet (see also: **WC** *mpl*)
WC *mpl* toilet (see also: **vécés** *mpl*)
WC *m* **à poser** toilet, floorstanding
WC *m* **autoportant** toilet, freestanding
WC *m* **chimique** toilet, chemical
WC *m* **compact avec broyeur integré** toilet, compact, with integral macerator
WC *m* **'gain de place', sortie horizontale** toilet, space-saving, horizontal outlet
WC *m* **suspendu** toilet, wall-mounted

Mécanismes & evacuation WC

WC cistern mechanisms

douche *f* **pour WC** spray attachment, WC
ensemble *m* **de mécanisme** flush mechanism, complete
manchette *f* **de réparation PVC** outlet sleeve, PVC, replacement
mécanisme *m* **à tirette, robinet**

Plomberie & Chauffage

flotteur à fermeture mécanique float valve and flush mechanism
pipe *f* **WC** outlet pipe
pipe *f* **WC souple extensible** outlet pipe, extendable
robinet *m* **WC** WC valve
  ~ droit ~ straight
  ~ équerre ~ angled
robinet *m* **WC d'arrêt** cistern stopvalve
robinet *m* **WC flotteur** WC float valve
robinet *m* **WC flotteur silencieux** WC float valve, silent
soupape *f* **WC** flush valve
soupape *f* **WC à tirette** flush valve, pull
soupape *f* **WC simple poussoir** flush valve, push

Robinetterie de salle de bain
Bathroom taps

cartouche *f* **céramique** ceramic disc seal
limiteur *f* **de température** temperature limiter
mélangeur *m* mixer, separate hot and cold taps
mélangeur *m* **bain/douche** mixer, bath/shower
mélangeur *m* **de baignoire** mixer, bath
mélangeur *m* **de douche** mixer, shower
mélangeur *m* **de lavabo** mixer, basin
  ~ bec bas ~ low spout
  ~ bec haut ~ high spout
  ~ bec mobile ~ swivel
  ~ moyen ~ medium height spout
mitigeur *m* mixer, single tap
mitigeur *m* **bain/douche** mixer, single tap, bath/shower
mitigeur *m* **de baignoire** mixer, single tap, bath
mitigeur *m* **de bidet** mixer, single tap, bidet
mitigeur *m* **de lavabo** mixer, single tap, basin
  ~ bec bas ~ low spout
  ~ bec haut ~ high spout
  ~ moyen ~ medium height spout
mitigeur *m* **mural deux trous** mixer, two-hole, wall-mounted
mitigeur *m* **thermostatique** mixer, thermostatic
  ~ de baignoire ~ bath
  ~ de douche ~ shower
robinet *m* **de lave-mains** washbasin tap
  ~ bec bas ~ low spout
  ~ bec haut ~ high spout

Plomberie & Chauffage

Cuisine
Kitchen

Robinetterie de cuisine
Kitchen taps

bec *m* spout
~ **col de cygne** ~ swan neck
~ **droit** ~ straight
~ **haut mobile** ~ high swivel
~ **incliné** ~ inclined
~ **rabattable** ~ swivelling
cartouche *f* **céramique** ceramic disc seal
mélangeur *m* **de cuisine;** ~ **d'évier** mixer, kitchen, two tap
mitigeur *m* **de cuisine;** ~ **d'évier** mixer, kitchen, single tap
~ **avec douchette** ~ with spray attachment

Eviers de cuisine
Kitchen sinks

bac *m* **à laver** washtub
bonde *f* waste outlet, sink
bonde *f* **à câble avec trop plein** waste outlet, cable-operated, with overflow
bonde *f* **à clapet rotatif sans trop plein** waste outlet, rotating, without overflow
bonde *f* **à panier en inox** basket strainer, stainless steel
~ **avec trop plein** ~ with overflow
bonde *f* **à tirette** waste outlet, lever-operated
~ **à bouchon** ~ with plug
~ **chaînette avec trop plein** ~ with plug on chain and overflow
ensemble *m* **complet avec trop plein** waste assembly with overflow
évier *m* sink
~ **en granit** ~ granite
~ **en grès** ~ sandstone
~ **en inox** ~ stainless steel
~ **en quartz** ~ quartz
~ **en résine** ~ resin
évier *m* **à poser** sink, surface-mounted
évier *m* **avec égouttoir** sink, with drainer
évier *m* **cuve** sink bowl
évier *m* **d'angle** sink, corner
évier *m* **deux bacs avec un égouttoir** sink, two bowl, with drainer
panier *m* **inox pour bonde tout-en-un** strainer, stainless steel, for sink waste, all-in-one
siphon *m* waste trap, sink
siphon *m* **avec prise machine à laver** waste trap, with washing machine connector
siphon *m* **d'évier extra-plat** waste trap, slimline
siphon *m* **PVC pour évier** waste trap, PVC
siphon *m* **réglable pour évier** waste trap, adjustable
tubulure *f* **de raccordement,**

Plomberie & Chauffage

deux cuves connecting tube, double sink outlet
vidage *m* sink waste
  ~ à câble ~ cable-operated
  ~ complet pour évier, deux cuves ~ two-bowl, with overflow
~ tout-en-un 'gain de place' ~ all-in-one space-saving

Chauffage électrique
Electric heating

convecteur *m* **électrique** convector radiator, electric
panneau *m* **rayonnant** radiant panel
plancher *m* **chauffant électrique** underfloor heating, electric
radiateur *m* **électrique à convection** radiator, electric convection
radiateur *m* **électrique à inertie** radiator, electric inertia
  ~ fluide ~ fluid
  ~ fonte ~ cast iron radiant/convection
  ~ pierre reconstituée ~ reconstituted stone heating element
  ~ pierre stéatite ~ soapstone heating element
  ~ sèche ~ dry
radiateur *m* **électrique à rayonnement** radiant heater
radiateur *m* **électrique chaleur douce** radiator, gentle heat

sol *m* **chauffant à pose collée** underfloor heating, for tiling

Chauffage d'appoint
Auxiliary heaters

chariot *m* **pour poêle à pétrole** trolley for petrol stove
chauffage *f* **d'appoint** auxiliary heater
chauffage *f* **d'appoint à brasero infrarouge** auxiliary heater, gas brazier, infrared
chauffage *f* **d'appoint à catalyse** auxiliary heater, gas catalytic
chauffage *f* **d'appoint à gaz** auxiliary heater, gas
chauffage *f* **d'appoint à infrarouge** auxiliary heater, gas infrared
chauffage *f* **d'appoint de terrasse** auxiliary heater, terrace
chauffage *f* **d'appoint de terrasse à gaz** auxiliary heater, terrace, gas
chauffage *f* **d'appoint de terrasse électrique** auxiliary heater, terrace, electric
cheminée *f* **électrique** flame-effect fire, electric
combustible *m* **liquide** fuel, liquid (for **poêle à pétrole**)
  ~ désaromatisé ~ dearomatized
  ~ extrêmement raffiné ~ extremely refined

Plomberie & Chauffage

~ **pétrole** ~ petrol derivative
~ **sans odeur** ~ odourless
convecteur *m* **mobile** convector heater, portable electric
générateur *m* **d'air chaud** propane heater, for building/work site
panneau *m* **rayonnant mobile électrique** radiant panel heater, electric, mobile
poêle *f* stove
poêle *f* **à gaz** stove, gas
poêle *f* **à mèche** stove, wick
poêle *f* **à pétrole** stove, petrol
~ **à injection électronique** ~ electronic injection
poêle *f* **effet feu de cheminée** stove, real fire effect
poêle *f* **infrarouge et électrique** stove, dual gas/electric
pompe *f* pump
pompe *f* **électrique pour pétrole** pump, electric, for refilling petrol tank
pompe *f* **manuelle pour pétrole** pump, manual, for refilling petrol tank
radiateur *m* **bain d'huile électrique** radiator/heater, oil-filled electric
radiateur *m* **soufflant électrique** radiator/heater, electric fan
~ **céramique** ~ ceramic element
~ **mobile** ~ portable
~ **salle de bain mobile** ~ bathroom, portable
radiateur *m* **soufflant électrique de chantier** radiator/heater, electric fan, work site
radiateur *m* **soufflant électrique salle de bain fixe** radiator/heater, electric fan, bathroom, fixed
radiateur *m* **soufflant électrique tour** radiator/heater, electric fan, tower unit
radiateur *m* **soufflant mobile** radiator/fan heater, portable

Chauffage central
Central heating

clé *m* **pour purgeur carré** radiator bleed key, square-shank
coude *f* **de réglage** lockshield valve
kit *m* **de fixation universel pour radiateur** radiator mounting kit, universal
purgeur *m* bleed valve
purgeur *m* **à volant mâle** bleed valve, finger-operated
purgeur *m* **automatique pour radiateur** bleed valve, automatic
radiateur *m* radiator
radiateur *m* **eau chaude** radiator, hot water
radiateur *m* **eau chaude acier** radiator, hot water, steel
radiateur *m* **eau chaude aluminium** radiator, hot water, aluminium

Plomberie & Chauffage

radiateur *m* **eau chaude bimétal** radiator, hot water, bimetal
radiateur *m* **mixte eau chaude/électrique** radiator, dual hot water/electric
radiateur *m* **sèche-serviette** radiator, towel
robinet *m* valve
robinet *m* **de radiateur** valve, radiator
robinet *m* **de radiateur à tête thermostatique** valve, radiator, thermostatic
robinet *m* **de vidange** valve, drain
robinet *m* **de vidange à boisseaux** drain valve, radiator
robinet *m* **de vidange à boisseaux orientable** drain valve, adjustable, for radiator
thermostat *m* thermostat
thermostat *m* **de haute precision** thermostat, high precision
thermostat *m* **digital programmable** thermostat, digital programmable
thermostat *m* **électronique** thermostat, electronic
thermostat *m* **électronique d'ambiance** thermostat, electronic room stat
thermostat *m* **électronique programmable radio/tél** thermostat, electronic radio/telephone control
thermostat *m* **mécanique** thermostat, mechanical
thermostat *m* **programmable** thermostat, programmable

Chaudières & accessoires
Boilers & accessories

ballon *m* expansion vessel (see also: **vase d'expansion**)
bouilleur *m* boiler (see also: **chaudière**)
brûleur *m* burner
chaudière *f* boiler (see also: **bouilleur**)
chaudière *f* **fonte chauffage seul** boiler, cast iron, heating only
chaudière *f* **murale** boiler, wall-mounted
chaudière *f* **murale à condensation gaz** boiler, wall-mounted condensing gas
chaudière *f* **murale avec ballon** boiler, wall-mounted, with expansion vessel
chaudière *f* **murale électrique** boiler, wall-mounted, electric
chaudière *f* **murale gaz** boiler, wall-mounted, gas
chaudière *f* **sol** boiler, floorstanding
chaudière *f* **sol à condensation** boiler, floorstanding condensing
chaudière *f* **sol avec ballon** boiler, floorstanding, with expansion

Plomberie & Chauffage

vessel
chaudière *f* **sol fioul** boiler, floorstanding, oil
chaudière *f* **sol gaz** standard boiler, floorstanding, standard gas
circulateur *f* circulation pump
clapet *m* **anti-thermosiphon** check valve (preventing thermosiphon effect)
fioul oil, for boiler
foyer *m* **fermé à bois pour chauffage central** fireplace insert, wood-burning, with boiler for central heating
gaz gas, for boiler
manomètre *f* **radial** pressure gauge
purgeur *m* **d'air automatique** air vent, automatic
servomoteur *m* actuator/servomotor
soupape *f* **de sûreté sécurité** safety valve
vase *f* **d'expansion** expansion vessel (see also: **ballon** *m*)

Chauffage au bois
Wood heating

adaptateur *m* **inox** adapter, to connect stove to flue pipe, stainless steel
aspirateur *m* chimney flue extractor, rotating
aspirateur *m* **de cheminée en béton** chimney pot/cap, concrete
aspirateur *m* **statique** chimney flue extractor, static
boisseau *m* **alvéolé** chimney flue block, terracotta
cadre *m* **de fixation raccord haut** fixing bracket, for upper chimney flue
chapeau *m* **de cheminée** chimney pot/cap
chapeau *m* **de cheminée pare-pluie** chimney pot/cap, rain
cheminée *m* chimney; fireplace
collier *m* **à pointe galvanisé** collar, galvanized steel, with screw fixing for wall
collier *m* **de fixation étanchéité** collar clamp, for sealing joint between lengths of flue pipe
collier *m* **mural** collar and wall bracket (metal flue)
conduit *m* **de cheminée** chimney flue
conduit *m* **de cheminée en aluminium** chimney flue, aluminium
conduit *m* **de cheminée en inox** chimney flue, stainless steel
conduit *m* **de cheminée isolé** chimney flue, insulated
conduit *m* **de fumée en terre cuite** chimney flue, terracotta block
conduit *m* **fumée** smoke pipe
conduit *m* **pour poêle, foyer et insert** conduit, for stove, fireplace and insert
elément *m* **de coude** flue pipe

Plomberie & Chauffage

connection, elbow
- **~ coude plissé aluminié 90°** ~ aluminium pleated, 90°
- **~ émaillé 45°** ~ enamelled, 45°

élément *m* **droit réglable soudé** flue pipe, straight, welded, adjustable

foyer *m* fireplace; hearth
- **~ en fonte** ~ cast iron

foyer-insert *m* (see also: **insert de cheminée**)

insert *m* **de cheminée** fireplace insert (see also: **foyer-insert**)

kit *m* **de fixation universel pour radiateur manchette droite** kit, stove installation, straight sleeve

manchon *m* **aluminé** flue pipe, connection sleeve

plaque *f* **d'étanchéité carrée** sealing plate, for chimney flue exiting roof

poêle *f* stove

poêle *f* **à bois** stove, wood-burning

poêle *f* **à granulé** stove, pellet-burning

raccord *m* **haut** connector, top of chimney flue
- **~ inox** ~ stainless steel flue

réduction *m* **conique** flue pipe, reduction, conical, stainless steel

sortie *f* **de toit** chimney stack, prefabricated

support *m* **de conduit** flue pipe bracket

té *m* **nu aluminié** tee connector, aluminium, for flue

té *m* **simple paroi** tee connector, single-wall

té *m* **tampon émaillé noir mat** tee connector, matt black enamel, for rear of wood stove

tubage *m* **de conduit flexible;**
- **~ flexible lisse** flue liner, flexible

tuyau *m* **aluminié** flue pipe, aluminium

tuyau *m* **émaillé noir mat** flue pipe, matt black, enamelled

tuyau *m* **inox** flue pipe, stainless steel

Production d'eau chaude sanitaire
Production of hot water

ballon *m* **d'eau chaude** hot water tank

ballon *m* **d'eau chaude électrique** hot water tank, electric

ballon *m* **d'eau chaude gaz** hot water tank, gas

chauffe-eau *m* water heater

chauffe-eau *m* **combi douche/lavabo** water heater, instantaneous, combination shower/basin

chauffe-eau *m* **électrique** water heater, electric
- **~ horizontal** ~ horizontal
- **~ mural** ~ wall-mounted
- **~ sous-évier** ~ under-sink

Plomberie & Chauffage

~ **sur évier** ~ over sink
~ **sur socle** ~ on vertical stand
~ **vertical** ~ vertical
chauffe-eau *m* **gaz instantané** water heater, gas instantaneous
chauffe-eau *m* **instantané**;
~ **rapide** water heater, electric instantaneous
chauffe-eau *m* **solaire** water heater, solar
chauffe-eau *m* **thermodynamique** water heater with heat pump
console *f* **d'accrochage plafond pour ballon d'eau chaude** ceiling attachment bracket for hot water tank
entonnoir *m* **siphon** funnel siphon for chauffe-eau
kit *m* (or **ensemble** *m*) ~ **sécurité/ raccordement chauffe-eau** kit, installation for water heater
~ **inox pour eau agressive** ~ stainless steel, for aggressive water
~ **sans soudure** ~ non-solder
~ **Téflon pour eau calcaire** ~ Teflon for hard water
manomètre *m* pressure gauge
mitigeur *m* **thermostatique anti-brûlure pour chauffe-eau** anti-scald mixer valve, thermostatic
pompe *f* **à chaleur air/eau** heat pump, air/water
réducteur *m* **de pression** pressure reducer

résistance *f* **de chauffe-eau** element, water heating
résistance *f* **de chauffe-eau blindée** element, water heating, reinforced
résistance *f* **de chauffe-eau stéatite** element, water heating, steatite (soapstone)
résistance *f* **de chauffe-eau thermoplongée** element, immersion heater
thermostat *m* **pour chauffe-eau** thermostat, for water heater
trépied *m* **chauffe-eau** stand for water heater
vase *f* **d'expansion sanitaire** expansion vessel, hot water

Climatisation & ventilation

Air conditioning & ventilation

aérateur *m* **d'air** extractor fan (see also: **extracteur d'air**)
climatiseur *m* air-conditioner
climatiseur fixe air-conditioner, fixed
climatiseur *m* **fixe réversible** air-conditioner, fixed, reversible
climatiseur *m* **local** air-conditioner, portable
déshumidificateur *m* dehumidifier
extracteur d'air extractor fan (see also: **aérateur d'air**)

Plomberie & Chauffage

goulotte *f* **pour climatiseur fixe** duct, fixed air-conditioner
humidificateur *m* humidifier
rafraîchisseur *m* **d'air** air freshener
saturateur *m* humidifier, radiator
tube *m* **condensat pour climatiseur fixe** condensation duct, for fixed air-conditioner
ventilateur *m* fan, electric
ventilateur *m* **de table** fan, electric, table
ventilateur *m* **sans pales** fan, electric, bladeless
ventilateur *m* **sur pied** fan, electric, standard

Traitement de l'eau
Water treatment

adoucisseur de l'eau *m* water softener
antibruit *m* **liquide pour chaudière** noise inhibitor liquid for central heating system
anti-calcaire *m* **magnétique** anti-hard water device, magnetic
  ~ **pour la douche** ~ for shower
  ~ **pour machine à laver et lave-vaisselle** ~ for washing machine & dishwasher
antigel *m* **chaudière** anti-freeze for central heating system
anti-tartre *m* **électronique** scale inhibitor, electronic
billes *f* **silico-phosphate anti-calcaire** anti-hard water silico-phosphate balls
cartouche *f* **filtrante** water filter cartridge
colmatant *m* **chaudière** liquid leak stop for central heating system
désinfectant *m* **pour adoucisseur** water softener disinfectant
disembouant *f* **chaudière** central heating boiler sludge remover
filtrante *f* **de l'eau** water filter
filtre *m* **anti-tartre pour machine à laver** limescale filter, for washing machine
inhibiteur *m* **chaudière** anti-corrosion/anti-scale liquid for central heating system
nettoyant *m* **chaudière liquide** central heating system cleaner
neutraliseur *m* **de calcaire** hard water neutraliser
pastilles *f* **de sel pour adoucisseur d'eau** salt tablets
poudre *f* **détartrante et dégraissante pour lave linge et lave-vaisselle** de-limescaling powder, for washing machine/dishwasher
sel *m* **régénerant pour adoucisseur d'eau** regenerating salt

Plomberie & Chauffage

Outils & accessoires pour la plomberie & le chauffage

Plumbing & heating tools & accessories

allume-brûleur *m* cup lighter for blowtorch
appareil *m* **à battre les collets** flaring tool and clamp
chalumeau (*pl* -**x**) *m* blowtorch
chalumeau *m* **monogaz** blowtorch, gas (butane or propane)
chalumeau *m* **soudeur** blowtorch, cutting (oxyacetylene or oxy-propane)
clé *m* wrench/spanner
clé *m* **à chaine** wrench/spanner, chain
clé *m* **à courroie en caoutchouc** wrench/spanner, rubber strap
clé *m* **à molette** wrench/spanner, adjustable
clé *m* **anglaise** wrench/spanner, monkey
clé *m* **de montage de radiateur** radiator valve mounting key
clé *m* **lavabo** wrench/spanner, basin
clé *m* **purgeur à radiateur** radiator bleed key
clé *m* **Stillson** wrench/spanner, Stillson
clé *m* **Suédoise** pliers, plumber's; tube tightening (see also: **serre-tubes Suédoise**)
collier *m* **à crémaillère à vis** hose clip, ratcheted
coupe-tube *f* tube/pipe cutter
  ~ **cuivre** ~ copper pipe
  ~ **PER** ~ PER pipe
déboucheur *m* drain clearing tool
  ~ **à piston** ~ piston-operated
  ~ **à pompe** ~ pump-operated
  ~ **à tambour** ~ spool type
  ~ **fléxible** ~ flexible
  ~ **fléxible à manivelle** (or **fléxible à crampons**) ~ flexible, cranked spring
  ~ **ventouse** ~ suction-operated
débouchoir *m* plunger
détecteur *m* **de fuites** leak detector
emporte-pièce *m* hole-making punch
flux *f* **décapant** flux
gabarit *m* **de pose tuyau** pipe-cutting gauge
joint *m* **d'étanchéité** gasket/seal
lampe *f* **à souder** blowlamp
lime *f* file
malette *f* **cintreuse** pipe bending tool (see also: **pince à cintrer**)
matrice *f* **et étrier** matrix and bracket, for flaring copper tube (use with: **toupie pour matrice**)
molette *f* **pour coupe-tube cuivre** pipe cutter, blade replacement
pince *f* pliers
pince *f* **à cintrer** pipe bending tool (see also: **malette cintreuse**)
pince *f* **à coupe tube multicouche**

pliers, pipe-cutting (multilayer pipe)
pince *f* **à siphon griptou** pliers, wide-jaw, adjustable
plomb *m* plumbline
pompe *f* **à vide** drain clearing pump
ressort *m* **à cintrer** pipe bending spring
rodoir *m* **et fraises** valve reseater and mills
scie *f* **à métaux** hacksaw
serre-tubes *m* pipe wrench
serre-tubes *m* **Suédoise** pliers, plumber's; tube tightening (see also: **clé Suédoise**)
toupie *f* **pour matrice** router for pipe-flaring matrix

Gaz & accessoires
Gas & accessories

bouteille *f* **gaz rechargeable** bottle, gas, rechargeable
bouteille *f* **gaz vide** bottle, gas, empty
butane *f* butane
cartouche *f* **jetable** gas cartridge, disposable
détendeur *m* **gaz** gas regulator
propane *f* propane
robinet *m* **relais gaz** gas regulating tap
tuyau *m* **à gaz** pipe, gas
tuyau *m* **flexible pour gaz naturel** pipe, gas, flexible, natural gas

Plomberie & Chauffage

Appendice

RÉFÉRENCE
REFERENCE

Référence

Les Numéros
Numbers

0 **zéro** nought
1 **un (une)** one
2 **deux** two
3 **trois** three
4 **quatre** four
5 **cinq** five
6 **six** six
7 **sept** seven
8 **huit** eight
9 **neuf** nine
10 **dix** ten
11 **onze** eleven
12 **douze** twelve
13 **treize** thirteen
14 **quatorze** fourteen
15 **quinze** fifteen
16 **seize** sixteen
17 **dix-sept** seventeen
18 **dix-huit** eighteen
19 **dix-neuf** nineteen
20 **vingt** twenty
21 **vingt et un (une)** twenty-one
22 **vingt-deux** twenty-two
23 **vingt-trois** twenty-three
24 **vingt-quatre** twenty-four
25 **vingt-cinq** twenty-five
26 **vingt-six** twenty-six
27 **vingt-sept** twenty-seven
28 **vingt-huit** twenty-eight
29 **vingt-neuf** twenty-nine
30 **trente** thirty
31 **trente et un (une)** thirty-one
32 **trente-deux** thirty-two
33 **trente-trois** thirty-three
34 **trente-quatre** thirty-four
35 **trente-cinq** thirty-five
36 **trente-six** thirty-six
37 **trente-sept** thirty-seven
38 **trente-huit** thirty-eight
39 **trente-neuf** thirty-nine
40 **quarante** forty
41 **quarante et un (une)** forty-one
42 **quarante-deux** forty-two
43 **quarante-trois** forty-three
44 **quarante-quatre** forty-four
45 **quarante-cinq** forty-five
46 **quarante-six** forty-six
47 **quarante-sept** forty-seven
48 **quarante-huit** forty-eight
49 **quarante-neuf** forty-nine
50 **cinquante** fifty
51 **cinquante et un (une)** fifty-one
52 **cinquante-deux** fifty-two
53 **cinquante-trois** fifty-three
54 **cinquante-quatre** fifty-four
55 **cinquante-cinq** fifty-five
56 **cinquante-six** fifty-six
57 **cinquante-sept** fifty-seven
58 **cinquante-huit** fifty-eight
59 **cinquante-neuf** fifty-nine
60 **soixante** sixty
61 **soixante et un (une)** sixty-one
62 **soixante-deux** sixty-two
63 **soixante-trois** sixty-three
64 **soixante-quatre** sixty-four
65 **soixante-cinq** sixty-five
66 **soixante-six** sixty-six
67 **soixante-sept** sixty-seven
68 **soixante-huit** sixty-eight
69 **soixante-neuf** sixty-nine
70 **soixante-dix** seventy
71 **soixante et onze** seventy-one

72 **soixante-douze** seventy-two
73 **soixante-treize** seventy-three
74 **soixante-quatorze** seventy-four
75 **soixante-quinze** seventy-five
76 **soixante-seize** seventy-six
77 **soixante-dix-sept** seventy-seven
78 **soixante-dix-huit** seventy-eight
79 **soixante-dix-neuf** seventy-nine
80 **quatre-vingts** eighty
81 **quatre-vingt-un (une)** eighty-one
82 **quatre-vingt-deux** eighty-two
83 **quatre-vingt-trois** eighty-three
84 **quatre-vingt-quatre** eighty-four
85 **quatre-vingt-cinq** eighty-five
86 **quatre-vingt-six** eighty-six
87 **quatre-vingt-sept** eighty-seven
88 **quatre-vingt-huit** eighty-eight
89 **quatre-vingt-neuf** eighty-nine
90 **quatre-vingt-dix** ninety
91 **quatre-vingt-onze** ninety-one
92 **quatre-vingt-douze** ninety-two
93 **quatre-vingt-treize** ninety-three
94 **quatre-vingt-quatorze** ninety-four
95 **quatre-vingt-quinze** ninety-five
96 **quatre-vingt-seize** ninety-six
97 **quatre-vingt-dix-sept** ninety-seven
98 **quatre-vingt-dix-huit** ninety-eight
99 **quatre-vingt-dix-neuf** ninety-nine
100 **cent** a hundred
101 **cent un** a hundred and one
200 **deux cents** two hundred
201 **deux cent un (une)** two hundred and one
300 **trois cents** three hundred
1,000 **mille** a thousand
1,000,000 **un million** a million

1er **premier** -**ière** 1st first
2e 2ème **deuxième** 2nd second
3e 3ème **troisième** 3rd third
4e 4ème **quatrième** 4th fourth
5e 5ème **cinquième** 5th fifth
6e 6ème **sixième** 6th sixth
7e 7ème **septième** 7th seventh
8e 8ème **huitième** 8th eighth
9e 9ème **neuvième** 9th ninth
10e 10ème **dixième** 10th tenth
1 1e 11ème **onzième** 11th eleventh
12e 12ème **douzième** 12th twelfth

Les Fractions
Fractions
un demi a half
un tiers a third
deux tiers two-thirds
un quart a quarter
un cinquième a fifth
un huitième an eighth
seizième a sixteenth

Pourcentages
Percentages
10%; dix pour cent 10% ten per cent
100%; cent pour cent 100% one hundred per cent

Les decimaux
Decimals
0,5 zéro virgule cinq 0.5; nought point five

Référence

Propriété
Property

à louer *adj* for rent
à vendre *adj* for sale
abri; ~voiture *m* carport
acheteur; ~euse *mf* buyer; purchaser
acte d'achat *m* conveyance of land transfer
acte de vente; ~ authentique de vente *m* deed of sale
acte notairé *m* property deed
appartement *m* apartment
appentis *m* lean-to
assainissement sanitation *m*
atelier *m* workshop
auvent *m* awning; porch
barrière *f* fence (see also: **cloture**)
bastide *f* country house (Provence); fortified village
bâtiment *m* building
bergerie *f* sheep barn
borne *f* boundary marker
bourg *m* small town; village (see also: **village**)
buanderie *f* laundry/utility room
bungalow *m* bungalow (see also: **pavillon**)
bureau *m* office
cadastre *m* land registry
cave *f* cellar
certificat d'urbanisme *m* planning certificate
chambre *f* bedroom
champ *m* field
chaumière *f* thatched cottage

chemin *m* path
cité *f* city
cloture *f* fence (see also: **barrière**)
comble *m* attic
compromis de vente *m* purchase agreement; contract of sale
cottage *m* cottage
cuisine *f* kitchen
débarras *m* junk room
dépendance *f* outbuilding
écurie *f* stable
escalier *m* staircase
escalier en colimaçon *m* spiral staircase
étable *f* pigsty; byre
étang *m* pond
fenil *m* hayloft
ferme *f* farmhouse (see also: **maison du fermier; maison paysanne**)
fermette *f* small farm; country/ weekend cottage
fossé *m* ditch
garage *m* garage
garde-manger *m* larder
gentilhommière *f* country manor
grange *f* barn
grenier *m* attic; granary
hameau *m (pl -***x***)* hamlet
jardin *m* garden
jardin potager *m* garden, vegetable
limite du terrain *f* boundary
location *f* rental; lease
longère *f* longhouse; Breton stone-built farmhouse
lotissement *m* plot of land; allotment

Référence

maison *f* house; home; abode; residence
maison bourgeoise *f* mansion
maison d'amis *f* ~ **de plaisance** weekend/holiday house
maison de banlieue *f* suburban house
maison de campagne *f* country house
maison de chasse *f* hunting lodge
maison d'habitation *f* dwelling house
maison de maître *f* gentleman's house
maison de rapport *f* apartment block
maison de repose *f* ~ **de convalescence** *f* rest home; convalescent home
maison de retrait *f* retirement home
maison de ville *f* town house
maison du fermier *f* farmhouse (see also: ~ **paysanne; ferme**)
maison meublée *f* furnished apartment
maison paysanne *f* farmhouse (see also: ~ **du fermier; ferme**)
maisonnette *f* small house
maisonnette du garde *f* gatekeeper's lodge
maisons doubles *fpl* semi-detached houses
mas *m* Provençal farmhouse
monument historique *m* listed building
niveau de la mer *m* sea level

pavillon *m* house; bungalow; pavilion; gazebo (see also: **bungalow**)
permis de construire *m* planning permission
pigeonnier *m* dovecote; pigeon tower
piquet de clôture *f* fence post
porcherie *f* pigsty
poteau télégraphique *m* telegraph pole
premier étage *m* first floor
propriétaire *mf* landowner
pylône *m* pylon
résidence primaire *f* primary residence
résidence secondaire *f* weekend holiday home
rez-de-chaussée *m* ground floor
rez-de-jardin *m* garden level
salle à manger *f* dining room
salle de bain *f* bathroom
salle de séjour *f* family room
salon *f* living room
source *f* spring
sous-sol *m* basement
système d'assainissement *f* drainage
terrain à bâtir *m* building land
toit roof *m*
toit-terrasse *m* flat roof
vendeur; ~euse *mf* vendor
vente aux enchères *f* auction
véranda *f* veranda
vestibule *m* entrance hall
village *m* village (see also: **bourg**)

Référence

Metiers
Trades

agent immobilier *m* estate agent
agriculteur; ~trice *mf* farmer
architecte *mf* architect
bricoleur; ~euse *mf* handyman/woman
carreleur *m* tiler
carrier *m* quarryman
charpentier *m* carpenter
chauffagiste *m* heating specialist
constructeur *m* builder
contremaître; ~esse *fm*; **maître d'oeuvre** *m* foreman/woman
décorateur; ~trice *mf* decorator
déménageur *m* removal company
dessinateur; ~trice *mf* draughtsman/woman
ébéniste *mf* cabinetmaker
électricien *m* electrician
ensemblier *m* interior designer
ferronnier; ~ière *mf* iron craftsman/woman
forgeron *m* blacksmith
garagiste *mf* mechanic/service station worker
géomètre *mf* surveyor
ingénieur *m* engineer
jardinier; ~ière *mf* gardener
maçon *m* bricklayer
maraîcher; ~ère *mf* market gardener
marchand; ~e *mf* shopkeeper; tradesman/woman
menuisier *m* joiner

métallo *mf* metalworker
métreur; ~euse *mf* quantity surveyor **notaire** *m* notary
ouvrier; ~ière *mf* workman/worker
paysagiste *mf* landscape gardener
peintre *m* painter
pépiniériste *mf* nurseryman
plâtrier *m* plasterer
plombier *m* plumber
plombier-zinguer *m* zinc roofer
quincaillier *m* ironmonger
ramoneur *m* chimneysweep
serrurier; ~ière *mf* locksmith
soudeur ~euse *mf* welder
tapissier; ~ière *mf* upholsterer
tapissier décorateur *m*; **peintre-décorateur** *m* interior decorator
travailleur; ~euse *mf* labourer
vidangeur *m* sewage tanker driver/cesspool cleaner
vitrier *m* glazier

Référence

Couleur
Colour

ambré, ~e *adj* amber
ardoisé, ~e *adj* slate
argenté, ~e *adj* silver/silvery
azur *m*; **azuré ~e** *adj* azure
beige *adj* beige
bicolore *adj* two-tone
blanc, blanche *adj* white
bleu, ~e *adj* blue
bleu ciel *adj* blue, sky
bleu marin *adj* blue, navy
bleu roi *adj* blue, royal
bleuâtre *adj* bluish
bleu-vert *adj* aquamarine
bordeaux *adj* maroon
brun, ~e *adj* brown (see also: **marron**)
cerise *adj* cerise; red, cherry
claire, ~e *adj* light
coloris *m* colour, shade of; tint; hue (see also: **teinte; nuance**)
couleur complémentaire *adj* colour, complementary
couleur fondamentale *adj* colour, primary
couleur secondaire *adj* colour, secondary
dominante *f* (paint) colour, main
doré, ~e *adj*; **or** *m* gilt; golden *adj*
foncé, ~e *adj* dark
fuchsia *adj* fuchsia
gris, ~e *adj* grey
gris acier *adj* grey, steel
grisâtre *adj* greyish
jaspé, ~e *adj* mottled
jaunâtre *adj* yellowish
jaune *adj* yellow
jaune citron *adj* yellow, lemon
jaune paille *adj* straw
lavande *adj* lavender
lilac *adj* lilac
marron *adj* brown (see also: **brun**)
mauve *adj* mauve
moucheté, ~e *adj* speckled
noir, ~e *adj* black
nuance *f* (see also: **coloris**)
nuancier *m* colour chart
orange *adj* orange
outremer *m* ultramarine
pâle *adj* pale
pastel *m* pastel
pourpre *adj* crimson (see also: **violet**)
rosâtre *adj* pinkish
rosé, ~é *adj* pink
rouge *adj* red
rougeâtre *adj* reddish
rousseur *f* russet
sable *adj* sand
saumon *adj* salmon
teinte *f* hue; tint (see also: **coloris**)
turquoise *adj* turquoise
unicolore *adj* colour, of a single
verdâtre *adj* greenish
vert, ~e *adj* green
vert bouteille *adj* green, bottle
vert émeraude *adj* green, emerald
vert jade *adj* green, jade
vert olive *adj* green, olive
vert pomme *adj* green, apple
violet *m*; **~ette** *adj* purple; violet (see also: **pourpre**)

Référence

Letters of the Alphabet
Lettres de l'alphabet

Letter	Pronunciation
a	ah
b	bay
c	say
d	day
e	euh
f	effe
g	jhay
h	ashe
i	ee
j	jhi
k	kah
l	elle
m	emme
n	enne
o	oh
p	pay
q	ku
r	erre
s	esse
t	tay
u	oo
v	vay
w	doo-bleuh-vay
x	eeks
y	ee grec
z	zed

Useful words & phrases
Mots & phrases utiles

Yes / No
Oui / Non

This / That
Ceci / Cela

Here / There
Ici / Là-bas

Please
S'il vous plaît

Excuse me...
Excusez-moi...

Excuse me... (to pass by)
Pardon!

Today
Aujourd'hui

Now
Maintenant

Tomorrow
Demain

Yesterday
Hier

Good morning
Bonjour

Good afternoon
Bon après-midi

Référence

Good evening
Bonsoir (after 6pm)

Goodbye
Au revoir / À bientôt

Good night
Bonne nuit

Good / Bad
Bien or *Bon / Mauvais*

Big / Small
Grand / Petit

Thank you (very much)
Merci (beaucoup)

How are you?
Comment allez-vous?

Can you help me?
Pouvez-vous m'aider

Do you speak (English / French)?
Parlez-vous (Anglais / Français)?

Sorry (for a mistake)
Je suis désolé

No problem!
Pas de problème

Can you say it again?
Pourriez-vous répéter?

I understand
Je comprends

I don't understand
Je ne comprends pas

I don't know
Je ne sais pas

How do you say this in French?
Comment dit-on cela en français?

What is this?
Qu'est-ce c'est?

I would like to order / buy…
Je voudrais ordonner / acheter…

Can you give me a quote?
Pourriez-vous me donner un devis?

I would like to enquire about…
Je voudrais me renseigner sur…

Do you stock…?
Est-ce que vous avez… / Avez-vous…?

My name is…
Je m'appelle…

Pleased to meet you
Enchanté (e)

How much is this?
C'est combien?

Coming soon from
Plátanos Publications

Two further titles in the *La Source!* series of English-French dictionaries by Richard Wiles:

Dictionary of French Gardening Terms
A bilingual sourcebook of plants, materials, tools & equipment for home-owners in France

Dictionary of French Culinary Terms
A bilingual sourcebook of ingredients, recipes, utensils & equipment for home-owners in France

"Essential guidebooks that help you experience the best of *La Vie en France!*"

Also by the author

Bon Courage!
A French Renovation in Rural France

Summersdale Publishers
Published 2003/2013
ISBN 978-1-84953-364-5
352 pages
Available on Kindle

A dilapidated, rat-infested stone barn might not be many people's vision of a potential dream home. But for Richard Wiles and wife Al, the cavernous, oak-beamed building in a sleepy hamlet in the Limousin region of France is perfect. Tussles with French bureaucracy and fierce storms do little to dampen their resolve as they immerse themselves in the quiet corner of France. Told by a well-intentioned if often hapless do-it-yourselfer, Richard's hilarious and heartwarming tale of a new life in France resounds to the Gallic refrain "*Bon Courage!*"

Bonne Chance!
Building a Life in Rural France

Summersdale Publishers
First published 2006
ISBN 978-1-84024-493-9
356 pages
Available on Kindle

Deep in the Limousin countryside, Richard Wiles bought his dream home. But little did he expect to be living full time in the dilapidated farmhouse and struggling to finish the conversion during the insect plagues of summer and the hard blizzards of winter. Watched by his bemused neighbours, Richard pursued his more unusual dreams of raising llamas, hot-air ballooning and marathon running while trying to keep the roof over his head. Told with unfailing humour and optimism, this is a unique tale of overcoming the challenges of building a home, and a life, in France.

Acknowledgements

The following websites were the source of invaluable research when compiling this book:

Brico Dépôt www.bricodepot.fr
Brico E.Leclerc www.e-leclerc.com
Bricoman www.bricomarche.com
Bricomarché www.bricomarche.com
Bricorama www.bricorama.fr
Castorama www.castorama.fr
Chausson Matériaux www.chausson-materiaux.fr
France Matériaux www.france-materiaux.fr
Gedimat www.gedimat.fr
Leroy Merlin www.leroymerlin.fr
Mr. Bricolage www.mr-bricolage.fr
Point P. www.pointp.fr
Screwfix www.screwfix.com
Système D.fr www.systemed.fr
Tool Finder www.toolfinder.co.uk
Tool-Net www.tool-net.co.uk
Tout Faire Matériaux www.toutfaire.fr
Weldom www.weldom.fr

Information on buying property, living or planning holidays in France:

About-France www.about-france.com
Anglo Info www.france.angloinfo.com
French Entrée www.frenchentree.com

Complete France www.completefrance.com
Subscribe to their magazines:
France Magazine
French Property News
Living France

English language newspaper www.connexionfrance.com
The Connexion

French-English dictionary app www.ultralingua.com

Printed in Great Britain
by Amazon